I0644273

By Touch Alone

Corporealities: Discourses of Disability

Series editors: David T. Mitchell and Sharon L. Snyder

Recent Titles

By Touch Alone: Blindness and Reading in Nineteenth-Century Culture
by Vanessa Warne

Down Syndrome Culture: Life Writing, Documentary, and Fiction Film in Iberian and Latin American Contexts
by Benjamin Fraser

Cripping Girlhood
by Anastasia Todd

The Disabled Child: Memoirs of a Normal Future
by Amanda Apgar

Blind in Early Modern Japan: Disability, Medicine, and Identity
by Wei Yu Wayne Tan

Cheap Talk: Disability and the Politics of Communication
by Joshua St. Pierre

Diaphanous Bodies: Ability, Disability, and Modernist Irish Literature
by Jeremy Colangelo

Embodied Archive: Disability in Post-Revolutionary Mexican Cultural Production
by Susan Antebi

Beholding Disability in Renaissance England
by Allison P. Hobgood

A History of Disability, New Edition
by Henri-Jacques Stiker

Vitality Politics: Health, Debility, and the Limits of Black Emancipation
by Stephen Knadler

Blindness Through the Looking Glass: The Performance of Blindness, Gender, and the Sensory Body
by Gili Hammer

HandiLand: The Crippest Place on Earth
by Elizabeth A. Wheeler

The Matter of Disability: Materiality, Biopolitics, Crip Affect
by David T. Mitchell, Susan Antebi, and Sharon L. Snyder, editors

Monstrous Kinds: Body, Space, and Narrative in Renaissance Representations of Disability
by Elizabeth B. Bearden

Autistic Disturbances: Theorizing Autism Poetics from the DSM *to* Robinson Crusoe
by Julia Miele Rodas

Foucault and Feminist Philosophy of Disability
by Shelley L. Tremain

Academic Ableism: Disability and Higher Education
by Jay Timothy Dolmage

A complete list of titles in the series can be found at www.press.umich.edu

By Touch Alone

Blindness and Reading in Nineteenth-Century Culture

Vanessa Warne

University of Michigan Press
Ann Arbor

Published in the United States of America by the
University of Michigan Press
First published July 2025

A CIP catalog record for this book is available from the British Library.

Library of Congress Cataloging-in-Publication Data

Names: Warne, Vanessa K., author. | Michigan Publishing (University of Michigan), publisher.
Title: By touch alone : blindness and reading in nineteenth-century culture / Vanessa Warne.
Other titles: Blindness and reading in 19th century culture | Corporealities.
Description: Ann Arbor : University of Michigan Press, 2025. | Series: Corporealities: Discourses of Disability | Includes bibliographical references (pages 193–202) and index.
Identifiers: LCCN 2024060639 (print) | LCCN 2024060640 (ebook) | ISBN 9780472077519 (hardcover) | ISBN 9780472057511 (paperback) | ISBN 9780472905089 (ebook other)
Subjects: LCSH: Blind—Books and reading—19th century. | Blind—Printing and writing systems—19th century. | Embossing (Printing)—19th century. | Braille—19th century. | Blind authors—19th century. | Literacy—19th century. | Literature, Modern—19th century—Social aspects.
Classification: LCC HV1721 .W37 2025 (print) | LCC HV1721 (ebook) | DDC 306.4/88087109034—dc23/eng/20250331
LC record available at https://lccn.loc.gov/2024060639
LC ebook record available at https://lccn.loc.gov/2024060640

The University of Michigan Press's open access publishing program is made possible thanks to additional funding from the University of Michigan Office of the Provost and the generous support of contributing libraries.

Cover image: Detail from the *Missionary Quarterly or Lutheran Herald for the Blind* (February 1939), published by the Evangelical Lutheran Synod of Missouri, Ohio and Other States. This image is reproduced by permission of The Lutheran Church—Missouri Synod. This book's cover features a photograph of a page of raised-print text written in Moon script. Moon script uses highly simplified versions of conventional ink-print letters. There is no ink on the photographed page; all the text is embossed. Sighted people can view the texture and shape of the letters embossed on this page but Moon script is not similar enough to standard ink-print letters for the words to be legible. The title of the book, *By Touch Alone: Blindness and Reading in Nineteenth-Century Culture*, is framed by a black circle at the center of the cover. The author's name (Vanessa Warne) is shared in a black rectangle at the bottom of the cover.

Authorized Representative: Easy Access System Europe, Mustamäe tee 50, 10621, Tallinn, Estonia, gpsr.requests@easproject.com

Contents

Digital materials related to this title can be found on the Fulcrum platform via the following citable URL: https://doi.org/10.3998/mpub.12860987

Figures

Acknowledgments

The research shared in this book was supported by the Social Sciences and Humanities Research Council of Canada and the Faculty of Arts at the University of Manitoba. I have many people to thank for their mentorship, advice, and encouragement. I would like to thank Martha Stoddard Holmes, Heather Tilley, Karen Bourrier, and Jennifer Esmail for the inspiration and insights of their scholarship on disability in nineteenth-century Britain. Thank you to colleagues Susan Prentice, Brenda Austin-Smith, Roisin Cossar, Fabiana Li, Shawna Ferris, and Krista Johnston for helpful feedback on early versions of chapters. Thank you to Arlene Young and Robert O'Kell for being caring mentors and for opening the door to our shared academic home to me. Thank you to my VSAWC friends, many of whom listened patiently as I worked through ideas at our annual conferences. Thank you also to all the members of the *Victorian Review* Editorial Team with whom I was fortunate to work, including Lisa Surridge, Kristen Guest, and Christopher Keep. I learned valuable lessons about academic writing from you. A special thank you to Ryan Stephenson for thinking about *Romola* and reading with me.

Academic writing coach Amy Benson Brown made me a better (and happier and bolder) writer and I am very grateful for her assistance. Librarians and archivists who supported this project with their expert help include Jan Seymour-Ford and Molly Stothert-Maurer (Perkins School for the Blind), Michael Hudson (American Printing House for the Blind), and, closer to home, Lyle Ford and Shelley Sweeney (University of Manitoba). Thank you also to Teresa Jaynes for lessons I learned from *The Moon Reader* and for permission to reproduce an image from the catalogue for her exhibition *Common Touch: The Art of the Senses in the History of the Blind*. I am indebted to former students who located sources that have shaped and enriched this project. They include Riley McGuire and Natalie LoVetri. Thank you also to Indiana Humniski for her assistance with proofreading.

At the same time that I was drafting chapters for this book, I was collaborating closely with four brilliant women. Thank you Andrea Korda and Mary Elizabeth Leighton, my Crafting Communities friends, for letting me make things with you and for time spent together. Thank you Hannah Thompson and Marion Chottin for all the opportunities you have shared with me and for the best picnic I will ever have on a train. And on the theme of brilliant women: thank you to Dana Medoro for consoling words, sage advice, and welcome company on this journey. Thank you to Alison Calder and Pam Perkins for the many gifts of your friendship and for comforting me with evenings on porches.

Thank you to my parents for a lifetime of kindness and for being proud of me. Thank you to Wendy for wisdom and support. I have been looking hard for the right words to thank my partner Brandon for his encouragement and kindness and hilariousness and companionship but I haven't found them yet. I hope he knows how completely and joyfully I love him. And on the theme of people I cherish: thank you to my daughters, Lucy and Alice, who are wonderful people. They have lived amiably and patiently with this project from its first appearance as a jumble of sticky notes pinned to a bulletin board in the attic. My daughters' belief in me kept me calm and made me brave. They make everything better. This book is for them.

Introduction

By Touch Alone

Soon after he learned how to read by touch, Henry Jones composed a poem about blind people's literacy. A member of the first generation of English-speaking people to learn to read with his fingers, Jones was passionate about the inkless books that had changed his life and that would, in the course of the nineteenth century, transform the lives of many blind people. In 1836, less than a decade after the publication of the first raised-print books in English, Jones traveled across England with his sighted teacher, Thomas Lucas, to raise money to fund the innovative printing processes that made reading by touch possible.[1] Sharing his poem with large audiences, Jones encouraged listeners to feel "wonder and amaze" when contemplating blind people's newfound ability to read (line 1). Regarding the invention of raised-print books, he asserted:

> The wisdom here display'd is vast,
> Which, while the course of time shall last,
>   No genius can exceed;
> By this, as yet, unrivall'd plan,
>   Not form'd alone by mortal man,
> THE BLIND ARE TAUGHT TO READ. (lines 7–12)

Across the Atlantic, Jones's sense of the significance of reading by touch was shared by students at The New York Institution for the Blind. In 1844, one of those students, Frances Jane Crosby, published a poem that described visitors' responses to the students' literacy. Crosby writes: "they could scarce believe it true, / That those on whom the orb of day / Had never shed its golden ray, /

By touch alone, were taught to read" (lines 64–67). Whereas Jones called on sighted people to appreciate a development that was transforming blind people's lives, Crosby gestures toward culture-wide consequences of the advent of reading by touch. They include revised perceptions of blind people's capabilities but also a new understanding of what it means to read, this as people, both blind and sighted, realized that an activity that had required visual acuity for the duration of its six millennia history could, in fact, be achieved, as Crosby states, "by touch alone."

Guided by the experiences of little-known blind commentators such as Jones and Crosby, *By Touch Alone* maps the emergence in the course of the nineteenth century of an inkless print culture shaped by blind people's preferences and needs. Following the publication of the first raised-print books in English in the late 1820s, thousands of blind people learned to read by touch. While some, like Crosby, studied reading in specialized schools, others, including Jones, learned to read with the help of teachers who visited their homes.[2] The inkless books that circulated among these readers were embossed in more than fifteen different scripts; some scripts were tactile versions of the printed alphabet used by sighted people, but others used dots, stenographic symbols, or radically simplified versions of the twenty-six letters of the Roman, or Latin, alphabet. The merits of these scripts were tested and debated; some fell quickly into obsolescence, while others, most notably Louis Braille's namesake script, gained popularity with readers over the course of the century. As scripts became fewer, the number of books published in raised print increased and blind readers could select from an ever more varied supply. By the early 1880s, libraries dedicated to blind people's print culture had opened in both the UK and the US. Founded in 1882, the Free Circulating Library for the Blind in Philadelphia mailed out copies of raised-print books to borrowers, this in addition to serving residents of Pennsylvania.[3] When the National Library for the Blind opened in London in 1887, it had 100 registered readers and 750 books, including novels, bibles, and textbooks. Less than a decade later, the library's membership had risen to 300 readers and its collection had grown to 3,200 volumes. Its holdings included raised-print editions of Alfred Tennyson's *The Lady of the Lake*, Benjamin Franklin's autobiography, a four-volume history of Ancient Rome, and scientific manuals on topics as varied as telegraphy and volcanoes.[4]

While literacy had, unfortunately, a limited impact on blind people's ability to secure paid employment, reading by touch transformed many people's experiences of education, faith, social inclusion, and privacy. Asked about his experience of reading at mid-century, a blind person from Edinburgh explained: "I commenced to learn to read [. . .] when I was about 69 years of age, with such success, that in a very few days I could read a chapter with tolerable ease. I can now read the whole Bible, I may say, with perfect ease and great comfort to myself" (Moon 139). A blind woman from Glasgow shared her experience: "I have found great pleasure in reading *The Pilgrim's Progress* [. . .]. I was so interested while reading it last Sabbath, that I did not eat my dinner till about seven o'clock at night!" (Moon 145). Also at mid-century, an anonymous reader described how receiving a package of raised-print books changed his experience of blindness: "[b]efore they came to hand, I had dull, desponding, and indolent feelings, with very dark prospects for this life; but when the means of improvement, comfort, and usefulness, was presented, they tended much to relieve my mind. I can now read very well, and had but little difficulty in learning" (Bull 212). Some readers compared their ability to read by touch to a cure for blindness. A volunteer teacher who taught students how to read a script named after William Moon, its blind creator, reported: "in speaking with an old man, who very much values the privilege of reading Moon's books, he said 'Yours is a glorious mission, giving sight to the Blind!'" (Moon 147).

Of course, reading by touch meant different things to different readers. The experience of reading raised-print books was shaped by class status and by gender, as well as by differences in readers' experiences of disability. Learning to read by touch was, for example, a different undertaking for blind people who had never been sighted than for people with acquired blindness; members of the latter group who had learned to read before becoming blind experienced reading by touch as a form of rehabilitation. Blind people valued reading for different reasons and, in some instances, they questioned its value. Some blind people were, at best, reluctant participants in reading classes; others, including well-educated blind people, opted not to learn to read by touch, preferring to listen to books read aloud. People who valued the ability to read by touch did not always agree on how best to support their fellow blind readers and improve their access to reading material. Differences in opinion fueled decades-long debates about printing techniques, script selection, book design, and the kinds of books that should be published in raised print. These debates would shape the development of a raised-print culture created for and by blind people. While it is difficult to determine how many blind people learned to read raised print in the course of the nineteenth century, what is certain is that reading by touch made unmediated access to written culture possible for a group of people who had previously required sighted people's assistance to access both printed and handwritten text.[5] Similarly certain is

Figure 1. "Blind Girl Reading," frontispiece to B.G. Johns's *Blind People: Their Works and Ways* (1867). Author's collection.

that the emergence of a new category of readers changed the composition of the reading publics of both Britain and America.

By Touch Alone explores blind people's experiences reading by touch as well as the sighted majority's response to this new skill. Whereas reading by touch changed blind people's experiences of visual disability, it also prompted sighted people to reimagine what it means to be blind. Sighted people had many opportunities to learn about blind people's literacy. In addition to staged demonstrations during school exhibits and fundraising events held throughout the UK and the US, some working-class blind people read from raised-print books in public thoroughfares to try to earn a living. Sighted people could also learn about reading by touch in books such as James Gall's *A Historical Sketch of the Origin and Progress of Literature for the Blind* (1834), Edmund Johnson's *Tangible Typography: or, How the Blind Read* (1853), or B.G. Johns's *Blind People: Their Works and Ways* (1867). Printed in ink, books of this kind shared both descriptions and images of reading by touch with sighted audiences. Johns's book includes, for example, a frontispiece depicting a young woman reading by touch (fig. 1). Sitting at a desk with her eyes and mouth closed, she reads silently to herself; the fingers of both of her hands touch the pages of a large book that lies open before her. This image announces Johns's focus on the education of blind people, including education in reading. Like book-length studies, articles in the periodical press played a critical role in raising awareness of reading by touch. Indeed, dozens of essays and announcements shared news about different innovations related to blind people's literacy, with many commentators speculating about benefits these innovations could secure for a marginalized group. A representative essay, published in 1854 in *Household Words*, celebrated blind people's entry into literacy while also taking undue credit for sighted people's contribution to raised-print culture. Harriet Martineau, a sighted author and deaf person, enthused:

> The blind can now read—a good many of them—and all will, by and by [. . .]. Their nice sense of touch, which used to be little more than an empty marvel to us, we have now learned to make use of in unbarring the doors which shut them out from literature. We now print books for them, in a type which they feel, instead of see; an embossed type which they learn to run over with their fingers with great readiness. (424–25)

Sharing Martineau's interest as well as her optimism, some sighted people were inspired by reading by touch to portray blind people reading in both sculptures and paintings.[6] Others chose to depict blind people's literacy in fiction. As this book demonstrates, literary works by authors, sighted as well as blind, can help us map how established ideas about blindness were challenged by reading by touch, a practice whose development supported the emergence of more progressive attitudes toward the experience of blindness than had previously existed.

Of course, reading by touch was not the first historical development related to blindness to attract sighted people's attention and to influence their perception of blindness. In the eighteenth century, in Europe, Britain, and North America, the development of successful surgical techniques to remove cataracts, a common cause of blindness, inspired sighted people to hypothesize about the cognitive and sensory lives of blind people.[7] The nineteenth-century invention of raised-print books functioned similarly, prompting sighted commentators to speculate about the experience of blindness and to conjecture about, for example, the degree to which the sense of touch might not only support blind people's intellectual pursuits but also open new professions to blind workers. However, as the chapters that follow demonstrate, reading by touch also provided some sighted people with new ways to sensationalize blindness. Whereas the late-century admission of blind students to non-specialized schools is indicative of the development of more progressive ideas about blindness, the circulation of apocryphal accounts of blind people reading books with their lips, instead of their fingers, or, similarly, of blind people identifying the color of threads by touch, exemplifies sighted observers' tendency to melodramatically embellish, mythologize, and misrepresent real-world developments.[8]

By Touch Alone demonstrates that, while changes both to the lived experience of blindness and to perceptions of blindness are the principal results of the proliferation of reading by touch, this new method of reading had culturally significant secondary effects. Reading by touch distanced reading from visual acuity, making the ability to see immaterial to the ability to read. Blind people's literacy, by which I mean the ability to read embossed text by touch, challenged established ideas about what it means to read and about the relationship between books and the bodies of their readers. Attentive to what I am terming raised-print culture, an understudied subsection of nineteenth-century print culture, I argue that the invention of new ways to make books together with the development of new scripts and orthographic practices for transcribing the English language demonstrated the adaptability of existing technologies of printing and bookmaking as well as established methods of written expression to the preferences and needs of blind people. It is thus the case that reading by touch did more than change the facts of blindness; reading by touch also changed the meaning and nature of reading.

To explore a sea change of importance to both the history of disability and the history of literacy, I engage a range of sources, including essays, letters to editors, speeches, and testimonials authored by the first generations of blind readers. These understudied sources allow me to challenge and revise current histories of nineteenth-century literacy, histories that have explored the experiences of sighted people in great detail but that have largely ignored the experiences of blind people. I also take up sighted people's commentary, including essays in the periodical press and books on blind people's education written for sighted audiences. In the chapters that follow, I pair exploration of press coverage of reading by touch with analysis of literary works by blind and sighted authors. I draw on nineteenth-century fiction and poetry to establish both the intensity and the diversity of literature's engagement with raised-print culture. I use both canonical and little-known works—poems, short stories, and novels—to trace cultural responses to reading by touch and to better understand the debates and technological developments that defined blind people's entry into literacy. Recognizing visually disabled people as both authors and consumers of literary works, not merely as characters portrayed by sighted authors, this book's focused and historically-informed study of nineteenth-century literature reveals how reading by touch transformed literary representations of blindness and blind people.

By pairing the study of historical developments related to blind people's reading lives with analysis of understudied literary texts, this book will, I hope, contribute not only to disability studies but also to Victorian studies, a field defined by its well-established interest in the portrayal of disabled characters and also by its growing awareness of the importance of the lived experience of disability and of disabled people's voices. While this study builds on several decades of disability studies scholarship, including research on the nineteenth-century history of disability, its approach is enriched by attention to the history of literacy as well as by emulation of the methods of book history. It is in this sense that *By Touch Alone* hopes to draw from, and contribute to, knowledge about visual disability, nineteenth-century literature, the history of literacy, and the history of the book, engaging both insights and unanswered questions from all four arenas. In the process, it surfaces the importance of reading by touch to such seemingly disparate objects of inquiry as a novel about interplanetary communication, debates about orthographic conventions, and the history of state-funded education.

In the sections of the Introduction that follow, I explore in more detail the relevance of histories of literacy, of book design, and of blindness to this book's arguments. Beginning with nineteenth-century investments in literacy and state-funded education, I explore how belief in the humanizing effects of reading shaped blind people's reading lives. I turn next to the history of raised-print books, using the career of blind person, inventor, and publisher William Moon to explore how the needs and preferences of blind readers shaped the design of raised-print books. My exploration of Moon's activism and innovation sets the stage for the next section's exploration of nineteenth-century attitudes toward blindness and blind people. It includes a discussion of important contributions to the scholarly study of the cultural history of blindness. I turn next to literary examples. Acknowledging a significant challenge for this book, namely the degree to which creative works by sighted authors far outnumber creative works by blind authors, I engage four literary works that sample the sighted majority's responses to blind people's literacy. I conclude this Introduction by outlining the arguments of each of the book's chapters and by offering a brief reflection on the relevance of the history of reading by touch to our own moment.

Uncommon Readers

A field of study initiated by Richard Altick's ground-breaking *The English Common Reader* (1957), the nineteenth-century history of reading has received significant scholarly attention.[9] Attentive to, for example, the role of public schools and libraries in the new literacy of working-class people, scholars have explored cultural values and social programs that supported dramatic increases in the proportion of the population who could read and write in the course of the nineteenth century. While scholars interested in the history of reading have looked closely at, for example, gender and class, the relationship between reading and disability has been comparatively neglected.[10] Yet, as Jonathan Rose astutely observed more than two decades ago, "The most difficult question historians of reading must confront is absolutely basic: Who read what, and how?" ("Education" 39). This book seeks to answer Rose's questions in regard to the first generations of people to read by touch, a group that, to adapt Altick's phrasing, could be usefully termed uncommon readers.

This group of readers was not a large one. Writing in 1913, Henry J. Wilson estimated the number of blind readers borrowing raised-print books from the National Lending Library in the UK at 6,000 (413). While imprecise, estimates like Wilson's are useful in that they give us a sense of the portion of blind people who could read by touch. Wilson's estimate of library use, when paired with a 1901 census record that put the number of blind people living in England and Wales at 25,317, suggests that, in the early twentieth century, at least one in four blind people living in the UK could read. What is certain is that nineteenth-century blind readers were vastly outnumbered by sighted readers. We can also say with certainty that they are proportionately understudied. While receiving little attention from contemporary scholars of literacy, they received significant cultural attention in their own moment. Their experiences can help us better understand both the social value placed on reading in nineteenth-century culture and the proliferation of reading among social groups historically excluded from literacy.

Consider, for example, the ways in which blind people's acquisition of literacy reflects a culture-wide belief in the humanizing effects of reading. For many commentators, a key benefit of reading was spiritual. Eager to secure a new set of readers unmediated access to scripture, religious organizations and individuals funded initiatives both to teach reading by touch and to publish raised-print editions of the Bible. Among those who donated to initiatives to publish raised-print bibles was Queen Victoria, who subsidized sighted Scottish printer John Alston's publication of a raised-print Old Testament and

New Testament with a gift of 400 pounds.[11] Completed in 1840, Alston's Bible was, like the effort that went into its creation, huge: it consisted of nineteen bulky volumes. *The Times* reported on this "great national work of printing," lauding Alston for having "for the first time in the history of literature, placed the complete Bible in the hands of the blind" ("Glasgow Asylum for the Blind"). The same report shared how, when Alston's students read from copies of the Bible at an event to celebrate its completion, "[t]he singular delicacy of touch and rapidity of manipulation exhibited by the boys and girls, together with the ease, fluency and accuracy of their reading, astonished every one in the room" (6). At the conclusion of the reading, the chair, a Dr. Symington, confided to the audience that "he was affected almost to tears" (6).

Commentators frequently highlighted the value of reading as a route to full membership in the human community. Indeed, for some commentators, the ability to read was a prerequisite of fully realized humanity. For Alston, the spread of raised-print books and of the skills needed to read them was, plain and simple, a "means of moral and intellectual improvement" ("On Printing" 242). Sighted commentator B.G. Johns, mentioned above, felt that, when "able to some extent to read the words of other men," a blind person "enters into the society of his fellow-men as fully and freely as if gifted with the keenest vision" (*Works* 189–90). An educator, Johns expects a great deal to follow from the entry into literacy of blind people. Regarding innovations that supported the printing of raised-print books, he wrote: "It is to be hoped that science, which has done so much for all other readers, will in due time provide for the dwellers in the land of darkness a literature and a typography which will help to make them wiser, better, and happier" (*Works* 117). The notion that reading could substantively transform the character as well as the daily habits of a blind person was frequently reiterated. In an 1842 letter, D. Macfarlan, Principal of the Glasgow Asylum for the Blind, wrote that blind people's ability to read has "not failed to produce marked and progressive improvement on their mental enjoyments and intellectual character" (Alston *Statements* 38). Belief in the humanizing qualities of literature supported investment not only in the publication of religious materials but also of novels and poems. As Heather Tilley has shown, Charles Dickens was one of several authors moved by these values to grant permission for the publication of their work in raised print; Dickens was similarly moved to donate toward the costs of the raised-print editions' publication.[12] Differentiated by the use of the sense of touch but energized by the same values that were motivating the expansion of literacy among sighted people, the reading history of blind people warrants more thorough study than it has received to date.

A New Kind of Book

Though reading was understood and valued as a normalizing practice, as something that lessened the cultural marginalization of blind people and their social distance from sighted people, the design and material qualities of the earliest books read by blind people alert us to important differences between reading by touch and reading by sight. Initiating a new chapter in the history of the book, raised-print books both feel and look different from ink-print books. While the replacement of inked text with embossed text is their most obvious difference, the absence of ink is only one of many noteworthy features. These books were, for example, made with paper that is heavier and stiffer than the paper used in books for sighted readers. These books also made less efficient use of paper, with less text fitting on a page than in an ink-print version of the same book, this because the script in which they are embossed needed to be large enough to ensure its legibility to touch and could, moreover, prior to the development of interlining techniques, be embossed only on one side of a page. The bulkiness of these books necessitated their division into many volumes and these volumes required more storage room than their ink-print equivalents. Consider, for example, a braille edition of Charles Dickens's *Dombey and Son* that consists of sixteen hefty volumes and fills three feet of shelf room.[13] Of course, both the kind of paper and the amount of paper used in raised-print books made them not only bulkier but far more expensive than ink-print books. In addition to having thicker and less flexible pages, which were further thickened by the addition of embossed text, the dimensions of early raised-print books differ from those of ink-print books. Books made for blind readers tend to have pages that are wider than the pages of ink-print books. The longer line of text that a wider page makes possible accommodates blind readers by lessening the frequency with which they need to locate the start of the next line of text.

While they share some common features, early raised-print books published in English were by no means homogenous. As mentioned above, the expensive and bulky books that circulated between blind readers were printed in a diverse array of scripts. Early in the English-language history of reading by touch, in 1832, Scotland's Society for the Arts held a gold medal competition to determine the best tactile script for blind people's use.[14] They received twenty-one entries, some for scripts that closely resemble the lettering used by sighted people and others characterized by radical breaks from the sighted status quo. Though competitions like this one demonstrate significant creative investment in the literacy of blind people, investments made both by blind

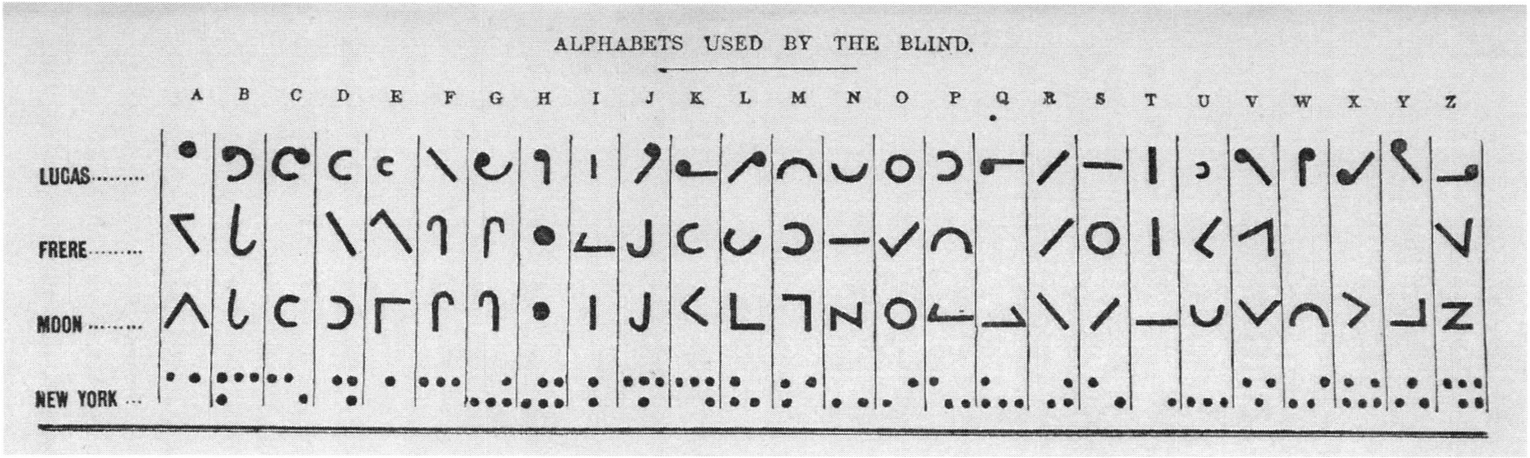

Figure 2. "Alphabets Used By The Blind," from T.R. Armitage's *The Education and Employment of the Blind: What It Has Been, Is, and Ought to Be* (1886). Source: Wellcome Collection. This image is a comparative chart of four so-called arbitrary scripts: Lucas, Frere, Moon, and New York Point. The name of each script is given on the left. In columns dedicated to each of the twenty-six letters of the Roman-letter alphabet, the chart shares the relevant sign or symbol for each letter. Lucas's symbols use combinations of straight lines, circles, and half-circles. Frere's script is notable for its use of shapes that resemble a shepherd's hook or walking stick. Moon's script is described in detail below. New York Point resembles the six-dot cell created by Louis Braille but differs in that the cell is wider than it is tall.

and sighted people, the proliferation of scripts was not without drawbacks for blind readers. Many blind readers believed the development of raised-print culture would benefit from the identification of a single script that could be universally adopted by printers and readers. That identification would allow for better use of limited resources that were, in an era characterized by the proliferation of systems, divided between rival scripts. The publication of the same book in different scripts was costly and, in the opinion of some observers, wasteful. Of course, another important resource was blind readers' time. Readers complained of learning one script only to have their supply of materials printed in that script dry up.[15] Writing in 1886, blind person and activist Thomas Armitage summarized the problem of the proliferation of rival scripts when he complained of the coexistence of a "Babel of systems" (*Education* 37).

Armitage's assessment is validated by a report of a reader's encounter with an early example of a raised-print illustration: an embossed portrait of Queen Victoria created for blind people's use. The proposal of new scripts was so frequent in the first years of Queen Victoria's reign that, in 1842, when a young blind woman was presented with a copy of the monarch's portrait, she concluded that it was a sample of a new script. Asked "what it was intended to represent,"

> [s]he hesitated for a long time, and felt the whole sheet of paper, till, discovering the word "London" in small raised characters in one corner of it, she hazarded the opinion that it was probably some, to her unknown, letters of the new London alphabet—a new alphabet for the blind of which she had never felt a specimen. ("Blindness and the Blind" 415)

While the confusion of raised shapes representing the Queen's body with a new tactile alphabet documents the failure of the portrait's creators to effectively adapt visual information for the sense of touch, it also documents a series of achievements. They include societal readiness to experiment with the tactile depiction of visual forms as well as significant investment, both financial and cultural, in the development of raised-print resources for blind people's use. While the development and coexistence of different scripts slowed the development of a print culture for blind readers, competition would, in time, clarify the needs and preferences of people who read by touch.[16]

With very few exceptions, proponents of scripts that resembled ink-print lettering were sighted people who felt a strong commitment to the sameness of blind and sighted people's books. They argued, for instance, that the use of the same script by blind and sighted people had practical benefits, allowing a sighted person with no special training to teach a blind person how to read. Countering this claim, champions of scripts that broke from the Roman (or Latin) alphabet argued that tactile versions of the ink-print alphabet were difficult for blind people to read because, even when enlarged, the embossed shapes of many letters in the Roman alphabet were hard to distinguish by touch (fig. 2). Many of these people, supporters of what were referred to as arbitrary scripts, were blind people who were guided by their personal experience of reading by touch. Unsatisfied with existing options for blind readers, William Moon (1818–1894), mentioned above, created a raised-print script that became popular with blind readers in both the UK and the US. Moon became blind at the age of twenty-one in 1840, a time when investment in blind people's reading lives in the English-speaking world was burgeoning.[17] Moon had studied a selection of scripts but had found them inadequately tactile. He worried especially about working-class blind people, the sensitivity of their touch having been lessened by callouses on their fingertips, a result of their participation in basket-making, brush-making, and similar tasks.

To develop his namesake script, which he debuted in 1845 and energetically promoted for decades, Moon drew on his knowledge of the shapes of the letters used by sighted people. He then identified seven simple and highly tactile shapes that could be flipped or rotated to represent all twenty-six letters in the Roman alphabet (fig. 3). Take, for example, the shape of the letter V: in Moon's script, it represents V in its standard ink-print orientation but is flipped upside down to represent an A and re-oriented with its open side to the right to represent K. The result is a script that Moon claimed was so tactile that it could be read with ease not only with the calloused fingers of a manual laborer but even with a gloved hand. Moon type became the script of choice for many English-speaking blind people in the second half of the nineteenth century and, to a lesser extent, in the first decades of the twentieth. Traveling across the UK in 1862, Moon gathered evidence of his script's popularity, which he published in a book titled *Light for the Blind.* In Cumberland, he listened to a three-year old blind girl read from a book printed in his type with what he termed "extraordinary facility" (37). In Liverpool, he discovered blind people's literacy in "a flourishing condition" (34): 268 people living in the city could, he reported, read his publications "with rapidity and ease" (34) and more than 400 people were learning to read Moon type in their homes using primers that were distributed by a network of home visitors, many of whom were blind. Moon visited the US in 1882 to promote

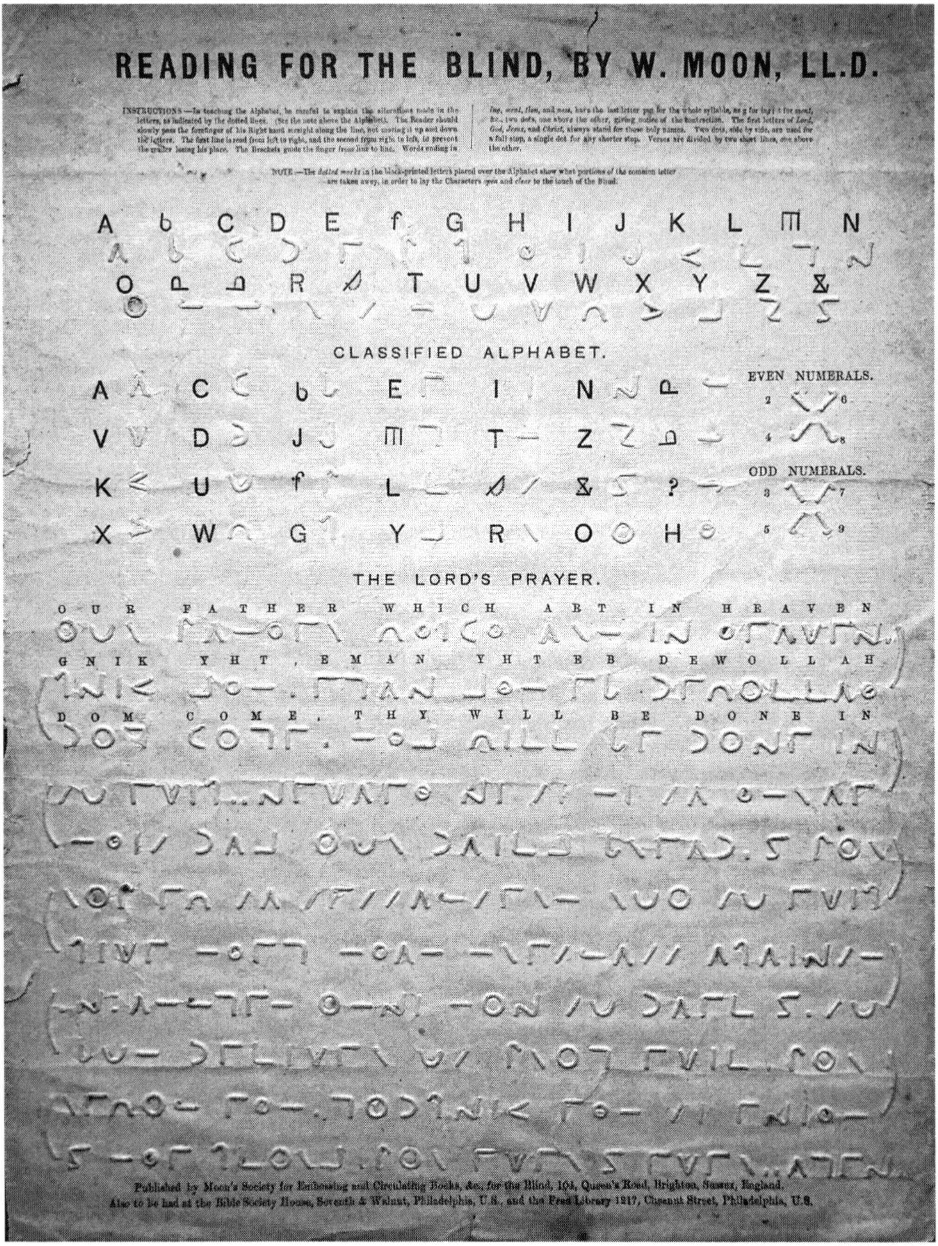

Figure 3. Detail of "Reading for the Blind, by W. Moon, LL.D," a primer of Moon script (n.d). Author's collection. A first lesson in Moon, this primer, made of cardstock, pairs raised-print text with inked text. It features two sets of Moon's version of the letters of the alphabet: a standard arrangement of letters from A to Z and a "Classified" alphabet that groups letters according to the shapes used by Moon to depict them. In both cases, letters printed in ink are paired with raised-print letters in Moon script. Below the alphabets, a portion of the Lord's Prayer is shared in both Moon script and inked text.

the adoption of his script among blind readers there; with the same aim, his son Robert Moon relocated to the US, where he served as secretary to the Pennsylvania Home Teaching Society. In 1904, the Society shared a report that it had 621 registered readers, among them a 70-year-old woman who "has become an exceedingly good and rapid reader" and a 75-year-old man who "mastered the alphabet" in two lessons (*Report* 4).

Prioritizing the needs and preferences of blind readers, Moon's script features versions of ink-print letters that are so radically simplified that text printed in them, while visible to sighted people, is not legible to them. Easy to read by touch, his script could only be read by sighted people who had invested time in training and practice. Notably, Moon's innovations were not limited to the shapes of his letters. One of the most radical choices Moon made as a printer was to break with the conventional left-to-right arrangement of both letters and words in printed English. Moon opted for a different approach, employing a boustrophedonic line, sometimes referred to as a return line, an arrangement of text on the page such that readers read the first line of text from left to right but the second line from right to left, the finger moving in two directions, alternating line by line. In other words, Moon script is arranged so that readers alternate the direction in which their fingers move, line by line. In, for example, the second line in a paragraph, "THE" would be printed "EHT" as readers would encounter the "T" before the "H" as their fingers moved leftward across the page. This change accommodated blind readers, freeing them from the task of tracking their fingers to the starting point of each new line of text on the left-hand side of the page, a process Moon argued was far slower for readers who use touch than for readers who use sight. With this and other adaptations, Moon accommodated people who used their sense of touch to read, pushing against conventions as ingrained as the reading direction of English-language text.

Opposition to systems such as Moon's was shaped by investment in the notion that blind people's literacy should be normalizing, minimizing their difference from sighted people. Critics of so-called arbitrary scripts argued, for example, that the use of Moon type or its rival braille would prevent correspondence between blind and sighted people, who would no longer have a writing system in common. Frank Rainey, an American opponent of arbitrary scripts, explained as late as 1893 that it was his wish "as far as possible, to untypify the blind, to unclass them, and represent them upon the world's canvas not as a distinct group, but in common with the human race as essential integrants of the people as a whole" (3). Worried in particular about the rising popularity of braille, he feared blind people would become "a class holding close communion, a mystery to all but themselves" (12). Rainey, a sighted person, would go so far as to speculate that, after death, a blind person educated only in braille might go "into the abyss of eternity without having the slightest idea of the characters and methods used by the seeing world; dying as a foreigner in the bosom of its family, save only in acquaintanceship, wondering what sort of character its mother used when reading a prayer" (13). For other critics, the visual appearance of arbitrary scripts was, ironically, a cause for concern. As I have argued elsewhere, the unfamiliar appearance of non-Roman-letter scripts prompted commentators to denounce braille, along with other arbitrary scripts, as barbaric, foreign, and coded.[18] Opponents were, it seems, challenged by arbitrary scripts' demonstration that the written Roman alphabet, a transcription system with a long history, was not the sole, natural, nor inevitable way of transcribing the English language.

To the disappointment of opponents of arbitrary scripts, and also, it should be noted, of proponents of Moon's script, by the end of the century, the majority of blind readers were reading Louis Braille's namesake script, a very compact and tactile script that had the great advantage over other scripts of being easily written with a stylus and slate or with a brailler, a keyed machine that resembles a typewriter. The widespread adoption of braille by English speakers was an achievement in which blind activists such as Thomas Armitage played an important role. Committed to self-determination and to research-based decision making, Armitage and his colleagues spent years testing readers' speed and accuracy when using different scripts. When, in 1881, Armitage launched Britain's first monthly magazine printed in braille, he very tellingly called it *Progress*. A few years later, in the second edition of his book *The Education and Employment of the Blind*, Armitage could reflect, "It is pleasant to note that the state of utter confusion which existed in 1869 has now to a great extent passed away. The Roman letter is all but abandoned in the United Kingdom for the purpose of reading" (45).

Though it was ultimately bested by braille, Moon's script, which is now very rarely read, has, like the larger topic of reading by touch, much to teach us. It instructs us in defining issues in the history of blind people's literacy. Designed by a middle-class man to be read by work-hardened hands, Moon's script reminds us that blind Victorians were not a homogenous group; their experiences of literacy were shaped by, for example, class as well as disability. What is more, the books that Moon made demonstrate the radical adaptability of core technologies of print culture—the written alphabet and the printing press—both of which were reimagined and transformed by blind readers. Highly innovative and highly tactile but outperformed by the invention of another blind innovator, the obsolescence of Moon script, like its design features, can help us better understand the emergence of raised-print culture. A participant in a decades-long competition between rival scripts, Moon's script typifies not only societal investment in raised-print culture but also, importantly, the persistence of blind activists and inventors who, in addition to competing with one another, pushed against ocularcentric values to successfully establish a reading culture shaped by the needs and preferences of blind people.

Notably, whether embossed in a Roman-letter script, in Moon script, or in braille, raised-print books have a prosthetic quality in the sense that raised print enables a human body to perform an activity that the body could not perform, at least not to the same level, without this material support. Not unlike eyeglasses, which increase a sighted person's visual acuity, raised print is an innovation that makes reading possible for blind people. Of course, all books have a prosthetic quality. Whether read by blind or sighted people, books share and store authors' words and ideas, allowing these words and ideas to have reach and longevity that they would not have otherwise. Contemporary observers were productively alerted to the prosthetic quality of raised-print books by the fact that reading did not become viable for blind people because of a change made to their bodies. What changed—what needed to change—was the design of books and the ideas that shaped, and in some cases limited, their design. It is in this sense that the material design of the first raised-print books published in English exemplifies a guiding insight of critical Disability Studies: that disability is not a problem of the body but a product of ideas, practices, and things that people make. The design features of nineteenth-century raised-print books exemplify, in other words, the shortcomings of the medical model of disability and its misleading identification of a bodily trait or condition as the cause of impairment. Blind people didn't need sight in order to read; they needed, and created, a new kind of book.

That said, a key effect of the proliferation of reading by touch was to draw attention to the body, specifically to the sense of touch, an historically underappreciated sense. Both blind readers and sighted observers responded to raised-print books with new awareness of how touch, a sense traditionally understood as inferior to both sight and hearing, might support cognitive processes. As I have argued elsewhere, increased appreciation of the role of touch in cognition was a lasting effect of blind people's literacy.[19] Curiously, the role of touch in reading also generated fear of a danger specific to blind people's reading culture. Because of the high cost of raised-print books, many blind readers shared books, borrowing them from one another, from charitable organizations, or from specialized libraries. Indeed, the circulation of books between readers was so central to the reading culture of blind people that legislation was passed in the UK and the US to significantly discount the cost of mailing raised-print materials.[20] The possibility that troubled at least some observers about the circulation of these books was the role that books exposed to prolonged touching might play in the spread of contagious disease. To limit the danger of borrowing raised-print books, touched by one reader then another, American librarians proposed the use of book ovens to kill off germs; they also recommended the strict quarantining of raised-print books that had been in the homes, and hands, of people who had been ill. An example of how reading by touch heightened awareness of risks of touch, as well as benefits of touch, the perception of books as carriers of disease demonstrates that a new way of reading prompted new ideas not only about the body's abilities but also about its vulnerabilities.[21]

Re-Thinking Blindness

The proliferation of raised-print books and the skills needed to read them co-existed with, and in some cases transformed, persistent and powerfully negative beliefs about blindness. The perception of blindness as a tragic condition, defined by limits placed on a person's capacity for pleasure as well as limits on their productivity, was as widespread in the nineteenth century as it had been in earlier eras. Influenced by biblical and classical depictions of blindness that equate sight with knowledge and blindness with ignorance, nineteenth-century Western culture tended, like the cultures of previous centuries, to identify blindness with inability and dependency, taking for granted that blindness was both a form of loss and the result of harm.[22] To use a term frequently used in the era, blindness was widely understood as a calamity. A passage from *The Youth's Magazine* from mid-century is representative of this assessment:

> There is no class of our suffering fellow-men, who meet with more universal sympathy than those who are deprived of their sight. When we consider all the sources of pure and exquisite pleasure of which the eye is the medium of communication to the mind, we can never attempt to realize the privation of the sense of seeing, without the utmost commiseration for those so afflicted. ("The Blind" 157)

Charles Bell Taylor, an eye surgeon, shared his perception of blindness as a tragic state when he shared information about eye surgeries: "it is quite certain that now and again apparently hopeless cases [. . .] may be restored to all the blessings attendant upon the exercise of that function without which life itself is worth little" (653). Charles Baker, a sighted expert on the education of blind people, described the experience of acquired blindness in ways that are wholly typical of the era: "The man who loses his sight after having had full use of it is profoundly to be pitied. He has lost not merely that great gateway of knowledge, but it frequently happens that the loss of sight, for a time at least, shatters and enfeebles mental energy, and weakens the remaining senses and powers" ("Blind" 224). Not limited to the loss of the ability to see, blindness initiates, in Baker's assessment, a web of crises. Many sighted commentators used imagery of imprisonment or of a living death to describe the state of blindness. Take, for example, Charles Dickens's now widely critiqued description of the deafblind American woman Laura Bridgman: "There she was, before me; built up, as it were, in a marble cell, impervious to any ray of light, or particle of sound; with her poor white hand peeping through a chink in the wall, beckoning to some good man for help, that an Immortal soul might be awakened" (40).[23]

Eager to correct the record, the blind author Alice King argued against the perception that "the blind man goes about the world shut up in a sort of terrible iron cage," explaining that "no idea is more mistaken than this. Blind men or women have to the full as much enjoyment, in their own peculiar way, of the glories and beauties of fair external nature, and of the sweetnesses of social intercourse, as those who can see" ("A Few Words" 189). Whereas King pushed back against both the imagery and ideas of the sighted majority, some blind people used the language of loss and deprivation to describe their experience of disability, especially in the context of appealing to sighted people for financial support. The phrase "Pity the Poor Blind" encapsulates widely held assessments of the experience of blindness. Written on signs held by blind people or labels worn by them, this phrase was also repeated aloud by blind people who tried to support themselves and their families as street sellers, street performers, or beggars. Charitable organizations also used the language of calamity or tragedy to try to secure financial support for blind people, who were, more often than not, perceived by nondisabled people as unfit for paid work. The persistence of powerfully ocularcentric assessments of blindness in the wake of the entry of blind people into literacy—or in the case of Dickens's description of

Bridgman, in direct relation to her literacy—is a measure of the tenacity of cultural perceptions of blind people as deserving objects of sympathy.

Though reading by touch did not cause people, blind or sighted, to abandon their assessment of blindness as a tragic state, it did challenge long established ideas about blindness and blind people. Blind people were, of course, prompted by the opportunity to read by touch to think in new ways about their own disability. Accounts emphasize the extent to which blind people felt, not surprisingly, better informed and more independent once they learned to read. For some, reading by touch was a catalyst to recognize and share an experience of "blindness gain," this more than a century before the coining of this term. Theorized by Hannah Thompson, blindness gain challenges the ableist and ocularcentric values implicit in the phrase "vision loss" and consists of a range of benefits created by blindness's sensory, cognitive, social, and cultural effects. As Thompson explains, "Blindness gain is the idea that rather than thinking of blindness as a problem to be solved, we think of blindness as a benefit." In the course of this book, I will explore how some nineteenth-century readers experienced blindness gain when they enjoyed a more attentive, informative, and engaged experience of reading when blind than they had had when sighted.

In complicated ways, as noted above, some blind people equated the ability to read with a kind of cure, not for blindness but for its accompanying social ills. W.W. Fenn, a professional author and blind person whose work is, like nineteenth-century experiences of blindness gain, explored in the chapters that follow, proposed in 1886: "[g]ive [. . .] the blind man in his fingers an equivalent for his eyes and the darkness in which he lives is dispelled" ("The Welfare" 478). *The Times* reported in 1870 that Armitage, the blind activist and braille proponent quoted above, went so far as to suggest blind people's physical health was improved by reading. In a public lecture at the Adelphi, Armitage remarked that "he had always found a great improvement in the physical, as well as in the mental, condition of the blind result from their acquiring the power of reading" ("Literature for the Blind," 27 Jan. 1870). What is more, for both blind practitioners and sighted observers, reading by touch demonstrated that sight was not necessary for the activity of reading nor for the pleasures and benefits—intellectual, spiritual, and social—that reading makes available. As noted above in regard to the design of raised-print books, a powerful secondary effect of reading by touch was the way in which it demonstrated how disability is not a reality of the body but a product of culture, including material culture. Transforming the experience of blindness without changing the body of the blind person, reading by touch alerted observers to the fact that features of the experience of blindness that some people felt were undesirable, such as lack of access to written culture, were not fixed and could, instead, be lessened or eliminated by technological innovation. To put this another way, the nineteenth-century history of reading by touch engages ideas of cure but does not posit the cure of a body by surgery, medicine, or miracle as the remedy to the perceived "problem" of disability.

Literature, a warehouse for nineteenth-century ideas about visual disability, primarily documents sighted people's perspectives, with sighted authors far outnumbering blind authors even in the context of the literary depiction of blindness. While the activity of reading by touch tended to promote messages about blindness very different from, and more progressive than, messages about blindness shared in literary texts by sighted authors, trends in the literary depiction of blind people by sighted authors provide us with a way to assess the extent to which reading by touch altered the sighted majority's attitudes toward blindness and blind people. The era's most influential portraits of blindness by sighted authors include portraits of blind villains, such as Charles Dickens's Stagg, Robert Louis Stevenson's Blind Pew, and Arthur Morrison's Blind George. There are, at the opposite end of the spectrum, highly moral blind characters such as Muriel from Dinah Craik's *John Halifax, Gentleman* (1856) and Bertha Plummer from Dickens's *The Cricket on the Hearth* (1845). More morally ambiguous are a trio of male characters from mid-Victorian literature whose experience of acquired blindness is chastening, correcting overly confident or morally flawed men. In Charlotte Brontë's *Jane Eyre* (1847), Rochester's partial blindness, together with the loss of a hand, make his marriage to Jane viable, as he is punished for past wrongs and deceptions and she, by extension, is licensed to marry by her adoption of the role of caregiver. In Charles Kingsley's *Westward Ho!* (1855), protagonist Amyas Leigh is blinded by lightning, his disability figured as one in a series of misfortunes that close the novel and his narrative. In Elizabeth Barrett Browning's verse novel *Aurora Leigh* (1856), Romney Leigh's blindness parallels, as many readers have noted, Rochester's in that it results from injuries sustained during the burning of his ancestral home and is part of a larger process of maturation that moves the male protagonist toward the reward of a happy marriage.[24] Notably, none of these well-known examples of blind characters from the nineteenth-century canon, nor the blind villains and blind ideals just named, are depicted reading by touch. Indeed, to take one character as an example, Rochester's reliance on Jane to read aloud to him is a defining feature of their marriage. When she famously addresses her audience, declaring "Reader, I married him" (395), the activity she evokes with the appellation "Reader" is one that her love object, and the object of her famously succinct sentence, can no longer perform.

Given the depth of Victorian literature's investment in depictions of blindness, it is not surprising that scholarly interest in nineteenth-century literary depictions of blind people has a history of its own. Close to a century of scholarship exploring representations of disability in Victorian literature has confirmed Julia Miele Rodas's description of Victorian literature as a body of literature in which "the disabled figure is an astonishingly important presence" ("Mainstreaming" 372). As early as 1930, Jessica Langworthy identified a range of blind character types: "the idealized and abnormally good; the repugnant and abnormally bad; the extremely clever; [. . .] the normal and well-described" and "the war-blinded" (271–72). This mix of character types continues to attract critics' attention. Martha Stoddard Holmes has, in her field-defining work on disability in British literature of the Victorian era, explored many facets of the depiction of blind people in literature and, more broadly, in culture. Particularly notable for her insights on life writing, melodrama, and the marriage plot, Holmes has given us new ways to read what she compellingly describes as "cultural scripts for disabled identity" (*Fictions* 9). In the American context, Mary Klages's groundbreaking *Woeful Afflictions: Disability and Sentimentality in Victorian America* (1999) takes nineteenth-century blind women and their bodies as its focus, demonstrating how institutions and authors relied on a sentimental framework to make sense of blindness. David Bolt's influential study of twentieth-century literature, *The Metanarrative of Blindness: A Re-reading of Twentieth-Century Anglophone Writing* (2014), draws on experiential knowledge of blindness to powerfully critique the literary depiction of blind people and to emphasize the real-world implications of literary misrepresentation for people with disabilities.

Like these scholars, whose work on the literary depiction of blindness guides my own, I draw on both the methods and findings of disability studies to explore the way reading by touch shaped nineteenth-century literary depictions of blindness and blind people. Specifically, with this study, I build on the work of Holmes, Klages, Bolt and others to show that, as tenacious as they are negative, conventions regarding the literary depiction of blind characters were, like real-world perceptions of blind people, challenged by blind people's highly publicized acquisition of the ability to read.

Of particular importance to my work is Heather Tilley's *Blindness and Writing: From Wordsworth to Gissing* (2018), which shares compelling insights regarding the importance of blindness to literary works authored by William Wordsworth, George Gissing, Charles Dickens, and Charlotte Brontë. In it, Tilley engages the medical history of blindness and eye surgery, paying particular attention to the influence eighteenth-century philosophical responses to medical cures for blindness had on the depiction of blindness in nineteenth-century literature. Tilley, who has also explored the history of blind people's literacy in curatorial work and in essays, productively engages the history of reading and writing by touch in *Blindness and Writing*, which includes a chapter dedicated to this topic. In addition to offering a detailed history of innovations in writing methods and tools used by blind people, Tilley argues for how "[t]he possibility of reading by touch emphasised how central the material form of writing was to textual meaning" (*Blindness* 69). She has also explored how "the history of printed books for blind people coexists with other important cultural and social narratives, which collectively reinscribe and reinstate the blind subject across the nineteenth century" (*Blindness* 96). My own work, focused on reading by touch, benefits immensely from her research and insights, which I engage more closely in the chapters that follow.

Blind Readers in Nineteenth-Century Literature

Literary descriptions of blind people reading books document both real-world changes in blind people's access to written culture and changes in sighted people's attitudes toward blindness and blind people. That said, literary representations of blind people reading by touch are, if nothing else, varied. Some authors chose to depict blind characters reading by touch as part of a realistic portrait of blindness that accurately documented the new reality of reading by touch. Wilkie Collins's 1872 novel *Poor Miss Finch* is a good example of this trend. The protagonist Lucilla Finch is a blind person who accesses text in two ways: with the help of sighted readers and by reading by touch. In recent decades, the novel has received significant attention from scholars who have explored its depiction of, among other topics, the surgical restoration of sight, the sexuality of blind women, and intersections between disability and race.[25] Yet, the fact that Lucilla is literate—that she has, as the novel's narrator explains, "learnt to read by touch (that is to say with raised characters)" (309)—has received comparatively little scholarly attention, this despite the fact that the novel is structured both by the circulation of letters and by journal writing. Able to write as well as to read by touch, "feeling her way on the paper with her finger" (309), Lucilla enjoys opportunities for privacy, independent action, and self-reflection that are not common among

Victorian-era blind characters. Importantly, she can write to other people; as she explains of a letter she writes, "Writing is long, long work for me. But this was a letter which I felt bound to write myself" (217). Given that literacy is the historical development that most significantly distinguishes Victorian depictions of blindness from that of other eras, it is noteworthy that Collins's novel contrasts Lucilla's experiences of reading and writing by touch with her experiences of these same activities during a period of temporary sightedness following surgery. As I will explore in chapter 4, Lucilla's literacy contributes to the novel's markedly positive approach to blindness, including the portrayal of a fully realized blind protagonist with personality traits, including flaws, that are not narrowly determined by her sensory experience. Regrettably, many of Collins's contemporaries were both less direct in their engagement with reading by touch and less progressive in their thinking about blindness. They allude to reading by touch while obdurately perpetuating negative stereotypes about blindness and blind people. This approach is exemplified by the emergence of a new object of literary interest in the Victorian era: the blind person's suicide note, an object that features in a surprising and troubling number of nineteenth-century short stories by sighted authors.[26]

Whereas Collins's engagement with reading features a blind person living in his own era, some nineteenth-century sighted authors play surprisingly fast and loose with the timeline of blind people's reading, portraying blind people reading or writing in ways that are temporally out of step with the era represented in the literary work. Take, for example, Rudyard Kipling's short story "They" (1904). Kipling's story features a wealthy blind woman who runs an estate, renting out portions of her large property to tenant farmers. A modern woman in a modern world, she admires the speed and design of a motor car that a visitor drives through her estate but this same woman lacks access to the decades-old technology of inkless books. Kipling depicts her using her fingers to read notches carved into wooden tally sticks: an antiquated record-keeping system that dates, not from her own time, an era of blind literacy, but from the medieval period. The blind woman describes her use of these records in conversation with the story's narrator, the motorist with whom she shares not just an admiration for automobiles but also an ability to perceive the presence on her property of ghost children who she hears and he sees. Though she is wealthy, intelligent, and psychically gifted (or, more accurately, compensated) by her ability to perceive not only ghosts but also the auras or energy fields of living people, this woman lacks basic literacy. When the narrator discovers a pile of tallies on her hearth, she explains:

"As I can't read or write I'm driven back on the early English tally for my accounts" (112). Holding a tally in her hand, she runs "her thumb down the nicks" (112), touching indentations carved in it that record a month's worth of data about milk production on her property. A wealthy blind woman living in an emphatically modern world, she uses her sense of touch to read an antiquated record-keeping system developed for sighted people by sighted people. That this system was associated with the illiteracy or at best very rudimentary literacy of agricultural workers adds to the complexity of Kipling's remarkably anachronistic portrait of a blind person reading by touch.

Equally anachronistic in its depiction of a blind character's literacy is Edward Bulwer-Lytton's best-selling (and now very seldom read) novel *The Last Days of Pompeii* (1834). Though shaped by its author's investment in historical accuracy, Bulwer-Lytton's novel features a blind person writing a letter, this despite the fact that it is set in an era that predates the advent of blind people's letter writing by more than a thousand years. Nydia, the character who writes the letter, is not a minor one; her depiction influenced ideas about blindness for generations of sighted people, including people who never read *The Last Days of Pompeii*. In elaborate stage adaptations of the novel and in works of visual art that include a celebrated mid-century statue by American sculptor Randolph Rogers, Nydia contributed to the identification of blind girls and women with selfless devotion and unrequited love.[27] Depictions of Nydia similarly promoted ideas about sensory disability and compensatory ability. Not reliant on sight, when Vesuvius erupts, she rescues sighted people who cannot find their way in the darkened ash-filled city by leading them safely to the sea. Prior to the volcano's explosion, Nydia attempts a different kind of rescue mission. Though jailed, she tries to save another person's life by writing a letter to a government official. Readers learn that Nydia "despite her blindness," had "acquired in childhood, though imperfectly, the art to write with the sharp stilus [sic] upon waxen tablets, in which her exquisite sense of touch came to her aid" (341). Her knowledge of written language, specifically of the shapes of letters and of conventions of spelling and transcription are, like her ability to write, by no means consistent with classical-era realities. They do, however, connect her, albeit fantastically, to nineteenth-century real-world blind people, her skills consistent with the abilities of what was, in 1835, a small but growing community of blind readers. In this early Victorian novel, a new innovation is imaginatively assigned a classical history, a new skill displaced in time to enrich and energize the literary depiction of a blind character.

What I am trying to demonstrate here is that both Kipling and Bulwer-

Lytton untether a blind character and blind people's literacy from history, either denying a blind character access to their era's technologies or granting a blind character abilities and methods that did not exist in the era depicted. These authors place people with disabilities outside of history, somehow unaffected by, for example, the history of education or technological developments in printing and bookmaking. Nydia can, without explanation, read and write; she can spell, she knows the shapes of the alphabet, and she can reproduce the letters of that alphabet with a stylus in wax, filling a tablet with text that she cannot read. Blindness, like other disabilities, has a history, but a character like Nydia exists outside of it. These authors' ahistorical texts are, I would argue, a prompt to literary critics to respond to them in historically informed ways. Reading by touch is a practice that demonstrates the extent to which both the lived experience and perception of blindness are historically specific. By reading literary depictions of blind people and their literacy in consciously historicized ways, we can both insist on and better appreciate visual disability's historically and culturally specific nature.

As examples shared in this section suggest, the literary record on reading by touch is largely a record of sighted people's responses. The extent to which literature preserves sighted people's ideas about blind people's literacy, whether accurate or fantastical, is a challenge for this project. Fortunately, though massively outnumbered by their sighted contemporaries, nineteenth-century blind authors did depict experiences of reading by touch. They include little-known figures such as Jones and Crosby, quoted above, and Edmund White, the author of a series of long poems, including his 1856 autobiographical poem *Blindness*. They also include better-known figures, such as George du Maurier, whose novel *The Martian* (1898) is shaped by du Maurier's personal history of partial blindness. My work on these texts in chapters that follow goes, I hope, some way toward creating a balance of perspectives between blind and sighted commentators. The same is true of my use of nonfiction sources to access blind people's perspectives. By framing readings of fictional work by sighted authors with readings of the life writing or activist writing of blind authors, I try to ensure that blind people are accurately represented as agents, specifically as both authors of literary texts and readers of literary texts, and are not confused with, or misrepresented by, characters in literary works authored by sighted people. In short, I engage a literary record unquestionably dominated by sighted authors' voices but I try to do so in ways that are guided by the perspectives of visually disabled people, including, importantly, blind authors. The analysis of George Eliot's *Romola* that follows is, I hope, representative of that approach.

On Not Reading in *Romola*

George Eliot's historical novel *Romola* (1862–63) suggests the complexity, both temporally and thematically, of nineteenth-century literature's engagement with reading by touch. This novel's fascination with, on the one hand, societal investment in literacy and, on the other, a blind character traumatized by his inability to read warrants in-depth consideration because it demonstrates not only the awareness of sighted authors of blind people's literacy but also the reluctance of sighted authors to revise their understanding of blindness as a condition defined by a tragic inability to access printed or handwritten text. Serialized in *Cornhill Magazine*, the novel is a study in acquired blindness, specifically the blindness of Bardo, the father of the novel's eponymous protagonist. Bardo is a citizen of fifteenth-century Florence, a scholar, and a collector of Greek and Roman manuscripts who, following the onset of midlife blindness, relies on Romola, his daughter, to read to him. Creating in Bardo an unquestionably tragic representation of blindness, Eliot draws on long-established cultural conventions related to the depiction of blind characters, conventions that predate her own era as well as the time period of her novel by centuries. She has, for example, Bardo walk with "the undecided gait of the blind" (55). Housebound, leaving his home only once in the course of the novel, to attend his daughter's wedding, Bardo slows the procession to the church. Embarrassed by his blindness, Bardo is reluctant to be seen standing or moving by visitors; Romola observes his "restless movement" in the library of his home, the space where Eliot consistently depicts him. Romola feels that her father's unusual gestures make him "look as if he were trying to get outside the prison of his blindness" (179). Predictably Bardo's blindness is compared to darkness, a "night" (53) that has descended on him, and a barrier, "a curtain" (56) that obscures his perception of the world. His eyes are described not just as unseeing but also as "silent" (48), a synesthetic image of their lack of communicative ability. Bardo blames his blindness for what is, in fact, a Casaubon-like, lifelong lack of scholarly achievement that predates his vision loss. He complains that "blindness acts like a dam, sending the streams of thought backward along the already-travelled channels and hindering the course onward" (52). Deepening the novel's association of blindness with loss, Tito, Bardo's secretary turned son-in-law, will betray Bardo, selling off the treasured collection of manuscripts and other artifacts that Bardo planned to donate to Florence as a posthumous gift.

Given these details of Bardo's depiction, it's not at all surprising that Eliot's portrait of a blind person has been criticized by readers, some of whom have noted how the life of John Milton influenced Eliot's portrait of a frustrated scholar who relies on a dutiful though unappreciated daughter to read and write for him.[28] While the novel engages Milton's life to create a Renaissance-era appropriate portrait of blindness, Eliot's novel also references the Victorian-era development of raised-print books, albeit in subtle and tentative ways. The reading that follows explores how Eliot's depiction of a fifteenth-century blind person is shaped by nineteenth-century blind people's entry into literacy, with important implications for cultural representations of blindness and blind people.

Exploring both *how* reading works and *why* reading is valued, *Romola* is deeply concerned with questions of literacy. As the novel's most memorable chapter title announces, reading is what happens when "The Black Marks Become Magical": when the inked text on a page mysteriously communicates meaning, when markings that indicate letters and words are first perceived by sight then understood (331). Eliot uses disability to study this magic, dividing the act of reading into its component processes, this by way of her plot's disabling of not just one but two classical scholars: Bardo, who becomes blind, and Baldassarre, Tito's adoptive father, who develops a cognitive impairment that prevents him from reading. In its paired depiction of two scholars who lose the ability to read, the novel insists on the dual nature of reading: on the extent to which reading requires both sensory input and cognition, or, to put it another way, both body and mind.

In their first scene together in the novel, which is set in Bardo's library of treasured manuscripts and parchments, Bardo, unable to perform the magic of reading, listens as Romola reads aloud to him. Tellingly, when Eliot selects a text from Bardo's collection for Romola to read, she reveals her interest in the symbolic power of blindness: the passage Romola reads to her father, who is deeply frustrated by his disability, is an account in Latin of the blinding of Tiresias, which Eliot gives at length in English. As Romola reads an account of blindness as a punishment to her father, doing so at his request, Eliot very efficiently imports into her novel messages about blindness that are both powerfully negative and culturally authoritative. Eliot borrows a second time from classical literature's depiction of blindness when Romola commissions a portrait of her father. Romola is an affectionate and loyal daughter yet she asks the artist to depict Bardo as an elderly Oedipus, a cultured choice but surely also a highly eccentric choice for a family portrait. Notably, the association of Bardo with Oedipus's error, ignorance, and punishment will go unchallenged by the novel's plot.

While Bardo treasures the books and scrolls in his collection for their content, he also values them as material things. Bardo knows the location of each of the many books and scrolls on the shelves of his library. He also has vivid visual memories of the appearance of these materials and of portions of them, confirming with Romola not just the content of a marginal note but also the location of the note on a page and the colour of the ink in which it is written. A measure of the strength of his visual memory, Bardo's remarks are also indicative of the intensity of his hunger for text. Given her interest in the endurance and intensity of a blind scholar's connection to his books, it is not surprising that Eliot consistently portrays Bardo in his library, a setting also depicted by Frederic Leighton in "The Blind Scholar and His Daughter," the first of twenty-four illustrations he created for the novel's serialization in *Cornhill Magazine* (fig. 4). The illustration shows Bardo seated with a closed book on his lap; Romola stands beside him, her gaze directed at a book that rests open on a lectern. Leighton signals Bardo's lack of vision through Romola's association with light, specifically with the sunshine that pours from the window behind her and with a lamp that she adjusts with her left hand. Leighton also communicates blindness by contrasting Romola's open eyes and open book with her father's closed eyes and closed book. In this illustration, as in the novel's text, the inability to read is depicted as the primary, and tragic, consequence of the loss of sensory function.

Significantly, both in Eliot's prose and in Leighton's illustration, Bardo's physical touching of books is emphasized. When Bardo asks Romola to retrieve a book for him, Eliot explains that Bardo waits with "his arms stretched out a little with nervous excitement to seize the volume" (50), eager to grasp a book he can hold but not read. In Leighton's illustration, Bardo's clenched fingers, on his chair's arm and on the edges of the closed pages of the book on his lap, feature prominently. His touching of the book on his lap signals frustration and loss; the content of the book lost to him, the book is reduced to a valuable and cherished but inscrutable material object. Leighton follows Eliot here. Drawing attention to the position of Bardo's fingers and his touching of the book, she explains, he "looked flushed and agitated as his hand explored the edges and back of the large book" (50). Importantly, Eliot has Bardo open the book. Romola will watch Bardo "passing his finger across the page, as if he hoped to discriminate line and margin" (50). In this moment, unable to see inked text on a page, Bardo feels for meaning, employing his sense of touch without success. The scene gains power from the fact that both his reaching for the book and his handling of it express a desire for unmediated contact, for a relationship to text that does not involve the mediation of a sighted person.

Figure 4. Frederic Leighton's "The Blind Scholar and His Daughter" (1862). Reprinted from *Cornhill Magazine*. School of Art Museum and Galleries, Aberystwyth University.

Moving his fingers across the open page of a book he cannot read, Bardo performs his own lack of access to ink-print culture in ways that contrast powerfully with the experiences of Eliot's blind contemporaries. As the chapters of *By Touch Alone* that follow will explore, the passing of fingers across pages yielded radically different results for an emergent community of real-world blind readers. It is in this sense that Eliot's literally gestural allusions to reading by touch demonstrate the tenacity of nineteenth-century literature's investment in the perception of blind people as tragic figures. Creating a doggedly tragic portrait of blindness, Eliot works at a distance from her own historical moment. That said, when she depicts a blind man touching a page of text with his fingers, she comes in closer contact with her own era and with the new realities of blind people. Portraying Bardo's failure to read by touch, she signals, in a proleptic gesture, a future moment, her own moment, in which touch allows blind people to read libraries full of books produced without ink. Eliot's bleak portrait of Bardo associates blindness with a triad of disempowerments—aging, an unrealized bequest, and, centrally, the loss of literacy. This portrait is, however, tempered, or at least complicated, by the novel's depiction of Bardo touching a book: a gesture that evokes a future for people with acquired visual disabilities defined not by illiteracy and loss but by literacy and possibility.

By Touch Alone

The first two chapters of this book explore reading by touch in disparate settings: public streets and domestic parlors. Chapter 1 analyzes the reading experiences of blind people who read aloud from raised-print books on streets and bridges. I argue that reading by touch as street performance publicized the new literacy of blind people while also exposing the limited capacity of reading by touch to ameliorate visually disabled people's social marginalization and poverty. To make this argument, I analyze poetry by Edmund White, a working-class man whose experiences of blindness as well as poverty shaped his depiction of blind street readers. I close the chapter with a reading of an anonymously authored short story, "The Poor Blind Woman," which depicts the reading of a raised-print Bible on a canal bridge as a valuable contribution to the reader's community. Chapter 2 considers blind people's experiences of reading by touch in more privileged contexts. It takes up the writing of Alfred Hirst, an essayist, activist, and blind person who argued that reading by touch is a more intellectually engaging practice than reading by sight and that blind people are consequently better readers of challenging literary works than sighted people. Focused on blindness gain and anchored by Hirst's arguments, chapter 2 argues that the perception of reading by touch as the superior mode of reading supported the emergence of a new representative figure of blindness: the blind scholar, a Victorian-era alternative to earlier blind types such as the blind seer. I supplement my analysis of Hirst's oeuvre with a literary case study: sighted author Grant Allen's *Linnet* (1898), an end-of the-century novel that imagines reading by touch as a skill that could be mastered and misused by sighted people.

The next two chapters extend the book's discussion of blind people's literacy to consider blind people's experiences as creators of written culture. Chapter 3 contrasts the history of close and productive collaborations between blind authors and sighted amanuenses with literary depictions of blind authors as dependent and exploited. I contrast the lived experiences of blind authors W.W. Fenn, Alice King, and Frances Browne with depictions of author-amanuensis pairings in fiction. They include the co-authored short story "Eyes that Saw not" by sighted collaborators Bertrand W. Babcock and Winnifred Eaton. I also offer a new reading of du Maurier's novel *The Martian* (1897), a novel shaped, as noted above, by du Maurier's lived experience of vision loss. Chapter 4 explores the impact of reading by touch on blind people's experiences of private correspondence. It explores the material history of blind people's letter writing, including the use of braille, stamps, and keyed writing machines. It offers a new reading of Collins's novel *Poor Miss Finch*, mentioned above, as well as case studies of how letter writing featured in the lives of two prominent blind Victorians: Elizabeth Gilbert, an activist and philanthropist, and Henry Fawcett, a political economist and parliamentarian. It argues that blind people's use of tools such as styluses and slates changed more than the materiality of handwritten letters; it initiated a non-visual culture of correspondence, one that rejected ocularcentric investment in penmanship in order to prioritize private communication by and between blind people.

The final chapter of the book explores a parallel development to the proliferation of reading by touch, namely, an increase in blind people's opportunities to touch non-textual objects such as natural history specimens, manufactured items, and paintings. I argue that public interest in reading by touch licensed the participation of blind people in nineteenth-century educational entertainments, changing their relationship to visually-oriented spaces such as museums and art galleries. I begin with a reading of an 1863 essay entitled "How A Blind Man saw the International Exhibition," an account of an anonymous blind author's experiences at London's 1862 Exhibition. I turn next to blind people's experiences as both users and curators of museum collections designed to be examined by touch. I close by taking up a recently exhibited and understudied artifact of the material culture of blindness: a tactile message pinpricked on the page of a raised-print textbook by an anonymous maker. By using the history of blind people's experiences of exhibitions to better understand a twenty-first-century exhibition of the material culture of blindness, I hope to demonstrate the importance of the sense of touch not only to the history of blind people's literacy but also to its ongoing study.

As a sighted person, I am conscious of my privilege in being able to work in ocularcentric spaces such as academic libraries and archives. I also recognize the role that sight has played in my ability to access many resources and records that were invaluable to this project, including records that make extensive use of visual images. Guided by the work of, among others, Georgina Kleege and Scott Wallin, I try to make visual material I have referenced and discuss in the chapters that follow accessible to all readers by offering detailed descriptions either in captions or, more often, as part of my analysis. More generally, I hope with both the methods and messages of this book to be an ally to visually-disabled people and to challenge, rather than affirm, ableist ways of thinking about blindness, both past and present-day.

While the history of reading by touch matters to our knowledge of the nineteenth century, it also matters to our present moment. Two centuries ago, reading by touch became possible because of changes to practices as ingrained as placing ink on paper to create a book. Today, the nineteenth-century proliferation of raised-print scripts has its equivalent in the proliferation of digital accessibility tools. While developments in refreshable braille signal the endurance of societal investment in reading by touch, screen reading tools play an increasingly central role in blind people's lives. As blind people actively assess the benefits and costs of the digitization of their reading lives, the value of reading by touch is debated anew. Whether accessed with a screen reader or as ink on paper, this book is an invitation to readers to actively support print-disabled people's right to read. Having explored the history of blind people's literacy, we will be better positioned to navigate, and shape, its future.

One

Reading in the Street

In 1874, a Londoner named William Hawkes was arrested for reading a raised-print Bible on Waterloo Bridge. Hawkes was a street reader, a blind person who made his living by reading aloud in public spaces. The *Morning Standard*, who reported on his arrest under the headline "A Case for Commiseration," described Hawkes as "a blind man, and very infirm" ("Case"). The newspaper explained that a witness, Montagu Williams, had disputed the judicial system's characterization of Hawkes as "a rogue and vagabond" ("Case"). Williams testified that "he had known the prisoner for years from seeing him sitting on Waterloo-bridge, tracing his fingers over a book designed for the blind to read, and in no instance had he seen him beg from those who passed by, so that he was practically doing no harm" ("Case"). Williams's defense of Hawkes had, it seems, little effect, as Hawkes received a four-month prison sentence.

Hawkes's arrest attracted the attention of John Ruskin, the sighted social commentator and art critic. Having received a clipping of newspaper coverage of Hawkes's case from a concerned correspondent, Ruskin reproduced news of Hawkes's arrest in *Fors Clavigera*, a series of pamphlets exploring contemporary social issues. Ruskin recommended both the clipping and the strongly worded letter that accompanied it "to the reader's most serious consideration" (118). D.O. Haswell, a blind person and activist, also took note of Hawkes's case. In 1876, Haswell published an essay in which he argued that Hawkes's arrest exemplified the extent to which London's blind residents are "exposed to the most cruel persecutions" (7). Haswell asserted that, if the mistreatment of working-class blind people was better known, the facts would cause "every manly heart to throb with honest indignation" (7).

This chapter explores the history of reading by touch by focusing on street readers and their treatment, both legal and literary. Highly visible figures in nineteenth-century British cities, street readers provided many sighted people with their first opportunity to observe reading by touch. Familiar to nineteenth-century city dwellers but largely ignored by scholars of disability history, Hawkes and his fellow street readers shaped the perception of blind people in complicated ways. Reading by touch outdoors and aloud, accepting the spare change of passersby, street readers raised the sighted majority's awareness of blind people's ability to read at the same time that they advertised the failure of reading by touch to ameliorate the poverty of working-class blind people. To put this another way, street readers alerted interested observers to the fact that, whereas many blind people gained the opportunity and the ability to read in the course of the century, this development did little to solve the problems of a large portion of Britain's blind citizens, problems that included underemployment and social marginalization.

In the same way that street readers alerted their contemporaries to limits on the transformative potential of literacy in blind people's lives, their experiences alert us to limits on the ameliorative impact of the invention of raised-print books. The experiences of street readers are consequently a useful starting point for this book's exploration of the cultural significance of the nineteenth-century proliferation of reading by touch. In what follows, I draw on press reports, the writing of educators and activists, an epic poem by working-class author and blind person Edmund White, and an anonymously authored short story to explore the role of street reading in the lives of its practitioners as well as the response of commentators, blind and sighted, to this practice. I argue for the influential role that street reading played in the public perception of reading by touch and I identify street reading as a practice that brought established ideas about blindness, including the longstanding association of blindness with begging, into dialogue with an emergent recognition of blind people as literate. I demonstrate that nineteenth-century responses to street readers engaged the question of blind people's ability to perform paid work at the same time that they raised questions about blind people's ability to read, with some observers speculating that street readers were only pretending to read raised-print books. I also explore how blind people's reading of portions of raised-print Bibles on bridges and streets confirmed some commentators' perceptions of blind people as exceptionally devout. While some observers, both blind and sighted, were troubled by street readers' use of Scripture to earn a living, others perceived street readers as uniquely positioned to have a positive moral influence on their communities. This is the case for the street reader depicted in "The Poor Blind Woman" (1881), an anonymously authored short story from the *Day of Rest*. Offering a more nuanced literary portrait of blindness than its title suggests, the story depicts a street reader's contribution to not only the soundscape but the moral tenor of the nineteenth-century city. Laying a foundation for the analysis of this story's portrayal of a fictional street reader, I open the chapter with the story of a real-world reader, a blind man whose mid-nineteenth-century interview with journalist Henry Mayhew documents both his easy acquisition of literacy and the difficult nature of his work.

Mayhew's Blind Reader

The presence of blind people reading Scripture in public spaces was an early and unintended consequence of the efforts of organizations such as the London Society for Teaching the Blind to Read, whose agents provided working-class blind people with both reading lessons and raised-print publications.[1] Having learned to read at home with the help of teachers who were eager to support their students' spiritual wellbeing, some blind people went public with their new ability, this in an attempt to meet bodily rather than spiritual needs. The streets of cities like London and Glasgow were a logical location for working-class blind men and women to try to support themselves by demonstrating a skill possessed by a small minority. In the course of the 1840s, street readers joined established communities of blind people who made their living as street sellers; they also joined blind entertainers who supported themselves by playing music, reciting poetry, cutting profiles in paper and, in at least one instance, imitating animal sounds.[2] Though only a small portion of, for example, London's literate blind population participated in street reading, the presence of readers on bridges, at intersections, and in public squares made street readers visually and audibly prominent representatives of blind people's literacy. While street reading by blind people seems to have lost its novelty by the mid 1850s, blind people continued to read in public spaces throughout the second half of the nineteenth century, albeit it in steadily declining numbers. The persistence of this practice over decades suggests that the public demonstration of the pairing of literacy with visual disability was, for at least some observers, a spectacle worthy of spare change.

The era's most detailed firsthand account of this work was solicited from an anonymous street reader by Henry Mayhew for *London Labour and the London Poor* (1851–61), Mayhew's encyclopedic survey of the occupations of London's working classes. This interview is one of a series of interviews with blind street people that Mayhew conducted. Indeed, as Martha Stoddard Holmes demonstrates, *London Labour and the London Poor* reveals not only Mayhew's interest in the daily lives of London's poorest residents but also his "utter fascination with blindness" (*Fictions* 143). Like his interviews with a blind needle seller and a blind boot-lace seller, Mayhew's portrait of a street reader offers an informative, albeit mediated, account of a nineteenth-century person's lived experience of blindness.[3] Mayhew, who does not name the street reader, prefaces the interview by explaining that: "An intelligent man gave me the following account of his experience as a blind reader. He was poorly dressed, but clean, and had not a vulgar look" (3:154). Mayhew's use of the phrase "blind reader" suggests that, at mid-century, at what was still an early point in the English-speaking history of reading by touch, street readers served as representatives of all blind readers and not just of those who read in the street. Thirty-eight-years-old, a husband and a father, the street reader, who had been blind for four years at the time he spoke with Mayhew, tells Mayhew that he began to "read in public" (3:154) out of financial desperation. Having lost his job as an office clerk when he lost his ability to see, the reader struggled to support his family: "we did as well as we could, but that was very badly, until every bit of furniture (and I had a house full of good furniture up to that time) went. At last I thought I might earn a little by reading in the street" (3:154–55). A reluctant participant in a new practice, the reader, who explains that he reads on Mornington Crescent and at Euston Square, both busy areas of Camden, estimates that "[t]here are now five or six blind men about London, who read in the streets" (3:155). He tells Mayhew that he reads Frere's books, portions of the Bible embossed in a raised-print script invented by James Hatley Frere, a so-called arbitrary script that the reader learned in only four lessons.[4] Notably, the reader only comments on the reading he does in public; his interview makes no mention of a private reading life nor of finding satisfaction, pleasure, or edification in reading by touch. Instead, the keynote of his account is the extent to which reading is difficult and poorly remunerated work.

Asked about his earnings, the reader tells Mayhew that he initially did quite well: "For the first fortnight or three weeks I took from 2s. 6d. to 2s. 9d. a-day—one day I took 3s. My receipts than [sic] fell to something less than 18d. a-day, and have been gradually falling ever since" (3:155). Estimating that he makes 2s. 6d. in a typical week, he continues to have occasional windfall days: "On Whit-Monday I made 2s. 01/2d., and that, I assure you, I reckon real good holiday earnings; and I read until I was hoarse with it" (3:155). The decline in the reader's average earnings suggests that public interest in the display of reading by touch declined as the novelty of the practice faded. It is possible that it might also, or alternately, be the case that charitable feelings toward street readers, either individually or as a category, lessened in the months this reader was at work in Camden. He compares his small and diminishing income to that of his wife, who makes "3s. or 4s. a-week with her needle" (3:155). He adds that only a portion of the people who pass him give him money: "Once I counted at Mornington-crescent, as closely as I could, just out of curiosity and to wile away the time, above 2000 persons, who passed and re-passed without giving me a halfpenny" (3:155). Finding his work far from rewarding, the demoralized reader tells Mayhew: "I am tired of the streets; besides, being half-starved" (3:155).

Though he learned to read by touch with ease, the reader is a tragic embodiment of blindness and of blind people's literacy. His work is a display of an ability that is simultaneously a display of the problematically yoked experiences of disability and financial desperation. Reading by touch may have provided Mayhew's interviewee with pleasure or spiritual consolation, but these experiences do not feature in the interview. There is, it seems, nothing enriching about this man's reading life. Reading by touch secures the "half-starved" interviewee a subsistence income but his new occupation is nowhere near as remunerative as the work he performed as a sighted person. What is more, as his awareness of the hundreds of people who pass him suggests, street reading likely heightened rather than lessened the social isolation he experienced as a working-class blind person. Offering valuable context for the analysis of the public perception of street readers that follows, this rare firsthand account of a street reader's work life introduces themes of importance not only to the history of the practice of this very public form of reading but also, more generally, to nineteenth-century attitudes toward blindness and blind people. They include blind people's relationship to begging and the role of Scripture in their lives, topics that engaged but also divided nineteenth-century commentators.

Begging and Reading

Mayhew's interviewee's meagre earnings raise questions about the extent to which reading by touch in public spaces constituted, or was perceived as, begging, a practice with which blind working-class people were closely identified in the nineteenth century as they had been for centuries prior.[5] It is difficult to know whether the money that street readers received from passersby was given in recognition of their achievement of literacy, as compensation for the labor of reading aloud, or as a charitable offering prompted by pity for the readers' visual disability. Mayhew, notably, includes his interview with the blind reader in Volume 3 of *London Labour and the London Poor*, the volume dedicated to "London Street-Folk;" Mayhew thus groups street readers not with beggars but with street laborers and sellers, workers who earned, or tried to earn, a living in London's public spaces.

To return to the example of William Hawkes, the variety of responses that Hawkes appears to have inspired in observers signals a division of opinions about street reading's relationship to begging. While his 1874 arrest indicates that some observers understood street reading as a criminal form of begging, for others, such as Hawkes's defender, Montagu Williams, the equation of street reading with street begging was by no means obvious. Other accounts of this practice suggest that street readers were more likely to be patronized than persecuted by the sighted majority. Periodical press references to a man who read on Waterloo Bridge for several decades in the second half of the nineteenth century make no mention of the threat of arrest. They suggest, in fact, that Hawkes was a local celebrity, both well known and well liked. For example, Joseph Ashby-Sterry, writing for the *English Illustrated Magazine* in 1888, observed that "Most Londoners know the Old Blind Bible reader on Waterloo Bridge" (802). Nostalgic in tone, describing the street reader on the bridge as a fixture of the city for decades, Ashby-Sterry asserts that the man on the bridge "has been there for more than thirty years" (802). He wonders, "What experiences he must have had, for London has changed wondrously in the last thirty years" (802). A second example, an essay on the history of Waterloo Bridge published in *Chambers's Journal* in 1878, also references the presence of a well-known street reader. Referring to the reader on the bridge as "Old Blind George," its author explains:

> Passengers who have gone backwards and forwards over the bridge cannot have failed to notice the old blind man who sits in one of its recesses day after day, reading aloud by the aid of his fingers from an embossed Bible. He has been at his post summer and winter for about twenty years, and is much respected and esteemed by all who know him. ("Waterloo" 751)

A living landmark, this street reader was, it seems, financially supported by Londoners to the extent that he continued his work in the same location for decades. Dutifully present at his post throughout the seasons and the years, worthy of notice both in print and by passersby, this street reader is portrayed in unambiguously positive ways.

The extent to which street reading was, for some observers, not only an accepted reality of urban culture but also a respectable form of work is signalled by a report on the social circumstances and occupations of Glasgow's blind residents. The report, created by the Glasgow Mission for the Blind, shares that, in 1869, fourteen blind people in Glasgow were street beggars; these people were part of a group that the Mission labeled "Not specially occupied" ("Circumstances"). In a different section of the report, one dedicated to employed blind people, the Mission reported that four men and one woman supported themselves by "Reading on the Street" ("Circumstances"). It grouped the five readers with other blind workers in the city, including a tea merchant, a teacher, and a bell ringer. This classification was, like the mixed treatment of the blind man on Waterloo Bridge, an indication of the existence of divided opinions on the activities of street readers and, relatedly, on what constitutes begging. In contrast, the sighted journalist Richard Rowe did not hesitate to identify street readers, together with other blind street people, as beggars. In an 1881 essay titled "Pity the Poor Blind," he asserted:

> The blind street musicians, monotonous blind readers on river and canal bridges, and blind sellers of small goods in the streets, are, in a strictly logical sense blind beggars. People don't buy the goods because they want them, or pay for the reading or music, as a rule, because they like the sound; but because they pity the blind sellers, readers, and musicians. (310–11)

Reading by touch is not, Rowe insists, a legitimate way to earn money because the reading is not valued by people who put coins in a reader's hat or hand. While street reading, by featuring the demonstration of a skill, differed from more straightforward forms of begging associated with blind people, for Rowe, it functioned the same way. Street readers did not rely on the repetition of formulaic phrases such as "Alms for the Blind" and "Pity the Poor Blind" to appeal to the public but, in Rowe's assessment, reading Scripture had the same effect. Reading by touch on a street or bridge, a blind person advertised the fact of his or her blindness in order to generate pity and prompt charitable giving.

Andrew Halliday, a sighted collaborator of Henry Mayhew, reached a similar conclusion about street readers but Halliday had, it seems, both more respect for their work and more sympathy for their circumstances. In the fourth volume of *London Labour and the London Poor*, published in 1861, Halliday wrote about a subgroup of street people he labelled "Bodily Afflicted Beggars." Troubled by the different "dodges" of London's beggars, many of whom, he asserted, misrepresented themselves by pretending to be disabled veterans, survivors of tragic accidents, or congenitally disabled people, Halliday supports the work done to expose deceptive beggars by London's Mendicity Society. Many contempories of Halliday were critical of the work of this charity, whose mandate was to end street begging by providing people in need with alternate forms of support.[6] Its critics included Haswell, the blind activist who objected to Hawkes's arrest. Whereas Haswell argued that the Society harassed working-class blind people instead of supporting them, Halliday understands the Society as a force for good. He explains, "The officers of the Mendicity Society have cleared the streets of nearly all the impostors, and the few who remain are blind men and cripples" (Mayhew 4:431). Halliday gives special attention to the street readers in this group who, having been deemed legitimately disabled, are allowed to continue their work in the streets:

> Many of the blind men are under the protection of a Society, which furnishes them with books printed in raised type which they decipher by the touch. Others provide their own books, and are allowed to sit on door steps or in the recesses of the bridges without molestation from the police. (Mayhew 4:431)

Referring here to a Society other than the Mendicity Society, likely a home visiting society such as the London Society for Teaching the Blind to Read, Halliday portrays street readers as an exceptional subset of street people. In a culture of begging that Halliday understands as newly cleansed of dishonest claimants, street readers are legitimate participants, tolerated by the police and deserving of the charity they receive. As Halliday explains, "It has been found on inquiry that these afflicted persons are really what they appear to be—poor, helpless, blind creatures, who are totally incapacitated from earning a living" (Mayhew 4:431). Of course, Halliday's belief that blind people, including literate blind people, are unable to perform conventional forms of paid work shapes both his perception and depiction of street readers. For Halliday, street reading is a legitimate form of begging because it is practiced by people whose blindness makes them, in his assessment, wholly dependent on charity. That reading aloud in the street could be prosecuted as mendicancy, characterized as work, or, in the case of Halliday, deemed a justifiable form of begging is a measure not only of the diversity of opinions about street readers but also of the tenacity of ideas about blindness, including the identification of blindness with ineptitude, that limited blind people's access to paid employment.

Halliday's depiction of street readers demonstrates that attitudes toward street readers, like nineteenth-century attitudes toward blindness and blind people more generally, were neither homogenous nor static. Halliday's comments also remind us that, for many sighted city dwellers, street readers were the public face of reading by touch. Of course, while Halliday's portrait of street readers offers insight into the relationship between, on the one hand, blind people's literacy and, on the other hand, their financial desperation and social marginalization, it is perhaps Mayhew's interviewee's description of himself as "tired of the streets; besides, being half-starved" (Mayhew 3:155) that most effectively signals the need for histories of reading by touch to acknowledge the experiences of readers who gained little from their new skill. The ability to read is, for good reason, associated with a sense of achievement, with social integration, and with pleasure. We might be predisposed by these associations to understand reading by touch as an uncomplicated boon to blind people. Yet the ability to read brought, it seems, none of those benefits to Mayhew's street reader. Knowledge of blind people's newly acquired literacy did not prevent Halliday from identifying blind readers as "poor, helpless, blind creatures, who are totally incapacitated from earning a living" (Mayhew 4:431). The proliferation of the skill of reading by touch was not, at least in the case of its most public practitioners, a development with the power to undermine the identification of blindness with both ineptitude and dependency.

"Better known to memory than to touch"

Suspicion of blind people, which can include suspicion of the claim to being blind, shaped the reception of street readers and, by extension, the reception of blind people's literacy. While Halliday is reassured that street readers "are really what they appear to be" (Mayhew 4:431), some observers doubted the legitimacy of street readers' claim to literacy. Take, for example, Alexander Brown, a sighted publisher and author who wrote under the penname "Shadow." Brown, who encountered a blind man reading on Glasgow Green in the 1850s, explains how:

> a poor blind man, dressed in homely fustian, claims our attention. He is seated upon the ground, reading aloud a portion of the Bible, from a book with raised letters for the blind. We are surprised by the apparent ease with which he manipulates. On close examination, however, we have suspicion that the tongue is greatly more nimble than the fingers, or that the Word is better known to memory than to touch. Accept-

> ing this exhibition, however, even as evidence of the tiring monotony of the poor blind man's work, we cannot fail to be deeply touched by it. (82)

Brown's observation of the street reader produces a mixed response, his feelings about the man shifting quickly from surprise to suspicion to sympathy. Doubting the blind man's skill as a reader of raised print, using the verb "manipulates" to refer to the reading of a book by touch, Brown suspects that the demonstration he witnesses is a demonstration of recitation from memory, not of reading. Though Brown does not specify if he is "deeply touched" by feelings of admiration or pity, his use of the phrase "poor blind man" strongly suggests the latter. Notably, for Brown, even pretending to read by touch seems laborious and worthy of the label "work" (82).

Brown was not alone in raising the possibility that street readers were not really reading. Indeed, the suggestion that street readers might be frauds features prominently in the commentary of two groups: middle-class blind people and sighted educators of blind people, both of whom opposed this practice. Invested in the respectability of reading by touch, both groups were troubled by how the highly public nature of this kind of reading tarnished the reputation of blind people who had no connection to street culture. For W.W. Fenn, an essayist and fiction writer who became blind in adulthood, street readers were beggars who misrepresented blind people's achievements and potential. In an 1885 essay titled "What Touch Does for the Blind," Fenn dismissed street readers as false representatives of the blind community. An educated person and a member of the middle class, Fenn laments the presence of blind beggars in British cities:

> Now as we must not judge of the characters and industrial capacities of the blind generally by the prowling, stick-tapping vagabonds about our streets, any more than we should of the rest of mankind by other mendicants, so we must not suppose that a fair example of their ability in reading an embossed Bible is afforded by the blind squatters here and there dotted about our pavements. (44)

No better than the "vagabonds" who circulate through the city, street readers are, for Fenn, "blind squatters," a label that proposes their presence in public space is as unlawful as it is unwelcome. Suggesting street readers are unskilled at reading by touch, Fenn, a blind person who made his living writing for sighted readers, both feels and promotes suspicion about the morality of street readers. Of the community of blind readers at work in his city, Fenn proposes: "Many of these, in all probability, have learned the passages by heart, and slip them trippingly off the tongue, as they would any other set, well-conned, high-sounding phrases" (44). Eager to distance street readers from "the blind generally," Fenn proposes that street readers are guilty of "pretending to fumble out with their fingers the Psalms or the Gospel according to St. John" (44). For Fenn, street readers pretend to be able to read by touch just as they also pretend to "fumble," playing up the difficulty of a skill that they do not, in truth, possess. To distinguish between legitimate and false displays of reading by touch, sighted people should, Fenn suggests, visit classrooms where blind students learn to read, spaces where, he asserts, neither fumbling nor spare change have a role.

B.G. Johns, a sighted educator of blind students, shared both Fenn's suspicions and his desire to distance street reading from a normative, non-commodified version of reading by touch. In his 1867 book *Blind People: Their Works and Ways*, Johns described the representative street reader as a man who:

> professes to be reading, in a loud, strong voice, some page of St. Paul, in Frere's system. Whether he *is* reading it or not is entirely another question. At all events, he has learned a good many pages by heart most correctly; and so reads on glibly enough in all weathers, rain, east wind, or snow, when the finger of an unprofessional blind boy would be utterly disabled. (84)

Like Fenn, Johns's suggestion that street readers are not really reading helps him to differentiate street readers from blind people who read under different conditions and for different reasons than a blind person standing on a street corner with a book. Johns's portrait of a street reader at work "in all weathers," in conditions which, Johns asserts, would disable the finger of an "unprofessional" reader, develops a contrast between a hypothetical amateur, "an unprofessional blind boy," and his counterpart, who reads for money on the street. Interested in where blind people read but also in why they read, Johns promotes a normative model of reading by touch, one that is not commodified and that does not expose the reader to weather and blind people to public derision. Troubled by the association of blind people's literary with poverty and dependence on charity, assigning public reading to a group of people they identify as having questionable reading skills and even more questionable morals, Johns and fellow critics of street readers work to distance street reading from the private reading of a blind majority.

An especially harsh assessment of both the literacy and the morality of street readers was shared by W.H. Levy, a blind person, author, and activist. Levy shared his thoughts on street reading in an encyclopedic study of blindness published in 1872. In it, he identifies reading by touch in the streets not as the sole or even the primary activity of blind beggars but instead as just one of a set of unethical activities blind beggars rotate between. For Levy, street reading is more than a false performance of literacy; it is, he claims, a performance of a false self:

> The most profitable qualification for a beggar is a faculty of lying, for it enables him to obtain donations with ease from persons of opposite characters. By day he can read the Scriptures, in the streets, and profess himself a thoroughly converted man, while at night he may play the violin, and sing immoral songs to extract pence and drink from company of the most abandoned kind. (469)

Regarding blind beggars, Levy adds: "the more hardened [. . .] generally settle at length in a large town, open lodging-houses for tramps, play, sing, and read the Bible from one public-house to another, and not a few become keepers of houses for abandoned women" (469–70). It is a surprising portrait of a community for whom Bible reading and brothel management are proximate occupations. Though deeply sympathetic to the plight of working-class blind people, to whose aid he devoted his career, Levy does not hesitate to vilify street readers.

Faith played a role in Levy's assessment, as it did also in other critics' responses. Making repeated mention of the role of the Bible in street readers' work, Levy is clearly troubled by the way in which reading Scripture misrepresents street readers as pious people who are "thoroughly converted" to the Christian faith. As we will learn, the relationship street readers had to Scripture registered very differently with the poet Edmund White, a working-class man whose Christian belief and experiences of both acquired blindness and poverty shaped his perception of street readers as well as his poetry.

"Nothing but the Scriptures"

Though a defining aspect of their work, the reading aloud of Scripture, instead of another genre of writing, was not a choice street readers made. Regarding his work in the streets, Mayhew's interviewee explained, "We can read nothing but the Scriptures, as 'blind printing'—so it's sometimes called—has only been used in the Scriptures" (3:154). By the early 1850s, raised print had, in fact, been used to publish a wide range of titles but it was highly unlikely that a working-class blind person, living in poverty, would have access to raised-print poetry collections or science manuals. Raised-print materials were costly and street readers, like other working-class blind people, relied on charitable organizations or generous individuals to supply the materials they read. The goal of many donors was the religious indoctrination of blind people and, indeed, the same might be said of Victorian culture's investment in blind people's literacy writ large. Not unlike nineteenth-century efforts to increase literacy rates among sighted people, investment in reading by touch was energized by a desire for as many people as possible to read and study the Bible. In the case of Mayhew's interviewee, the two raised-print books he reads, one containing the Gospel of St. John and the other the Gospel of St. Luke, were gifted to him, one by the Society for the Indigent Blind and the other by his brother-in-law. Limited to reading Scripture, the street reader's work is distinct from that of other street performers, such as blind musicians, in that the reader's work is linked to spiritual edification instead of entertainment. The nature of the text he reads makes his reading not only a demonstration of his own religious belief but also a prompt to piousness in passersby. Notably, Mayhew's interviewee, in addition to reading from the Bible, writes out passages of Scripture that he hands to passersby. "I believe," he tells Mayhew, "I am the only blind man who writes in the streets" (3:154). This activity extends his circulation of Christian messages in the space of the city from oral performance to textual record.

Clearly, as Levy's comments on street readers indicate, an association with Scripture did not exempt street readers from either suspicion or censure. Whereas some critics, like Levy, believed that street readers misrepresented themselves as devout, others objected to the reading of Scripture for financial gain and even to the style in which street readers read sacred text. The activist, doctor, and blind person Thomas Armitage gave a speech in Paris in 1878 in which he complained that blind people "sit in the streets, reading the Bible in a loud voice, to attract the sympathy of passers-by" (*On the Means* 10). In a different context, Armitage suggested that the typical street reader begins to read in "a loud voice as soon as he hears a footstep approaching" (*The Education* 59). Similarly troubled by street readers' demeanour, the sighted commentator Rowe characterized the reading performed by street readers as "monotonous" (310); the blind author Fenn worried that the Psalms and the Gospels "slip . . . trippingly" from the readers' mouths ("What Touch Does" 44); and, sighted educator Johns used the word "glibly" (*Blind People* 84) to describe a street reader's irreverent style. Only attentive to their books of

Scripture in the presence of an audience, boisterous and glib in their reading of the Bible, street readers have, their critics proposed, an improper relationship to sacred text. Both their reading material and their manner of reading scrutinized, street readers' presence in public spaces placed their work at the center of conversations about blind people's literacy as well as their spirituality, a small group of very public readers standing in for a diverse and growing community of people who read books by touch.

Whereas Fenn, Armitage, and Levy were blind people who objected to the ways in which street readers misrepresented, in their assessment, the achievements and potential of blind people, Edmund White, a person who had, like Mayhew's interviewee, lost his job when he lost his ability to see, identified quite closely with street readers. Feeling empathy for readers and hoping to promote public sympathy for them, White not only commented on street reading but composed poetry about it. Deepening our knowledge of blind Victorian authors' attitudes toward this practice, White's writing is of interest not only for what it says about this much-debated practice but also for what it shares about his own experience of acquired blindness.[7]

White began to write and publish poetry when he lost his job as a railway guard in midlife. Inspired by the example of John Milton, White authored long poems, which he, like Milton, dictated to his daughters. His 1856 poem *Blindness; A Discursive Poem in Five Cantos*, which White published by subscription, combines memoir, biblical narrative, allegory, and social critique in a generically complex exploration of White's experience of acquired blindness. Written in rhyming couplets, the poem, which is over one hundred pages in length, is supplemented by several pages of endnotes that detail, among other things, the role that a violent workplace accident played in White's loss of the ability to see. White had, he explains, intervened when a passenger attempted to board a moving train; as White looked on, the passenger fell on the tracks and was killed. White experienced a short period of blindness immediately following the accident; his blindness became permanent several months later. As White explains in both his poem and its endnotes, he applied to his former employer, the Great Western Railway Company, asking, unsuccessfully, for financial help. He also wrote letters to wealthy individuals but was refused.

Like his understanding of the cause of his blindness, White's poem is both compelling and unconventional. Consider, for example, the fact that *Blindness* explores White's experiences of acquired blindness by re-telling the story of Adam and Eve. Though structured by biblical narrative and populated by Britannia, Caledonia, and Hibernia, among other personifications of nations, White's poem makes space to explore lived experiences of blindness, including the experiences of street readers. Finding common ground with street readers, White argues that their poverty and social marginalization are, like his own experiences of job loss and mistreatment, cause for national shame. While he regrets the presence of blind readers in public spaces, he develops a thoroughly compassionate portrait of them. According to White:

> . . . our towns and cities [are] all dispread
> With poor blind mendicants, whose daily bread,
> The dole of charity at times supplies;
> At others, all unheeded are their sighs.
> Hence, in our streets we hear the blind men read
> The Sacred Scriptures for their daily bread. (5.239–44)

For White, it is precisely the ability of street readers to embody and publicize the poverty of working-class blind people that makes them worthy subjects for poetic representation. White does not object to street readers' solicitation of money; instead, he objects to the fact that the money they receive from the sighted majority is insufficient to their needs. His poem calls for increased generosity toward working-class people with acquired blindness, a group whose experiences of financial distress and unemployment he shared. The presence of street readers in a city is, he argues, a measure of the inadequacy, as well as the unpredictable delivery, of limited financial support for working-class blind people. To make this case, White engages the sound of the readers at work but, notably, his depiction of street readers is written in the voice of a sighted observer. White describes, for example, the gestures of street readers as they call out to sighted people who pass them:

> [. . .] we behold them turn their sightless eye
> Up from their books, and to each passer by,
> Exclaim in doleful accents, friends, I read,
> By sense of touch or feeling, strange, indeed. (5.245–48)

The turning of a "sightless eye" upward, a gesture of supplication, is emblematic for White of street readers' piety as well as their financial desperation. In this exchange, in which readers invite sighted people to observe them, the readers' posture, their faces turned away from their books' surface, advertises their sensory difference from their sighted observers. In White's poem, the sighted passersby agree that reading by "touch or feeling" is "strange, indeed" but they are not moved to assist street readers when they ask for help:

> 'Tis very strange, remarks some looker on,
> While others nod assent, and one by one,
> They leave the blind man in this hapless state
> Of poverty: a sad disastrous fate. (5.249–52)

For White, the shame associated with the neglect of street readers is heightened by the fact that street readers bring to the space of the city both the stories of the Bible and its "glowing language" (5.257). Though inadequately compensated by sighted observers, street readers continue to share Christian messages:

> Still they read on, and in a loud clear voice,
> Tell how Our Heavenly Father doth rejoice,
> Over one sinner that repenteth, more
> Than ninety-nine, who never err'd, or pour
> In glowing language forth, the precious streams
> Of mercy, that poor sinful man redeems,
> And from his fallen state, to realms of bliss,
> Calls him away. Oh, what a scene is this. (5.253–60)

White concludes his portrait of this mistreated group with a reflection on society's failure to fulfill its Christian duty of charity. Street readers are clearly, in White's opinion, figures of ability and resilience. Modern-day martyrs, they share the word of God but they suffer for it. For these reasons, White embraces the street readers' potential to represent working-class blind people. Offering an assessment that differs from that of other blind commentators both in tenor and genre, White's long poem shares a blind working-class person's understanding of reading by touch in public spaces as an ethical albeit ineffectual way to appeal for charity. As the next section explores, White's recognition of blind readers as subjects with literary potential was shared by at least one other writer, the anonymous author of an 1881 short story whose portrait of a blind reader reached a much wider audience than White's poem did.

The Street Reader as Ideal

Both the public and the private life of a street reader are explored in an anonymously authored short story published in *Day of Rest*, a monthly magazine. Titled "The Poor Blind Woman," the story was the first in a set of twelve anonymously authored sketches of ideal human beings commissioned by the magazine. Appearing in January 1881, it was prefaced by a note from the editors explaining that all twelve stories would be written by "Eminent Authors" but that the authors' names would be withheld. The idea was, the editors explained, to "[allow] the reader to settle for himself which among the characters represents the ideal of Charles Reade, of Mrs. Oliphant, of Anthony Trollope, of George MacDonald, or of the others" (51). While the identity of its author remains unknown, there can be no debate about the richness of this story's contribution to conversations about the legitimacy of street readers' work. Taking a blind woman and street reader named Matty as its central figure, the story is noteworthy not only for its compelling assertion of the social value of Matty's work but also for the way it moves beyond the public space of the street to consider her domestic life.

The story is narrated by an unnamed middle-class man whose route to and from work in London includes the bridge where Matty, whose full name is Martha Anson, reads. Consistent with the account of people passing Mayhew's interviewee, the narrator passes Matty twice a day for several years before he begins to notice her but, once aware of her, he is intrigued by her. The story begins with a portrait of Matty, a sentence fragment whose grammatical structure signals the limited nature of the narrator's knowledge of her: "A single human figure, poorly-clad, elderly, blind, always keeping one attitude,—the sitting posture,—and beheld ever in the same spot, under the sheltering wall of a railway bridge" (51). Confessing himself "fascinated" by this woman's life, he wonders if his readers will be as interested in the life of "a blind woman begging in a London street" (51) as he is. Developing his portrait of Matty, he draws attention to both her posture and the book she holds; she sits, he explains, "with uncomfortable squareness against the massively-riveted iron wall, while in her lap unfailingly lay open the finger-worn pages of an embossed-printed Bible" (51). Very closely echoing descriptions of real-world street readers shared above, the narrator notes that "[s]he had taken up this post summer and winter, in all weathers, for so many years that to the eyes of the habitual users of the thoroughfare Matty had become a part of the bridge itself" (51). He also describes her as reading in a "monotonous, sing-song drone" (52) and explains that at night, when darkness makes it difficult for sighted people to see her and, similarly, for sighted people to read printed text, she can still be heard, "her loud strong voice reading on, all unhindered by the half-concealing dimness" (51).

Interested in her ability to read without light, the narrator takes careful note of the movement of her fingers and hands. He describes, for example, watching Matty "[p]ushing her finger-tips over line-after-line of the raised letters" (52), her touch changing the surface of raised-print pages he describes as "finger-worn" (51). The narrator, who watches Matty closely as she reads, seems equally fascinated by her actions when she pauses in her work. Passing her one morning, he notices how:

> She was not reading at this moment, although her fingers still lay on the raised letters where she had just stopped. You not infrequently came upon her in this arrested condition. The reading machinery, well-habituated as it was by years of practice, now-and-again abruptly ceased, and remained perfectly quiet for a time. (52)

Her lack of movement prompts the narrator to think of Matty as a stalled machine and, equally evocatively, as a piece of statuary, specifically as an "effigy" (53). He explains, "she had the aspect of a piece of cleanly-chiselled sculpture—though the material was bronzed flesh, not stone" (53). His tendency to equate Matty with non-living things dehumanizes her at the same time that it identifies her with the bridge on which she sits. The narrator's interest in her dates to a morning when he watched Matty move temporarily to a different spot on the bridge so that the men who maintain it can paint over what they call Matty's "portrait": "a patch of less faded colour on the iron rivet-headed wall, showing unmistakably a kind of caricature-outline of the blind woman's thick waist, square shoulders, and large bonnet" (52). Prompted by this scene to develop an understanding of Matty that goes beyond a "caricature-outline," the narrator decides to make a "keener observation of blind Matty," a phrase that reveals the extent to which his interest in Matty is shaped by her blindness (52). In time, he becomes so interested in Matty's life that he visits the bridge just to see and hear her: "Again-and-again I left my house in the evening, and went back to the bridge to get another glimpse of her, and to catch the words she might be uttering" (56). As the narrator explains, "Matty haunted me" (56).

The narrator tries to make sense of his fascination with Matty by developing a metaphor of the city of London as theater and casting Matty as a performer in it. For the narrator, the drama of Matty's disability gains piquancy from her poverty: "A fellow-being, with two square feet of space for a stage, and an ever-passing London crowd to serve as a chorus, I found could give the spectacle of a human drama, when a fight of duty is being actually waged from day to day under the pressure of hard circumstances" (51). While interested in her poverty, Matty's perceptual life is the focus of the narrator's attention. He brings a series of conventional beliefs about blindness to his observation of Matty, explaining, for example, that he "had read and heard of the sharpening of the other bodily faculties in those persons who had lost any of them" (52). He wonders especially about Matty's perception of the city. He doubts that she can understand the "wonderful daily panorama of metropolitan life ceaselessly passing before her darkened eyes" (52). Here and elsewhere, his choice of metaphors is a measure of his investment in visual perception. Though he thinks almost obsessively about the experience of blindness, he struggles to understand it: "I tried to imagine what a blind person's conceptions of the scene, so near to them and yet so veiled from them, might be. [. . .] But, fancy as I might, Matty's world remained black and nearly quite vacant to me" (52). Importantly, as the story progresses and the narrator becomes friends with Matty, he refines his understanding of her perceptual life. In time, he also reconsiders assumptions he made about the social isolation he assumes Matty experiences as a result of her blindness. He foreshadows the revision of his erroneous understandings of both blindness and blind people very early in the story when he notes, "[b]y-and-by, I discovered that Matty was not the wholly passive personage I then pictured her as being" (52). Using an evolving portrait of a street reader to map the evolution of a sighted person's conception of blindness, the story engages widely held ideas about blind people's lives as tragically limited in order to challenge those ideas.

Matty's fulfillment of her role as the story's ideal has a great deal to do with her reading of the Bible. Hearing Scripture read aloud by Matty complicates the narrator's experience of London and his sense of time and place. When, for example, Matty reads aloud about Bethlehem, the narrator feels disoriented: "the strangeness was fully with me, as I hastened on, of that fragment of Syrian history being called out in a noisy London crowd nineteen centuries afterwards" (52). Whereas the narrator is disoriented by Matty's reading, other passersby are disturbed by the choices she makes, specifically by Matty's decision to use Scripture to speak very pointedly and directly to their individual circumstances. Matty, the narrator realizes, has detailed knowledge not only of Scripture but of the moral failings of her fellow city-dwellers. A clergyman, who has, like the narrator, closely observed Matty over the course of months, asks the narrator: "Did you ever hear her launching what she calls her 'arrows in the dark'?" (55). The clergyman uses the phrase to refer to instances when Matty suddenly recites Scripture from memory, this regardless of the raised-print text that happens to be beneath her fingers when people pass. The clergyman gives as an example a time when a judge crossed the bridge on horseback on his way to court. He explains how Matty

> checked herself in reading from a chapter in the Revelation, and just as he was passing on her side of the road, she uttered the words, 'With what judgment ye mete, it shall be meted to you again.' The arrow hit, for the Judge so tightly pulled the rein that his horse reared. (55)

Whereas critics of street readers whose opinions were explored earlier in this chapter insinuated that street readers recited biblical passages because they lacked the skills needed to read by touch, this story portrays Matty's break from the raised-print page on her lap as not only deliberate but admirable. Interested specifically in "the curious way in which she is, as it seems to me, made use of in scattering the Scripture abroad" (55), the clergyman is, like the story's narrator, a sighted, middle-class man who finds himself fascinated by Matty and, more narrowly, by the possibility that her work has divine purpose.

It isn't long before the narrator witnesses Matty shooting "arrows in the dark" and is obliged to recognize her as a person with deep knowledge both of Scripture and of the people who pass by her. When a banker crosses her bridge, Matty pauses in her reading to recite a verse about the hoarding of wealth. The narrator is also present when Matty recites a biblical passage about a woman's sexual immorality, this as a sex worker and her client pass. Matty's identification of the moral weaknesses of the people who cross her bridge prompts the narrator to re-imagine Matty as a kind of blind seer, the moral conscience of the city's inhabitants. He explains: "I felt a kind of awe as I looked on the dark, rusty-clad figure, thinking of those strange warnings it could wake up and utter as it were oracularly" (55). Evoking a conventional perception of blind people as clairvoyant, the narrator's use of "it" to describe the body of Matty, a body that inspires awe, clearly dehumanizes her. It's worth noting that the narrator's awe verges on fear. At an early point in his observation of Matty, the narrator realizes he is, in fact, being closely observed by her. Noticing that he has paused on the bridge, Matty addresses him as "Sir" and asks if he has lost something, offering to help him find it with her sensitive sense of touch. He fails to answer her and, when she senses that he is not, in fact, stooping in search of some lost item, she resumes her reading, "pushing her fingers along the lines" (53). Both her observation of him and her offer of assistance trouble the narrator. He explains,

> I felt as if somehow Matty's blind eyes wrapped me in a keen, all-revealing illumination, in which, as I stood, I was suddenly being

> observed behind and before and on all sides together. She had somehow divined my sex, my exact spot of standing, my very attitude. (53)

A close observer of a blind person who discovers that he is, in turn, observed by her, the narrator is too surprised to speak. After placing a penny in her hand, an act that arguably serves to counter her offer to help him by asserting his position as the more able figure, he ends their unexpected and unsettling exchange by walking away from her "at a brisker pace than usual" (53).

This challenge to the narrator's perception of blind people as unaware or unobservant is just one in a series of challenges Matty presents to his conception of blindness. His perception of blind city dwellers as socially isolated is another idea that he abandons as he gets to know Matty better. He comes to a fuller appreciation of both her connection to other members of the community and her awareness of her surroundings when he watches her greet a policeman and a nurse-girl, both of whom she recognizes by the sound of their footsteps. Revising his bleak perception of her perceptual life, he concedes: "It was plain that inside Matty's head, behind the darkened eyes, there was a world somehow corresponding to the outer one" (54). His newfound awareness of Matty's "inner world" (54) prompts him to think differently about the value of sight. He proposes that, for example, "her quick ears in not a few matters were worth more than other persons' eyes" (54). He goes so far as to suggest the sighted people who move freely about the city do "not know so much of what happened about them as Matty who sat on fixedly upon the bridge from morning to night" (54). Spending time with Matty, the narrator learns to think differently about not just blindness but sightedness. While reading by touch is the activity that initiates the narrator's interest in Matty, the narrator's contemplation of Matty engages aspects of the daily lives of blind people wholly unrelated to reading by touch.

The narrator's understanding of blindness and blind people continues to evolve, for example, as he learns about Matty's role as a giver, rather than a recipient, of charity. He witnesses Matty sharing her earnings with a sighted watercress-seller named Brisket, a man who is "deformed in his shoulders, as well as being crippled in one leg" (53). He also learns that Matty is a caregiver who nurses and houses people in her home. When he visits that home for the first time, the narrator discovers that Matty is sheltering a dying woman: the sex worker who passed her on the bridge months earlier. The narrator learns even more about Matty from the clergyman, who shares details of her past. He tells the narrator that Matty became blind from smallpox soon after her marriage and that she became a street reader when her husband died, explaining that she went "into an Institution, and there was taught to read the raised letter; then she came out, and had ever since sat daily upon the bridge" (55). Earning her status as the story's ideal, Matty does more than support herself; she is a positive influence in the lives of people in a wide range of social positions, from banker to beggar.

When Matty is missing from the bridge one morning, the narrator visits her home. He learns that she has died and he views her body, which has been prepared for burial. He notices that her raised-print Bible is lying open beside her bed. The narrator observes, as he stands beside Matty's body, that: "A chair was near, on which was the embossed Bible, open from her last reading in it. There was a specially worn passage on the left-hand page, and we found it was the text: 'In Thy light shall we see light'" (58). Matty, who read by touch for money on the streets, also read by touch in private and for her own spiritual edification. Indeed, reading by touch seems to have been her final act. Adding to a dense web of commentary about the reading of Scripture by blind people for money in public spaces, the story imagines the highly public and commodified activity of street reading as complemented by, and perhaps also expunged by, a blind person's private and devout reading practice.

While "The Poor Blind Woman" maps the evolution of a sighted person's opinions about a blind person and casts a street reader as a positive social force, its author's depiction of a sighted person's growing knowledge of a blind person reveals some noteworthy gaps in knowledge, specifically in the anonymous author's knowledge of the material realities of raised-print culture. These gaps suggest that the story's author had, at best, very limited contact with members of the blind community. For example, the suggestion that a raised-print Bible could exist as a single volume, kept at Matty's bedside on a chair, signals the author's lack of familiarity with blind people's books. The author of the story is unaware, it seems, of just how large a raised-print version of the complete Bible would be. As noted in the Introduction, because of the thickness of the paper required for embossing, the texture of raised print, and the size of tactile scripts, a raised-print edition of the Bible could not be contained in a single volume. Indeed, most nineteenth-century editions of raised-print bibles consisted of between fifteen and twenty bulky volumes. That was the case for the first complete version of a raised-print Bible printed in English. Published in 1840, the work of the sighted printer and educator John Alston in 1840, its raised-print Old Testament consisted of fifteen volumes. The New Testament was published in an additional set of four volumes, for a total of nineteen large books.[8] The author of "The Poor Blind Woman" mistakenly assumes that Matty has access to the whole of the

Bible in a single volume that she can carry to the bridge and home again. The story makes no mention of the costly and bulky set of books that Matty would have needed in order to access the whole of the Bible in her home, a collection that a person living in poverty could only dream of owning.

A second example of the author's limited knowledge of blind people's books is the narrator's reference to a "specially worn passage on the left-hand page" (58) of Matty's open Bible. Referring to a left-hand page, the author reveals their conflation of the design of books for blind people with the design of books read by sighted people. The vast majority of the books made for blind readers in nineteenth-century Britain were printed only on the right-hand side of the open folio as, historically, raised-print text was embossed on only one side of each sheet of paper. This was especially the case for books that could be read by a sighted person with no special training, a person like the narrator. This reality would change in time with the late-century popularization of braille and of interlining, a practice which allowed braille text to be embossed on both sides of a sheet of paper. But in the case of a book that used a Latin (or Roman) script, which is the case for Matty's book, a left-hand page in raised-print would only exist if the reverse sides of two sheets of raised print had been glued together to create a page that more closely resembled the pages of the books of sighted people, an undertaking that added significantly to the cost and bulk of a book with no practical benefit to the blind reader.

Interested in, but not knowledgeable about, the material realities of blind people's books, the author of this story is not unlike its narrator: fascinated by blindness and blind people but limited in his or her understanding of the realities of blind people's reading lives. Assuming that books for blind people were inkless, textured versions of books for sighted people—that, for example, a book propped on a blind person's lap could contain the whole of the Bible—the author of this story writes at a distance from blind people and the raised-print culture they created. It seems that this author had watched a street reader at work but had not gone so far as to talk with a blind person about their books. Of course, what matters most about Matty's book of raised-print Scripture for this author is that the book is open beside her bed. The facts of blind print culture are less important than the goal of establishing Matty as an ideal: as a person who both read the Bible in the streets to improve other people's lives and read it at home for her own spiritual consolation, even in her final hours.

Fascinated by reading by touch but limited in its knowledge of blind people's books, this story documents sighted culture's interest in raised-print books as well as the sometimes limited nature of sighted people's knowledge of these books. Imagining a sighted narrator's gradual penetration of a public figure's private life, this story does more than complicate widely held perceptions of street readers as a problematic if not immoral presence in the nineteenth-century city. Using a portrait of a street reader to both ask and answer questions about the social, perceptual, and religious lives of blind people, "The Poor Blind Woman" is, as upcoming chapters will demonstrate, just one example of how nineteenth-century authors relied on depictions of reading by touch to imagine, and re-imagine, blindness.

Looking at Street Reading

Like many stories about blind people published in nineteenth-century magazines, "The Poor Blind Woman" was illustrated (fig. 5).[9] Not unlike its letterpress, its sole illustration documents both realities of street readers' lives and sighted creators' attitudes toward this subgroup of working-class blind people. The engraving positions Matty, a middle-aged woman dressed in a dark cloak and bonnet, seated on the bridge, with her back against its guardrail. Her left hand is touching the left-side page of the open book on her lap; her right hand rests on the shoulder of a young boy huddled beside her. The boy, referred to in the caption as a "dirty urchin," is identified in the letterpress as Diver. He looks in the direction of a policeman who approaches them. The story's narrator explains that Matty will convince the policeman to let Diver stay with her and "earn a penny honestly" (56). The image, which depicts Matty's hands prominently, positions her so that she faces straight ahead, toward the center of the bridge. Unlike Diver, whose highly expressive posture clearly indicates that the policeman is the subject of his thoughts, Matty does not have a communicative posture. She does not turn her face toward the boy she touches nor toward the policeman who approaches them. Instead of using her book, whose pages are not visibly textured, to signal Matty's blindness, the illustrator uses Matty's body, both her rigid posture and her expressionless face, to represent blindness.

Other visual records of street reading in nineteenth-century cities are similar in their investment in the body of a blind person and their comparative lack of engagement with material features of the raised-print book they read. An engraving of a drawing by W.D. Almond of the reader on Waterloo Bridge, from the 1888 issue of *The London Illustrated Magazine* quoted above, shows a man wearing a heavy coat and a hat, a large placard reading "BLIND" hanging from his neck (fig. 6). He sits in a stone recess, his feet on

Figure 5. "The dirty urchin was crouching at the side of her stiff, upright form." Illustration to "The Poor Blind Woman" (1881). Author's collection.

a small wooden stool. The book from which he reads is open on his lap but its edges are covered by his cloak while its pages are concealed by his large and prominently depicted hands. Whereas the sign that reads "BLIND" in large Roman-letter capitals is at the center of the portrait, the raised print of the book on the reader's lap is only gestured at, the pages largely hidden. An earlier image, from 1871, depicts a street reader seated and reading on Waterloo Bridge as part of a scene that also features five pedestrians (fig. 7). This group of people, whose clothing identifies them as middle-class, pass between the viewer and the street reader. One of them, a child, holds a coin in her fingers; an adult woman beside her gestures toward the street reader, guiding the child to give him the coin. Depicted with the river and the skyline of London visible behind him, the reader sits in an erect posture, actively reading the book he holds open on his lap. He wears a top hat not dissimilar from that of one of the pedestrians and there is no sign of a placard identifying him as blind. Once again, it is the body of the reader, his immobility in a space characterized by movement, and his handling of an open book in public space, rather than the book's design or features, that signal he is blind.

These images, like the literary works explored in this chapter, date to the

Figure 6. "On Waterloo Bridge. From a Drawing by W.D. Almond," *English Illustrated Magazine* (Sept. 1888), p. 799. Internet Archive.

second half of the nineteenth century. The decline in literary and visual references to street readers in the twentieth century reflects the decline in the number of street readers in public spaces. Whether reading by touch became more widespread and consequently less engaging, whether arrests like that of William Hawkes forced readers to abandon this work, or whether readers gave up this work for better opportunities, street readers were not a defining feature of the post-Victorian city. That said, nineteenth-century street readers, such as the readers depicted in these illustrations, continue to have a visual presence of sorts in modern-day London. Brightly coloured fiberglass statues displayed outside charity stores operated by the Greater London Fund for the Blind recall a community of street people who were described as statue-like by nineteenth-century commentators, as fixtures in the Victorian cityscape. One of these statues, installed outside the charity store on Fulham Road, depicts a neatly groomed blind boy dressed in colorful mid-twentieth-century clothing: a white shirt, red tie, blue shorts, yellow sweater, and white knee-high socks (fig. 8). A book with a bright red cover lies on his lap and his

Figure 7. "Blind Bible-Reader on Waterloo Bridge" (1871) by M. Ralston. Collection of Mary Evans Picture Library.

Figure 8. Statue belonging to the Greater London Fund for the Blind; Fulham Road, London (2015). Author's photograph.

eyes are closed. As is also the case with similar statues distributed throughout London, the book the boy holds is hollow: it is a receptacle for the spare change of passersby. There is a coin slot just above the child's fingers, which are positioned as though he is reading by touch, this despite the fact that the book is closed.

These statues, which are chained to the doors of charity shops throughout London, include written messages for sighted audiences. The statue on Fulham Road asks people, in bold lettering beneath the boy's feet, to "PLEASE GIVE TO THE BLIND." Both the statue and its lettering powerfully evoke a now absent and little studied presence: blind Victorians who read by touch in public spaces in exchange for sighted observers' spare change. Holding a book, displayed on a sidewalk, these human-shaped coin receptacles connect reading to blindness to begging in a chain of association that necessarily commodifies reading by touch. Revisiting and re-energizing connections between blindness, reading, and poverty that pre-exist their display by more than a century, these fiberglass statues do little to change or challenge the perception of blind people as tragic figures. Specters of the flesh-and-blood street readers of earlier eras, these blind boys and their hollow books signal the endurance of societal attitudes that continue to limit blind people's access to employment, to social inclusion, and to cultural influence.

This chapter has mapped the ways in which the practice of street reading publicized a progressive development in blind people's lives while also affirming the identification of blindness with dependency. Whereas for some observers, the blind street reader was a beggar, for others, the reader was a worker; while for some commentators, the street reader was deserving of charity, for others, the reader was a criminal presence. Equally divisive was the question of whether street readers were really reading or just reciting text and, relatedly, whether their reading (or recitation) of Scripture was indicative of piety or immorality. Whereas the presence of blind people reading in the street was a measure of the success of educational initiatives, it was, in equal measure, an indication of the limitations of literacy's ameliorative power. As the next chapter demonstrates, street readers were representative figures of blind people's newly acquired literacy who shared space in the nineteenth-century cultural imagination with a contemporaneous representative of a very different blind identity: the blind scholar, a skilled practitioner of literal and figurative close reading whose academic potential was purportedly increased by the scholar's freedom from the distractions of visual experience.

Two

Difference as Advantage

In 1837, James Gall, a sighted publisher of books for blind readers, offered an assessment of reading by touch that was both pragmatic and progressive:

> If there are advantages possessed by those who see over the Blind in reading, it must be confessed at the same time, that the Blind possess other advantages, which those who read with their eyes cannot have. They need no candle. They can read by night as well as by day. Even in bed, when sickness would prevent him from sitting up, the Blind person can take his Bible to bed with him, and read with his book beneath the bed-clothes. (*Account* 62)

Promoting reading by touch by drawing attention to the dependency of sighted readers on light, be it daylight or candlelight, Gall was not alone in contrasting blind people's experiences of reading in bed with those of sighted people. Indeed, reflections on nocturnal reading were a mainstay of Victorian-era depictions of blind people's reading lives.[1] An 1882 essay imagined blind people taking a book "into their quiet room, and even into bed with them, to while away the hours of the night, and there open, literally with their own fingers, the door of some new, strange chamber in the domain of science, or history, or fiction, or poetry, or philosophy, or religion!" (Clark 131). The same essayist enthused, "They need to pay no gas-bills, and even the electric light is of no concern to them. This is one of the compensations of their condition" (131). A student of the London Society for Teaching the Blind to Read described a similar scene of reading when she proposed that "the one great advantage that blind people have over others is, that they can read comfortably in bed" ("Blind Guy Fawkes" 256). She told a sighted contributor to the weekly magazine *All the Year Round*:

> You [. . .] are uncomfortable when you read in bed—you know you are. You are obliged to hold the book up till you are tired, and then have to twist yourself about to get the light, and catch cold in your shoulders. If it is night-time you must be very naughty to light a candle, which is sure to gutter down and set the house on fire. Now when I take a book to bed, I bury myself under the clothes, book and all, and read away as fast—as fast—till I go fast asleep. ("Blind Guy Fawkes" 256–57)

Cataloguing, among other hazards, the nonblind reader's exposure to cold, this student identifies sighted reading with discomfort, effort, and risk. Eager to extend the advantages of reading by touch to sighted people, in 1866, a contributor to *Golden Hours* offered the following recommendation:

> My advice to every one is, to learn to read in embossed characters whether blind or not; keep the Book by the bedside, and read during sleepless hours; there is no fear of taking cold, for the letters can be felt under the bedclothes. This occupation of mind may shorten many weary hours of sickness at a future day, besides preparing you to do good to others. (M.M.)

In preparation for future sickness, in pursuit of comfort, the sighted are encouraged to follow the example of blind people and to learn, by choice rather than necessity, a new way to read.

This chapter examines a range of advantages that commentators, both blind and sighted, associated with reading by touch. Attentive to benefits of greater consequence than the cost of electricity, it explores nineteenth-century blind readers' perception of their mode of reading as more engaging, more accurate, and more informative than reading by sight. Anchored by the autobiographical writing of Alfred Hirst, a largely forgotten activist, author, and blind person, the chapter opens with a discussion of the prominent role John Milton's poetry played in Hirst's work and, more generally, in nineteenth-century discourse on blindness. I explore how acquired blindness, an experience Hirst had in common with Milton, shaped Hirst's assessment of reading by touch as a practice that facilitates readers' comprehension of sophisticated literary works as well as increasing their pleasure in them. I also consider how re-reading contributed to perceptions of reading by touch as superior to reading by sight. I show that the restricted supply of raised-print books, a reality of blind people's lives, was understood by some observers as advantageous in that it obliged blind readers to study a small set of texts closely. I propose that assessments of reading by touch as uniquely advantageous supported the emergence of a new archetype of blind identity: the blind scholar, a person whose visual disability is not perceived as a barrier to advanced study but instead as a desirable qualification for it. The chapter ends with a reading of Grant Allen's *Linnet: A Romance* (1898), a late-Victorian novel whose sensational depiction of sighted men reading with their fingers raises questions about the information-gathering power of touch and about the appropriation of blind people's reading methods by nonblind people. Taken as a whole, the chapter demonstrates that the assessment of reading by touch as a uniquely beneficial way of reading shaped both lived experiences of blindness and literary depictions of it.

Alfred Hirst on Milton

Alfred Hirst, a wool merchant and world traveler, became blind in midlife. An avid reader of raised-print text, Hirst authored essays and speeches that championed the development of a raised-print culture created for and by blind people. Hirst wrote at length about his experiences reading by touch, sharing, for example, his thoughts on reading in bed in an 1897 essay for *The Sunday Magazine*. He explained, "It troubles me little to wake at one or two o'clock in the morning. I simply turn on to my back and prop myself up, and pass an hour with Milton or Shakespeare, or Wordsworth or Burns, or Keats, or some other of the immortals" ("My Dark World" 14). Hirst, who described literature as "the blessed and unfailing light of my dark world" ("My Dark World" 14), was particularly passionate about the work of Milton, whose poetry he turned to in the first days of his blindness. As Hirst explains, "my knowledge of Milton came to my aid, and I determined, like him, not to: '. . . bate one jot / Of heart or hope, but still bear up and steer / Right onward'" ("My Dark World" 5). Hirst went on to acquire both raised-print editions of Milton's poems and the skills required to read them. "I cannot," he wrote, "put into words what a pleasure and profit the study of Milton has been to me during nearly twenty-two years of blindness" ("A Plea" 14).

Given the difference Milton made to his life, it is not surprising that Hirst was eager to add blind people to the celebrated seventeenth-century poet's already significant readership. As he explained in an 1896 essay titled "A Plea for the Study of Milton by the Blind," "It is not my present purpose [. . .] to recommend the study of Milton to the sighted, but rather to advocate and encourage it amongst those who like myself are 'Dark, dark, dark! amid the blaze of noon: / Irrevocably dark'" (4). In it, Hirst argues that Milton's poetry is of special interest to blind people and is, moreover, a powerful support to their wellbeing. Hirst urges schools for blind students to offer classes dedicated to the study of Milton's poems; he also identifies passages of particular relevance to blind readers. He notes of the first 55 lines of Book Three of *Paradise Lost* that "no blind boy or girl should be allowed to pass through our schools without having committed it to memory" ("A Plea" 12). He recommends with equal passion the study of Milton's three sonnets on blindness, widely regarded in the Victorian era, as in our own, as stylistically complex and difficult to parse. Rejecting the view that "the blind cannot learn or appreciate these sonnets" ("A Plea" 10), Hirst insists on the importance of these poems in the daily lives of blind people, including working-class adults. He notes with admiration that the sign of a blind basket-maker's shop in his village includes a quotation from one of these sonnets. He adds that a "successful piano tuner in an important northern watering-place [. . .] knows every one of them by heart, and probably has a better critical knowledge of them than any other person, clerical or lay in the place" ("A Plea" 10). Confident in blind people's ability to read poetry and, what is more, to appreciate poetry, he rejects the possibility that Milton might not appeal to some people: "My experience has proved to me that if they have the chance, the blind, as a class, take to Milton like ducks to water" ("A Plea" 4). And the benefits of studying Milton extend, in Hirst's experience, far beyond the development of literacy skills and literary knowledge: "Where the experiment has been tried upon members of this afflicted class, it has produced almost magical results, putting into them, as it were, mental bone and muscle, and life and mettle" ("A Plea" 4). Here and elsewhere, Hirst assigns the study of Milton's poetry a transformative role in blind people's lives.

For Hirst, blind people are able to achieve a deep understanding of Milton's work not only because of their shared experience of blindness but also because they read by touch, a method that, in Hirst's assessment, makes blind readers more engaged, careful, accurate, and cognizant readers of text, including challenging literary texts, than sighted people. Well-positioned as an educated person with acquired blindness to compare reading by sight to reading by touch, Hirst proposes that blind readers:

> have in some respects the advantage of the seeing, for let physiologists explain the phenomenon as they may, it is undoubtedly the fact that information which reaches the brain through the fingers and arms is much more likely to stick there ("like burrs in wool," as Bunyan has it), than when it arrives at its destination by the eye. ("A Plea" 5)

This observation exemplifies Hirst's perception of reading by touch as a reading method with affordances not shared by reading by sight. For Hirst, differences between the two reading modes favor the blind reader, the use of touch making a blind person a more receptive reader than their sighted counterpart, and, consequently, a more successful reader of challenging literary works. Rejecting a rhetoric of equivalence, epitomized by oft-repeated phrases such as "fingers for eyes," an equivalence noted in the Introduction to this book, Hirst argues in favor of an appreciation of the differences between the two reading modes, differences that made him prize his ability to read by touch.

Hirst's characterization of blind readers as exceptionally capable is grounded in his own experiences of careful and perceptive reading, including his discovery of errors in the work of respected sighted authors. Hirst finds fault first with Sir Walter Scott, who, he argues, misquoted Milton in his novel *The Antiquary*. Observing that Scott "was fond of quoting Milton, but rarely does so correctly," Hirst explains how reading by touch facilitated his discovery of Scott's errors: "I had often read *The Antiquary* in my days of sight, and I had had that favourite story read to me more than once since I became blind, but it was not until I read it with my fingers that I detected these errors" ("A Plea" 11). Turning next to historian and biographer James Anthony Froude, Hirst queries Froude's handling of Milton, suggesting that Froude relied on Scott rather than consulting an edition of Milton's work when he quoted the poet: "The student of literature will be interested to find abundant evidence in Mr. Froude's twelfth lecture on Erasmus that the historian took his Milton from the novelist" ("A Plea" 11). Hirst, himself an adept "student of literature," discovers a chain of misquotation, his use of the sense of touch revealing the failure of two highly respected sighted authors to treat a blind poet's work with due care. It is, notably, the experience of reading "with my fingers" that enables Hirst to read carefully and productively; this method alerts him to details he did not notice when he read with his eyes nor when he listened to others read aloud. For Hirst, blind people's lives are enriched by reading Milton's poetry, but they are also enriched by a reading mode that allows them to read expertly by improving their retention, encouraging attention to detail, and facilitating discovery.

Hirst, who repeatedly and strategically engages Milton in his writing, was by no means the only commentator on blind experience to re-engage the work of a long dead poet. When Hirst named and quoted Milton in his essays and speeches, he contributed to an already massive stockpile of references to Milton in Victorian-era commentary on visual disability. Indeed, it would be difficult to overestimate the frequency with which Milton, a seventeenth-century poet, features in nineteenth-century writing about blindness and blind people.[2] Whatever their genre, whatever the venue, if their topic is blindness, nineteenth-century writers repeatedly evoke Milton and his blindness. Take, for example, a fundraising speech Sir John Coleridge gave in 1859 in support of the West of England Blind Institution. Reporting on the speech, *The Times* summarized what Coleridge said but quoted, word for word, a passage from Milton that Coleridge had shared: a 16-line excerpt from Book Three of *Paradise Lost* ("Sir John Coleridge on Blind Institutions"), a passage much admired by Hirst. The same passage appealed to British eye doctor William Lawrence, who quoted from Book Three of *Paradise Lost* in his lecture on diseases of the eyes, which was published in *The Lancet* in October 1825.[3] And the very same passage is reproduced, yet again, in the collection *Dark Days Brightened: A Selection of Poetry about and by the Blind*, published in 1881. That collection, published in support of the Royal Blind Asylum Bazaar, not only features an engraving of a portrait of "Blind Milton" on its first page but also opens with a 185-line dramatic monologue by W.E. Aytoun. Titled "Blind Old Milton," Aytoun's poem adds to what Milton himself wrote about blindness, ventriloquizing the long dead poet so as to share more than Milton chose to share about his experience of vision loss. With public interest in blindness energized by the new literacy of blind people, Milton's poetry acquired the status of an ur-text of blind experience, his writing about blindness, especially acquired blindness, influencing not only Victorian-era thinking about visual disability but also, as the example of Hirst suggests, lived experiences of it.

The misattribution of texts about blindness to Milton is a measure of the intensity of both blind and sighted readers' appetite for Milton's writing on blindness. Blind author W.H. Levy's encyclopedic prose study of blindness, *Blindness and the Blind: or, A Treatise on the Science of Typhlology* (1872), is one instance. Levy, whose respect for Milton is signaled by his book's frontispiece, a dual portrait of Milton and Homer, quotes accurately and at length from Milton throughout his book. Unfortunately, Levy also incorrectly credits Milton with two pieces of writing about blindness. The first is a paragraph-long prose passage Levy publishes under the title "The Sacredness of the Blind." Levy asserts that the passage was recently discovered and describes it as "taken from a manuscript copy," adding that he believes it "has not yet appeared in any edition of Milton's writing" (217).[4] The second piece, a poem titled "Lines by Milton in his Old Age," was, Levy explained, "discovered about the same time" and "published in an Oxford edition of the poet's work" (217). In fact, the poem, which opens with the words "I am old and blind" (1), is the work of sighted nineteenth-century American poet Elizabeth Lloyd Howell, its proper title reading "Lines On Milton in his Old Age."[5] While accurate citations of Milton's work far outnumber errors of this kind, the misattribution of texts signals the intensity of blind authors' desire to engage with Milton's oeuvre. One can't help but wonder what Hirst, an enthusiastic and careful reader of Milton, might have thought of the misattribution of a contemporary poem by a sighted person to the blind poet he revered.

"Quite a new or additional significance"

Hirst's identification of reading by touch as a form of reading that facilitates a deep appreciation and detailed knowledge of a text was, like his tendency to quote Milton, shared by other commentators, many of them people with acquired blindness. Baron Hatherley (William Page Wood) was among them. Hatherley served as Lord High Chancellor of Great Britain from 1868 to 1872, retiring from that office because of problems with his eyesight. Moved by his personal experience of visual disability to support the efforts of charitable organizations that supported blind people, Hatherley gave speeches at public meetings of London's Society for Teaching the Blind in 1873 and 1874. Hatherley had, "when nearly wholly deprived of sight," learned how to read Moon's script by touch, acquiring that skill in only three hours ("Lord Hatherley"). He would express thanks, in June 1874, for "the great mercy which had been vouchsafed to him in the restoration to sight" ("Education of the Blind"), but a year earlier, in May 1873, it was reading by touch that secured his gratitude. He enthused that, having learned to read Moon's script by touch, he "was now never at a loss to read the type used by the blind" ("Lord Hatherley"). Hatherley also spoke publically about how reading by touch deepened his appreciation of texts that were familiar to him from his life as a sighted reader:

> There was, he thought, a good deal of advantage in reading the Scriptures slowly, as was necessarily the case when the touch was the only sense employed, for he had often found that in passages which he thought he understood very well and knew much better he came across words and phrases which had quite a new or an additional significance to him. ("Lord Hatherley")

His understanding deepened by a change not in what he read but in the sense he used to read, Hatherley, like Hirst, read with greater profit when he read by touch.

Hatherley's perception of reading raised-print Scripture as more informative than reading Scripture printed in ink was shared by working-class people. Their experiences are preserved, albeit in mediated form, in William Moon's fundraising publications, in which teachers of Moon's system share students' testimonials with the goal of increasing public support for Moon's work. A teacher based in Barnstaple gave the following report in 1872 about a jeweler who had become blind: "He told me he had read John 3 several times, and 'never did that chapter seem so beautiful before.' He had often spoken upon it to others; but as he lay in his bed, and read it verse by verse, it seemed more precious to him than ever" (Moon 137). Another testimonial featured a student who felt he had gained a deeper understanding of the Bible by reading raised print: "I understand it far better than when I read it with my eyes" (Moon 138). The student's teacher proposed that this was a "result partially owing, probably, to the reading of it rather slowly, and not passing over a single word without thought" (Moon 138). A teacher named Brown, based in Edinburgh, contributed the following testimonial of a man who had been blind for five years and whose "chief enjoyment" (Moon 145) was reading: "Before I lost my sight I had read a great deal of the Bible; but it is only since I have read with my fingers that I have felt the power and comfort of God's Word; and now it is my daily companion" (Moon 145). More than a substitute for reading by sight, reading by touch was for these readers, as it was for Hirst and Hatherley, more engaging and more informative than reading by sight. Connected by a shared experience of acquired blindness, be it permanent or temporary, readers with very different levels of social privilege attested to having, when reading by touch, increased appreciation of their text, whether that be of the typographical errors in a literary text or the power of a Bible verse. Literally close to the book, touching text instead of viewing it, readers of raised print with acquired blindness repeatedly assert that they practice a form of reading that is superior to the reading they did while sighted.

We are, I propose, justified by more than Hirst's love of the study of poetry to think of the kind of reading that Hirst both practiced and promoted as closer reading: a kind of reading both literally and figuratively closer than the reading performed by sighted people. Closer reading is a compelling example of "blindness gain," a concept developed and promoted by scholar Hannah Thompson. Influenced by fellow disability studies scholars' insights, including Georgina Kleege's conception of "gaining blindness" and Rosemarie Garland-Thomson's idea of "disability gain," Thompson proposes a radical re-evaluation of blindness: "Blindness gain is the idea that rather than thinking of blindness as a problem to be solved, we think of blindness as a benefit"

("Blindness").[6] As she adds in an essay co-authored with Marion Chottin, "Instead of subscribing to dominant conceptions of blindness as a problem, deficit, or lack, we choose to position blindness as a solution, benefit or 'gain'" (Chottin and Thompson 33). Thompson's revaluation of blindness prioritizes gains related to blindness that are most significantly felt by blind people but, she argues, "blindness gain is also about how blindness can benefit nonblind people" ("Blindness"). While a blind person may experience blindness gain in the form of, for example, a richly non-visual engagement with a cultural work or the natural world, a sighted person experiences blindness gain when they benefit from the adoption of tools, methods, or approaches to daily life associated with blindness, such as listening to the audio description of a theater performance, participating in a touch tour at a museum, or reading an audio book.

The applicability of Thompson's ideas to Hirst's experience of reading by touch is palpable. Identifying benefits specific to reading by touch, Hirst and his contemporaries share experiences of blindness gain that add depth and sway to the suggestion, quoted in the introduction to this chapter, that sighted people should learn to read by touch as well as by sight. This chapter will revisit that suggestion in its final section but, for now, it adds to knowledge of the reading lives of nineteenth-century blind people by exploring how blind readers experienced the re-reading of a limited selection of raised-print books as yet another advantage unique to reading by touch.

The Blind Reader as Re-Reader

British student and blind person Robert Edgar was an exceptional reader: exceptional in the sense of being skilled but also in the sense of being unconventional in his engagement with text. Edgar, who became a student at Edinburgh's Royal Blind Asylum and School in 1870, was initially refused a place at the school because he was deaf as well as blind. He quickly became a model student, learning to read six different tactile scripts. According to the Asylum's superintendent, Gilbert Macculloch, Edgar was such an avid reader that he "mastered, in the space of but a few months, well-nigh all the books, alike sacred and secular, contained in the school library, and would have read many more could they have been obtained for him" (12). Edgar was also, the superintendent observed, a re-reader: "Not a few of the volumes were perused several times over, till at last they were got off by heart" (12). Similarly noteworthy was Edgar's attention to details other readers ignored. As Macculloch explains, Edgar found new ways to engage and appreciate a collection of books that he had read many times:

> he would often, to amuse himself and others of the boys, endeavour to test their knowledge of different books and subjects by proposing to them what he termed "puzzlers." For example, he would ask which is the shortest verse in such a book, or which the longest? How many words are contained in the preface to Dr Moon's "Natural History?" &c. (26)

An exceptionally close reader, engaged by what could be dismissed as inconsequential or trivial details, Edgar not only memorized the words on the page but also textual details such as the number of words on a page. When Edgar became seriously ill at the age of sixteen, he continued to read; reading by touch was "his almost constant occupation, night and day, for the last few weeks of his life" (37). In words that bring to mind the death of the fictional Matty, whose depiction was explored in chapter 1, Macculloch describes Edgar on his deathbed: his "thin, wasted finger still tracing the pages, up, I may say, to the last" (33). Accomplished and persistent, Edgar read and, importantly, re-read raised-print books, his pleasure in them a defining feature of his short life.

While Edgar's death in his teens is unquestionably tragic, the degree to which his school's limited library failed to satisfy his appetite for books is, in its own way, troubling. Edgar's re-reading of books is an expression of his love of reading but it is also a measure of the inadequacy of his access to reading material. That being said, re-reading is an activity closely associated with academic study and, more generally, with mastery of a text and its messages. Commentators likely had that association in mind when they proposed that the re-reading of a small and select body of texts was advantageous to blind people's intellectual development. Take, for example, French scholar and author Pierre Villey; Villey was a blind person and an expert on the writings of Michel de Montaigne. Villey proposed that the limited availability of raised-print reading materials might benefit blind readers, specifically by protecting them from periodical literature. Finding advantage in what could be construed as lack, Villey, writing in 1909, wonders in regard to blind readers if "their infirmity protects them from the invasion of the magazine? The substitution of the magazine for the book, of miscellaneous facts and patchy articles for the long matured work, seems in our age to be one of the obstacles to intellectual progress" (691). The limited availability of books is perceived by Villey as protective. Less promiscuous in their reading than sighted people, blind people are able to devote themselves to re-reading and deep study. Unaffected by the deluge of text available in ink, the blind person is encouraged, or more accurately, obliged to re-read authors such as de Montaigne or Milton, this instead of reading inconsequential literary newcomers. Their reading choices curated by both the high cost and the limited supply of raised-print books, blind readers necessarily read a select canon. Proposing that what could very reasonably be termed a shortcoming of raised-print culture might actually be an advantage, promoting a perception of blind readers as not only avid readers but discriminating readers, Villey contributes to the characterization of the reading lives of the first generations of blind readers as distinct from, and better than, the reading lives of sighted people.

To return to Alfred Hirst, Hirst also wrote about his pleasure in his small library and about what he personally gained from the frequent re-reading of familiar texts. Estimating that he owns no more than 50 raised-print volumes, he strikes a similar note to Villey: "It will be seen that I have but few books, and yet I am never at a loss for good reading. I think there is something to be said for excellence of quality rather than excessive quantity" ("The Need" 120). Yet, Hirst also worried that limits on the supply and variety of raised-print books necessarily limited blind people's intellectual development and also, importantly, their pleasure in reading. While Hirst views re-reading as pleasurable and productive, he celebrates the expansion of blind people's choices, lauding in particular the work of the British and Foreign Blind Association, an organization he credits with the publication and sale of "more than 100,000 volumes of high-class literature" ("The Need" 120). Hirst, who was grateful for the steady expansion of the raised-print canon in English in the course of his career as a blind reader, actively campaigned for the publication of literary works, versus religious publications, for blind people. His desire for an expansion in blind people's choice of books is, for example, clearly signaled by a lecture he gave in 1902 on "The Need of More and Cheaper Literature for the Blind in 'Braille' Type." While advocating for the re-reading of books, and specifically of books that he perceived as "high-class literature," Hirst worked to increase the range of reading materials available to blind people, a development that would make re-reading a choice rather than an inevitability.

The work that Hirst did to expand blind readers' libraries was literally hands-on. A volunteer proofreader, he read and re-read new raised-print books, offering feedback on ways different publications might be improved. His appreciation of the affordances of reading by touch is, in fact, closely bound up with his appreciation of the correctness of raised-print books, especially of books printed in braille. He shared some thoughts on his personal history with braille in 1897, explaining that he had been blind for two years when he learned about "the wonderful invention of the illustrious Frenchman, Louis Braille" ("My Dark World" 6). Initially worried that braille's raised dots would be too small for him to distinguish by touch, Hirst mastered this script quickly. He reports: "within three days I could both read and write it" (6). A vocal advocate for the wide adoption of braille by blind readers, he describes it as a "great gift which a benign Providence has made us" ("The Need" 119). Hirst even imagines Milton, who is never far from his thoughts, reading braille:

> I sometimes wonder what Milton would have thought if he could have had his favorite Greek authors in this blessed and wonderful type. A friend of mine suggests that probably in that case we should not have had such matchless blank verse as we now possess in 'Paradise Lost.' ("My Dark World" 7)

This scenario places a blind person's poetic production in competition with an imaginary—and, what is more, a proleptic—experience of reading, the composition of a great work made possible by its blind creator's lack of access to raised-print reading materials. While curious about Milton as a hypothetical reader of raised print, what Hirst values is the opportunity to read what Milton wrote. He praises editions of Milton's works in braille published by the British and Foreign Blind Association (BFBA), comparing them to ink-print editions and noting they "contain fewer errors than the printed copies sent out by the best publishers" ("A Plea" 5). That the BFBA's braille edition of Milton's work is affordable, costing only "a few shillings" ("A Plea" 4), adds to Hirst's admiration. Working to secure the high quality and increased supply of blind people's reading materials, Hirst experiences the publication of works of literature in raised print as a form of social progress: "thus," he explains, "the blind are placed on an equality with the seeing" ("A Plea" 4). While he understands reading by touch and reading by sight as different and unequal modes, he works to secure an equivalent library for blind and sighted readers in no small part to secure their social equality. The problem to be solved in Hirst's assessment is not blindness but a material limitation experienced by blind people who lack the variety of books available to the sighted majority and who desire both a more varied, and a more affordable, supply.

The Blind Scholar

The rise of the blind scholar as a representative type occurs in parallel with, and was supported by, perceptions of blind people as readers with unique advantages. Whereas Hirst is interested in reading by touch and in ways in which, in his assessment, the inevitably careful and thorough process of reading raised-print books enriches blind people's lives, for other Victorian-era commentators, it was freedom from the sense of sight that was blind readers' primary advantage over their sighted peers. Articulating their perception of yet another example of blindness gain related to reading by touch, these commentators identify blindness as an experience that increases the intellectual potential and productivity of blind people by freeing them from the distractions of visual information. The sighted educator B.G. Johns proposed, for example, that blind readers are more engaged than sighted readers by the books they read because of their lack of sight. Johns, who authored a number of essays on blind people's cognitive lives, proposed: "on whatever subject—the blind man thinks with greater concentration and individuality of purpose than the student who has eyes; if he loses the help of external objects in forming certain conceptions or ideas, he gains by not being liable to their intrusion in tangible and solid reality, when not wanted" ("The Blind" 31). Johns fleshes out his claims regarding blind people's superior powers of concentration with a hypothetical scenario that contrasts the experiences of two fictional readers: Mr. Cassio Brown, whose eyes are "as keen as a hawk's" and Mr. Octavius Smith, who is blind ("How the Blind Dream" 315). Johns's description of Brown lists ways in which visual information, including visual memories, distract him:

> It is a winter evening, and Mr. B sits reading in his library. He has mastered a chapter of metaphysics, and now shuts his eyes to ponder on the final and toughest morsel. As his bodily eyes close, his mental eyes open; and the very objects at which he but just now gazed reappear, almost as they fade. He can, *if he will*, still see the printed page; opposite, over the fire-place, still appears to hand that incomparable likeness of him as President of the Pedlington Archery Club; he can still *see* the ruddy fire; and the shadow on the wall still seems to flicker in the uncertain light, on whichever of these points his thoughts chance to dwell,—metaphysics, archery, his own noble mien as "Sagittarius," the price of coals, or the theory of shadows—of that very one may his eyes, though closely shut, still behold a visible symbol. ("How the Blind Dream" 315)

Here, Johns is not concerned with the mode of reading, be it touch or sight; he is interested instead in how different readers process what they have read. Even when the unfortunate Brown closes his eyes to try to better understand the chapter, he continues to be sidetracked by visual information. Smith, who reads a book "under precisely similar circumstances, save that he is blind," is more successful:

> He, too, reads, and is given to meditation; he leans back in his chair, and thinks. He has been blind these forty years. He cannot, with any approach to accuracy, recall the outline of any single object of sight [. . .]. [. . .] He is fairly acquainted with the main features of the room in which he sits, can find almost any volume that is wanted, and is aware of the portrait over the fire-place. But when he leans back to muse on that last tough chapter, no sudden change takes place further than this: that a moment ago he was reading—now he is thinking of what he read. But no visions of shadow on the wall, of printed type or page, of portrait, or of archery are ready to spring up at a moment's notice, to be scanned or dismissed at will. ("How the Blind Dream" 315)

In the comfort of their middle-class, book-lined rooms, the two men have very different experiences: one distracted, the other focused. While these paired portraits are progressive in their insistence on what these equally prosperous, independent, and curious men have in common, they are radical in that their differentiation of Brown and Smith positions Smith as intellectually more fortunate and more effective.[7]

Johns's assessment of a representative blind reader as having an intellectual advantage over a sighted reader aligns closely with the conclusions of Pierre Villey, who argued that "sight [. . .] is the sense of distraction. The less one is distracted, the less the internal reverie is interrupted by accidental happenings without, the more one is concentrated on himself, the more one takes time to mature one's reflections, to weigh the pros and cons of one's deliberations" (691). Villey, whose essay "Intellectual Work Among the Blind" is quoted above, assigned reading a special role in blind people's lives when he proposed, "In general the blind are very fond of reading, much more so at least than those of the same intellectual level who can see" (690). He argued, moreover, that "This taste for reading, this need for mental diversion, constitutes, if I am not mistaken, an intellectual advantage of much importance to the blind and favors their development" (691). Villey's perception of blind people as temperamentally suited to reading and, relatedly, as highly motivated readers differentiates blind people's reading from sighted people's reading not only in terms of intellectual potential but also in terms of pleasure.

Drawing perhaps on his own experiences as a respected expert on the essays of Michel de Montaigne, Villey argues that "Intellectual recreation is, indeed, especially dear to the blind" (690); he also asserts that a principal advantage of blindness is "a tendency to reflection, to the concentration which is so noticeable among so many of them" (691). His claims recall Hirst's use of the phrase "profit and pleasure," quoted above, to describe his reading life. Able to achieve greater understanding than the sighted majority, blind readers have the additional boon of a special fondness for reading, a shared taste for it. Or so these commentators claim.

While a comparative reading of Hirst, Johns, and Villey reveals continuities between blind and sighted people's beliefs about reading by touch and, similarly, between Anglo and French perspectives (Villey's work was translated into English in 1909, very soon after its publication in French), it is hard to ignore how readily these commentators generalize about the experiences of blind people. A diverse group of individuals whose experiences of both disability and literacy were shaped by gender, age, class, and race, as well as other factors, such as an individual's access to schooling or their appetite for epic similes, nineteenth-century blind readers' primary commonality may well have been the experience of being generalized about. While sweeping claims about blind people's appetite for reading and their skill as readers served commentators in their pursuit of specific goals, such as Hirst's advocacy for a role for literary studies in schools for blind students, generalizations necessarily elide the diversity of blind people's experiences. Assigning a socially marginalized group specific talents and tastes, commentators on blind people's reading lives add new items to an already long list of conventional traits associated with blindness, such as piety or musicality. While Hirst, Johns, and Villey record their own reactions to the advent of raised-print books, and also, no doubt, document the realities of some readers' experiences, they do not question the idea that blindness is a determinant of identity with the power to predispose people to avid and engaged reading, be it of Milton, de Montaigne, or metaphysics.

Generalizations about a marginalized group's skills and preferences are particularly potent when they amalgamate into an archetype. Well-known examples of blind archetypes include the blind beggar, a figure of blind inability explored in chapter 1, and the blind seer, a person who lacks literal vision but has the compensatory gift of prophecy, or second sight. These two representative figures of blindness have long histories in Western culture and a not insignificant presence in Victorian culture.[8] It is my contention that, in the second half of the century, as public awareness of reading by touch grew, these two types kept increasingly frequent company in the popular imagination with a new representative figure of blind identity: the blind scholar.

While the history of blind people's education has been very extensively documented,[9] very little attention has been paid to the rise of the blind scholar as a representative identity that developed in parallel with and was supported by the recognition of blind people as readers and, more specifically, by the perception of blind people as readers with unique advantages. One indicator of the rise of the blind scholar as a type is the development of a subgenre of books that feature accounts of blind people's exceptional intellectual achievements. In the course of the Victorian period, both blind and nonblind people authored and published laudatory studies of blind scholars, scientists, literary critics, and historians. Some studies, such as sighted author John Plummer's 1868 *The Story of a Blind Inventor*, a biography of scientist, educator, and blind person James Gale, focus on a single figure's intellectual achievements. Other studies group together the biographies of highly successful blind people. Many of these books about blind people's achievements were authored by blind people but were, notably, printed in ink and were thus aimed at sighted audiences. William Artman and L.V. Hall, the blind co-authors of *Beauties and Achievements of the Blind* (1854), which was printed in ink, explained: "It has been our object in the present work, to point out to the blind, and the public in general, the achieving abilities of our order" (12). Though their book prioritizes the accomplishments of blind authors, including contemporary poets Frances Browne and Alice Holmes, Artman and Hall's book also includes a section titled "Achievements of the Blind in the Learned Professions," which explores blind people's success in the realms of science, law, and medicine. For his book *Heroes of the Darkness*, likely published in 1911, sighted author John Bernard Mannix gathered biographies of accomplished blind people, dedicating chapters to individual achievers and finding in their accomplishments evidence of "compensations for loss of sight" (12). Sharing life stories that he believed demonstrated that blind individuals have in them "the making of a hero—a sightless superman" (12), Mannix authored chapters on, among others, scientist François Huber, professor and parliamentarian Henry Fawcett, and, unsurprisingly, poet John Milton. The first chapter, titled "Helen Keller: A Genius," introduces Mannix's claims regarding "compensations for the loss of sight," namely that: "Increased powers of concentration are certainly a concomitant, and as a secondary result there is an improved retentiveness of memory" (12). His highly laudatory descriptions of Keller's schooling and accomplishments, as well as of the accomplishments of Laura Bridgman, typify sighted interest in the intellectual lives of people with sensory disabilities in the wake of the advent of schools for blind students and the related proliferation of reading by touch.

Several real-world blind scholars drew on their personal experiences to assert the intellectual potential of blind people in an era of blind literacy. A letter to the Editor of *The Times* from June 15, 1874 written by Herbert J.R. Marston adds to our understanding of the blind scholar as both an historical reality with a public presence and a societal ideal. Marston was prompted to write when *The Times* reported he was the runner-up candidate for the Classical Scholarship at the University of Durham. He explains, "I should not have ventured to intrude myself thus upon public notice, were not the circumstances sufficiently peculiar and the object sufficiently important to justify the action" (Marston). Marston, interested in how academic opportunities for blind people level the playing field between blind and sighted scholars, nodded to changes in the educational landscape that had facilitated his scholarly achievements:

> Of those circumstances I need say nothing more than that hitherto it has been comparatively unusual for blind persons to enter into successful competition with sighted candidates for honours and emoluments. Recently, however, owing to the untold advantages enjoyed by the students at the Worcester College for the Blind, such cases have been more frequent. (Marston)

Marston attributes his success to the education he received at Worcester College for the Blind Sons of Gentlemen, a secondary school founded in 1866 that provided academic, versus vocational training, for blind students. Given that English-speaking blind people had only had the opportunity to learn to read by touch for less than four decades when Worcester accepted its first students, the rate at which blind people's access to higher education had improved is, indeed, newsworthy. Marston's achievement is a personal one, but it is also one that signals a larger shift in the lived experience of some blind people, a shift that, in turn, shaped the perception of blind people's academic potential.

Also of note are the experiences of another Victorian-era winner of academic honors, the Canadian scholar and author Edgar Robinson. Born in 1872, Robinson, a prize-winning undergraduate at the University of Toronto, was educated at the Ontario Institute for the Blind in Brantford, Ontario, Canada.[10] In 1896, Robinson published *The True Sphere of the Blind*, a book dedicated not to the career of a specific blind scholar but instead to the idea of the blind scholar. In it, Robinson promotes a new perception of blind people as characterized not by inability or limitation but instead by intellectual potential. As he explains, "I believe 'The True Sphere of the Blind' to be in those vocations which require mental activity rather than manual skill for their successful prosecution" (v). He offers what he describes as a "careful psychological analysis" of how "blindness renders possible a more intense mental life" (v). Robinson asserts that:

> The general tendencies of the effect of blindness upon the psychical life is to intensify and strengthen all those mental activities which depend more for their existence upon the internal and higher processes of knowledge than on the external and immediately sensuous elements. (19)

He is succinct in his claims when he proposes of blind people that "their very blindness makes possible a more fruitful mental life" (193).

Robinson's book, whose thesis is also summarized by his assertion that "blindness clears the way for a more intense mental life" (20), includes a chapter on the transformative impact on blind people's intellectual lives of "Tangible Print." Like his contemporary Hirst, Robinson believed blind people's access to reading materials was essential not only to their education but also to their wellbeing. He was personally responsible for the creation by hand, either with a stylus or with a brailler, of dozens of copies of braille books; Robinson also founded, in 1906, the Canadian Free Library for the Blind.[11] Robinson died in 1908 but his library survived and became, in time, the library of the Canadian National Institute for the Blind. In his career, as in his monograph, Robinson insisted on the importance of access to raised-print reading materials and rejected the perception of blindness as a limit to intellectual achievement. Robinson, like Villey and Marston, was not only an embodiment of the academic potential of blind people in an age of raised print, he was also a person who pushed for public recognition of that potential. Supported by the invention of raised print, both his academic success and his championing of blind people as intellectual workers supported the emergence of the blind scholar as an ideal: a new stereotype of blind identity that, while preferable to both the blind seer and the blind beggar, nonetheless generalized about the interests and aptitudes of a diverse community of people. Turning from real-world and first-hand accounts to the speculative and sensational, the final section of this chapter takes up sighted author Grant Allen's novel *Linnet* and finds in it a very different expression of interest in advantages of reading by touch, advantages that sighted people might access if they learn how to read by touch.

Grant Allen's *Linnet*: Taking Advantage

The prolific novelist Grant Allen, best known for his New Woman novel *The Woman Who Did* (1895), was no stranger to sensation. His twenty-eighth novel, *Linnet: A Romance* (1898), features two characters who read by touch, a choice that allowed Allen to explore the narrative potential of this practice. What makes Allen's engagement with reading by touch noteworthy is that both of these characters are sighted. The author of what might be the century's most fantastical depiction of reading by touch, Allen proposes that advantages associated with reading by touch might be felt by sighted people and, indeed, be exploited by them. Villainizing a sighted person's appropriation of reading by touch, Allen's novel signals, on the one hand, the ubiquity of the perception of reading by touch as uniquely advantageous and, on the other, the development of a vein of uneasiness about who merits access to experiences of blindness gain.

Linnet maps the rise to fame of its title character, a talented singer whose international success brings her into contact with both fans and fellow performers. The main plot's focus on choral performance is re-engaged by Allen in a secondary storyline featuring Joaquin Holmes, a charismatic American mesmerist on tour in London. Both Holmes's name and his nationality suggest that Allen found inspiration in the life and career of the real-world spiritualist D.D. Home, who held séances throughout Europe, making his living by demonstrating psychic skills. In Allen's novel, the fictional Holmes does as the real-world Home did, giving demonstrations of mind-reading at private parties. At one such event, his performance is scrutinized by Florian Wood, a British gentleman who is more than a little skeptical about Holmes's claims. To convince his audience of his possession of psychic powers, Holmes invites guests to write phrases of their own selection or composition with pencils on slips of paper and then seal their notes in envelopes, which he provides. Holmes then asks to have the electrical lighting in the room dimmed, explaining that light "confuses and distracts one by revealing to the eye so many surrounding visible objects" (182). With his sighted audience's ability to see lessened, Holmes collects the envelopes, holding them to his forehead and stating aloud the messages they contain. The novel's narrator explains that one audience member "had never before seen anything that looked so like a genuine miracle" (184); another observer remarks aloud, "The man has eyes in the back of his head" (185). Wood, more skeptical and better informed, arrives at a different conclusion. He proposes that it would be more accurate to say that Holmes "has eyes in the tips of fingers" (185–86).

Sure that Holmes is a fraud, specifically that he is a finger reader rather than a mind reader, Wood invites the mesmerist to his house. It isn't long before Holmes confesses his use of the sense of touch to read messages he claimed to read with his mind. The top opening of the envelopes that contain the handwritten notes are, he explains, carefully sealed by audience members but the envelopes, which Holmes prepares ahead of time, are only partly sealed on one side. Assisted by dim lighting, Holmes pulls the slips of paper out of the side of each envelope and reads with his fingers the messages written in pencil, or more accurately, he reads the indentations made by a writer's pencil on the back of the paper.

Holmes is able to trick his audiences in this way because of a personal history with visual disability, a history that he does not disclose. Only when he is confronted by Wood will Holmes reveal that he was blind as a child and that he learned to read by touch, a skill he retained and continued to develop after the surgical restoration of his sight. Regarding his highly refined sense of touch, Holmes tells Wood:

> it's bred in the bone with me to some extent; but all the same, it's cost me fifteen years of practice to develop it. I come of a blind family, I do; father was blind, and mother as well; made their match up at the Indiana State Asylum. Grandfather was blind in mother's family, and two aunts in father's. *I* was born sighted; but at five years old I was taken with the cataract. They weren't any great shakes at the cataract in Colorado where I was raised; I was fifteen year old before they tried to couch it. So I learned to read first with embossed print on Grandfather's old blind Boston Bible. I learned to read first-rate; that was as easy as ABC, for the tips of my fingers were always sensitive. (193)

Holmes, a sighted charlatan, is by no means a representative figure of blind literacy yet his life story engages common threads in the educational, medical, and familial lives of nineteenth-century blind Americans. Just as the Indiana School for the Blind, founded in 1847, was a real-world residential state-operated school, the blind Boston Bible was a celebrated and early example of an American raised-print book. It was published in eight volumes between 1836 and 1842 by the American Bible Society under the direction of Samuel Gridley Howe, a sighted educator now best known as the teacher of

Laura Bridgman. Similarly, the surgical restoration of sight was also a very well-publicized innovation not to mention a medical reality for some blind Americans. All of these details, from the naming of a school onward, lend Allen's depiction of a formerly blind person both depth and plausibility. The accuracy of his portrait matters because it will predispose his reader to accept his novel's highly implausible depiction of reading by touch.

Holmes's skills are not, it turns out, limited to the reading of either raised-print bibles or tactile impressions made with pencils on paper; Holmes can also use his sense of touch to read books printed in ink. An inveterate showman, he demonstrates the full extent of his skills for Wood, picking up an ink-print book from a table in Wood's study, opening it to a random page, and turning it face down. The narrator explains how, "passing one finger almost imperceptibly over the face of a page, he began to read, as fast as the human voice can go, the very first verses he chanced to light upon" (192). Commenting on the speed and precision of his reading, the narrator adds, "He read it like print" (192). And, of course, in this highly fanciful depiction of reading by touch, Holmes *is* reading print: he is using his fingers to read text transcribed in ink, text that was created for sighted people to read with their eyes. Portraying a sighted man reading by touch and, what is more, reading a book printed in ink by touch, Allen pushes a real-world skill, acquired by thousands of blind people, first into the domain of the sighted majority and then into the realm of the superhuman. Allen offers no explanation for the tactility of inked text, of whether the printing press leaves a perceptible depression on the surface of the page or if the residue of ink is somehow legible in relief on the page. What interests Allen is the idea that a sighted person might use the sense of touch to read a book that was designed to be read by sight. Reading by touch is distanced from the lived experience of blindness but what is more, in this fantastical scenario, the method of reading by touch is separated off from the material realities of reading by touch, namely the raised-print books read by a real-world blind person, such as Alfred Hirst.

In a demonstration of the intensity of Allen's interest in sighted people's use of touch to read, Allen grants a second sighted character the ability to read by touch. Wood, the skeptical witness of Holmes's performance, can also read by touch, though he has a less developed skill set than Holmes. Wood can identify the suit and number of standard issue playing cards with his fingers but he relies on sight to read ink-print books. Unlike the showman Holmes, Wood, sighted throughout his life, does not have first-hand experience of blindness. He does, however, have visually disabled relatives and, inspired by their example, has taught himself to read raised print. Wood tells

Holmes that his fingers have an unusually high level of sensitivity, a sensitivity he believes he inherited from a blind uncle and from his blind grandfather. A sighted person who can read by touch, he is uniquely positioned to identify another person with the same highly uncommon pairing of abilities. Indeed, it is Wood's own ability to read by touch that makes him suspect the showman's deception.

Holmes, the more skilled and less honest of the two, already knows all about reading playing cards by touch; before he began his career as a mesmerist, he made his living as a card sharp, reading the ink on the face of playing cards with a brush of his finger as he dealt them. As the novel draws to a conclusion, Allen disposes of this unusually skilled and thoroughly unsavory character with a plot development that signals the danger implicit in the secret practice of a prodigious skill. As public interest in displays of psychic ability declines, Holmes, obliged to return to card sharping, dies a violent death in Monte Carlo, stabbed through the heart by a card player who notices him feeling the faces of cards. Of course, readers of Victorian literature would be hard pressed to feel surprise at the villainization of a character with a personal history of disability or, relatedly, at the violent removal of a disabled villain from the plot.[12] It is instead the vilification of reading by touch—an ability heralded by many as an improving influence on the intellectual, cultural, and moral lives of visually disabled people—that is surprising.

What does Allen's fictional and fantastical depiction of reading by touch communicate about blindness and blind people? Holmes is a sighted man whose personal history with blindness leaves no visible trace; having regained sight, he hides his history of blindness, including his experiences of blindness gain. Holmes is consequently able to misrepresent a form of literacy as a psychic power, passing off a skill as a marvel. Of course, Holmes's skill is exceptional in the sense that he can read inked text by touch, something that real-world blind people who read by touch cannot do. Holmes has an extraordinary ability yet he opts to misrepresent that ability as unrelated to blindness.

Of course, Grant Allen is also in the business of misrepresentation. When he transforms reading by touch, a reality of blind people's lives, into a fantasy of superhuman haptic sensitivity, Allen de-normalizes an emergent mode of reading and the people who practice it. What is more, when he separates the method of reading by touch from the medium of the raised-print book, Allen authors a fantasy of extreme ability and hyper-sensitivity. The skills required to read a purpose-made raised-print book by touch are not transferable to reading ink by touch. Allen's novel places these very different achievements, reading raised-print by touch and reading ink by touch, on a continuum of ability, thus legitimating an implausibility. To put this another way, Allen blurs the real and the unreal: living in an era of blind literacy, he ignores the material realities of reading by touch in favor of a fantasy of superhuman ability. Allen's portrait of a formerly blind conman also links the practice of reading by touch, and by extension, blindness and blindness gain, with deception. Keeping his personal history of disability a secret, retaining an ability linked with blindness after he regains sight, Holmes misuses a skill possessed by blind people to defraud sighted people who pay him for psychic knowledge he doesn't possess. In this way, Allen depicts an undisclosed personal history of disability as an unfair advantage. Thus, while his portrayal of sighted people reading by touch is both unusual and fanciful, the connection Allen makes between disability and villainy is thoroughly conventional.

To return to the first section of this chapter, Allen's fictional portrait of reading by touch obviously differs radically from Hirst's contemporaneous first-person experience of literacy. Still, there are revealing points of resonance between them. Hirst's autobiographical writing and Allen's novel are, for example, connected by their exploration of an individual's changing relationship to blindness. Whereas Hirst shares an experience of acquired blindness, Allen's portrait of Holmes imagines the aftermath of the surgical restoration of sight. Both the non-fictional and the fictional narrative also engage questions of ability and advantage. For Hirst, the advantages of reading by touch are linked to attentiveness and comprehension, to a careful and close form of reading that facilitates personal development as well as pleasure. For Allen, reading by touch is a skill that advantages an unethical practitioner so that he profits financially, not intellectually, from its surreptitious use. Allen's novel engages the kinds of experiences Hirst explores, such as learning to read by touch in an institutional setting, but, whereas Hirst celebrates how reading by touch enriches lives, Allen villainizes a reader who employs touch instead of sight to read at the cost of his life.

Depicting a sighted person who profits from the secret practice of a blind person's skill, the novel itself profits from its engagement with blindness, using the life experiences of a real-world blind community to lend credibility to a fictional, and fanciful, portrait of a formerly blind person. Allen's reader is not a blind scholar but a sighted charlatan, an unethical man who profits monetarily rather than intellectually. Allen and Hirst are both, to put it simply, interested in how reading by touch advantages its practitioners. The same historical development that motivated Hirst to campaign for the publication of more books in braille prompts Allen to speculate about what might happen if sighted people learned to read by touch and then did so surreptitiously, not for the kinds of profit and pleasure that Hirst described, but to secure an unfair advantage.

Perhaps the most surprising point of resonance between Hirst and Allen is their shared interest in extreme forms of ability. In Allen's novel, extreme ability takes the form of the ability to read not just handwriting but inked text by touch. In Hirst's writing, extreme ability is by no means his keynote though it does have a presence. In his 1897 essay "My Dark World," Hirst compares his own experiences as a reader of raised print with an account of an unnamed blind reader's exceptional skill at reading braille, which had, by century's end, been interlined, allowing text to be embossed on both sides of a single sheet of paper, thus reducing the cost and bulk of books while also bringing blind people's books into closer resemblance with those of sighted people. Hirst writes: "I know one ex-pupil of the Royal Normal College who can with his left hand read aloud the left-hand page, whilst with a finger of his right he can to himself read the right-hand page, and tell the listener what the latter contains immediately he had completed the reading aloud of the opposite page" ("My Dark World" 7). Enthusiastic about reading by touch and eager to promote it, Hirst shares a portrait of an ambidextrous reader with an extraordinary ability, his account of the simultaneous reading of different passages distancing reading by touch from reading by sight.[13] The result is a portrait of a supercrip reader, a kind of portrait that, as disability studies scholar Eli Clare has argued in a different context, invests in extreme achievement at the cost of attention to "material, social, [and] legal conditions" (Clare 3) that limit possibilities for people with disabilities.[14]

Making a remarkable claim about a remarkable skill, Hirst's portrait of the extraordinary skill of an ambidextrous reader of braille participates in a larger social identification of disability with extreme ability at the same time that it is consistent with other claims Hirst makes about blind readers in that this highly skilled blind person benefits from the difference in his reading mode, from the difference between fingers and eyes. He can, Hirst insists, direct the fingers of his two hands toward two pages of a book: a cognitive juggle and sensory challenge for a person reading by touch but an impossibility for a sighted reader who cannot independently direct the gaze of each of their eyes. Whether Hirst's account of the ambidextrous reader is an accurate record of extraordinary achievement or merely a fantasy of blind ability doesn't matter. What Hirst insists on is possibility, both sensorial and cognitive possibility, in the context of the proliferation of a new reading mode. When Hirst writes about blind people's reading, his message is consistent: reading by touch is a uniquely enabling practice.

This chapter has engaged the work of Alfred Hirst, an understudied but energetic advocate for reading by touch and its advantages. Using Hirst's enthusiasm for Milton as a starting point, it has explored how experiences of blindness gain and perceptions of blind readers as uniquely capable contributed to the emergence of a new representative figure of blind ability: the blind scholar. As both Allen's novel and this closing reflection on supercrip readers suggest, the reality of blindness gain shaped some unrealistic depictions of reading by touch, this in addition to playing a role in generalizations about the tastes as well as the skills of blind people, a community of readers who gained a shared reputation, in the age of raised print, as uniquely avid and capable. As the next chapter will show, the work of sighted people who read to or took dictation from blind people retained its importance in the lives of some blind people even in an era of raised print. Taking the experiences of blind authors as its focus, that chapter will add to existing knowledge about blindness and authorship in the nineteenth century by asking how the delegation of tasks to a sighted assistant shaped not only the experiences of blind authors but also the literary depiction of blind authors by their sighted peers.

Three

Authors and Amanuenses

After graduating from New York's Institution for the Blind, William Artman and L.V. Hall coauthored *Beauties and Achievements of the Blind* (1854), a book celebrating the creativity and cultural influence of blind people. In it, Artman and Hall reject the notion that blindness is an obstacle that blind creators must overcome. Refuting, for example, the idea that blind poets are disadvantaged by their inability to compose poems on paper, Artman and Hall explain that a "supply of stationery" is only necessary to those who "hew and carve poetry, as a toy-maker whittles out his articles" (12). In the case of a "true poetic spirit" (12), transcription is immaterial to the creative process. Transcription was, however, a precondition for the publication of their book and so Artman and Hall, like other blind authors of their era, worked with sighted amanuenses. The frontispiece to *Beauties and Achievements of the Blind* shows them dictating to these assistants; the men stand at a table at which two women are seated, the gendered division of their tasks reflective of centuries-old conventions that pair blind men with nonblind female helpers (fig. 9). The men face the women while the women look toward the sheets of paper on which they write, the position of the four figures indicative of the transmission of ideas from the authors' minds, through the amanuenses' bodies, to the page. Tipped in between the frontispiece is a sheet of raised-print text, the only page in this book that can be read by touch (fig. 10).[1] A single paragraph of raised print followed by chapters of inked print, this addition is, not unlike the image of Artman and Hall at work, emblematic of nineteenth-century blind people's reliance on sighted assistants for access to print culture, even in the case of a book authored by, about, and for blind people.

Guided by the insights of contemporary Disability Studies scholars, this chapter explores relationships between nineteenth-century blind authors and their sighted amanuenses. Taking up the experiences of four understudied

Figure 9. Frontispiece to *Beauties and Achievements of the Blind* (1879 edition). Author's collection.

authors, W.W. Fenn, Frances Browne, Edmund White, and Alice King, it demonstrates the surprising degree to which raised print was peripheral to the careers of nineteenth-century blind writers. I show that the persistence of blind authors' work with sighted assistants decades after the advent of reading by touch was particularly challenging for working-class authors whose resourcefulness in securing assistance is a measure of their determination to both access ink-print culture and contribute to it. Turning from lived experience to the literary record, I share a reading of "Eyes that Saw not" (1902), a co-authored short story by sighted spouses Bertrand W. Babcock and Winnifred Eaton. Their story pairs an inept blind author with a sighted secretary who, unbeknownst to him, thoroughly revises his compositions before publishing them. The result, an ableist depiction of a blind man as untalented and unwitting, sensationalizes the author-amanuensis relationship by emphasizing the vulnerability of the blind partner to deception. My second literary case study, George du Maurier's novel *The Martian* (1897), engages themes of blindness, authorship, and assistance in a more creative and progressive manner. Shaped by du Maurier's personal experience of blindness in one eye, *The*

Figure 10. Photograph of a sheet of raised-print text that has been glued between the frontispiece and title page of *Beauties and Achievements of the Blind.* The frontispiece is covered by a tissue guard; the raised-print page shares a quotation from the Book of Isaiah embossed in Kneass's script and framed with a tactile border. Author's collection.

Martian is a fictional biography of Barty Josselin, a partially blind person who finds success not as an author but as an amanuensis. To the surprise of Victorian and contemporary readers alike, Barty transcribes books that are dictated to him by an extraterrestrial being. Decoupling blindness from authorship, linking it instead to the work of transcription, du Maurier casts a blind man as a provider of secretarial assistance rather than a recipient of it. Attentive to ways in which gender shapes ideas about both blindness and authorship, I argue that du Maurier's novel engages the conventional, and historically factual, pairing of a blind male author with a sighted female assistant in order to radically transform it. I conclude the chapter by exploring parallels between du Maurier's unconventional novel and the contemporaneous emergence of a new group of office workers: blind amanuenses who, in a symbolically potent, real-world reversal of cultural expectations, used typewriters to take dictation from sighted people. Whether engaging lived experiences or the literary record, this chapter demonstrates that author-amanuensis relationships are ideologically generative pairings of blind and nonblind people that both map and query the persistence of limits on blind people's access to written culture.

Caring and Pairing

As recent work in the field of Disability Studies has shown, the provision of care is a useful lens for the analysis of relationships between disabled and nondisabled people. In *Communities of Care: The Social Ethics of Victorian Fiction* (2021), Talia Schaffer defines care as both an emotion and a set of actions. She turns to Victorian literature for insight into the history of care relationships but also for guidance on how care might shape actions not normally associated with caregiving, such as the analysis of literary texts. Proposing that good kinds of care are fluid and multidirectional, Schaffer explains that "[t]he care dynamic is a complicated, flexible set of actions among multiple actors in a social relationship" (6). She argues for increased recognition of how "carer and cared-for roles slip around" (6), with the person in the position of the carer at some times also being, or becoming, the cared-for in the course of a relationship or even in the duration of a single social interaction. Schaffer's insights both add to and build on the work of scholars who share her interest in Victorian literature's fascination with the pairing of a disabled character with a nondisabled character. Martha Stoddard Holmes's seminal study *Fictions of Affliction* (2004) explores both literature and drama's shared investment in, among other relationships, the pairing of a blind woman and a sighted sister figure, a relationship that, given the historical expectation that young women's lives move them toward the reward of marriage, sets up a comparison of the two women's "physically, emotionally, and socially divergent fates on the basis of blindness and sight" (5). Karen Bourrier, in *The Measure of Manliness* (2015), explores Victorian literature's depiction of close friendships between disabled men and nondisabled men; by contrasting the two men's abilities and personalities, these friendships contribute to the establishment of masculine norms of behavior, especially in the context of male-dominated spaces such as public schools or workplaces. Though they engage different scenarios, both Holmes and Bourrier demonstrate the capacity of paired characters positioned as foils to communicate messages about disability and disabled people.

I propose that blind authors and sighted amanuenses are another example of an ideologically generative pairing, or, to put this differently, of a relationship that contrasts its participants in ways that influence both perceptions and experiences of disability. A core message communicated by author-amanuensis relationships is the interdependence of blind and sighted people, with both participants in the relationship depending on one another to have their needs met. Some of the needs that shape these relationships are emotional in nature but tangible exchanges also structure them, with, for example, a blind author receiving the secretarial assistance she or he requires and the sighted amanuensis receiving either monetary payment or, in the case of a spouse or child, compensation in the form of a share of the author's earnings. Thus, while the author-amanuensis pairing of a disabled and nondisabled person has traits in common with the pairings Holmes and Bourrier explore, this relationship, whose *raison d'être* is the production of written expression, possesses unique attributes, its emphasis on interdependence, reciprocity, and productivity promoting different and potentially more progressive perceptions of disability than the pairing of sister figures in a marriage market or of male friends who engage in a competitive public sphere in dissimilar ways. Portraying disabled people who contribute to the public sphere and who engage, to borrow from Schaffer, in a two-way flow of care, both relying on others and providing for others, these literary depictions of blind authors and their sighted assistants are not so much about the different fates or futures of disabled and nondisabled people as they are about what disabled and nondisabled people might create by working together.

Of course, because a wide range of nineteenth-century people, including sighted writers, worked with paid or unpaid assistants, only a portion of the era's author-amanuensis relationships were initiated or structured by blindness. Sighted author Wilkie Collins described his work with an unnamed assistant in the 1871 preface to his novel *The Moonstone*. Experiencing "a double calamity," first anticipating then grieving his mother's death at the same time that he was "crippled in every limb by the torture of rheumatic gout" (5), Collins dictated from his bed, authoring the portion of his novel that was, he proposed, the "most successful in amusing the public" (5).[2] Henry James worked with three professional secretaries between 1897 and his death in 1916; all three secretaries used a typewriter to take his dictation.[3] William Makepeace Thackeray also employed amanuenses, even taking them with him when he traveled. In addition to working with paid assistants, Thackeray dictated fiction to his daughter Annie Thackeray Ritchie, who went on to have a literary career of her own.[4] Importantly, while working with an assistant was an option for sighted authors, an arrangement they might opt in or out of in the course of their careers or even in the course of a project, for the entirety of the nineteenth century, assistance was a fixed feature of blind authors' working lives. Their use of secretarial assistance is consequently a valuable context for investigating the history of ideas about blindness, including ideas about blind people's literacy.

Writing about It; Doing without It

The careers of a representative sampling of blind authors from the second half of the nineteenth century indicate that, while the development of raised print and the spread of the skills required to read by touch revolutionized many blind people's experiences of reading, these developments did not transform the working lives of blind authors. The proliferation of raised print did not, for example, provide authors with unmediated access to publications that were useful to them in their work. With very few exceptions, nineteenth-century blind authors relied on sighted people to read aloud works of contemporary literature, reference materials, and the content of the periodical press. What is more, as the case of Artman and Hall reminds us, even the work of nineteenth-century blind authors, including books by blind authors about blindness, were printed in ink, with raised print largely reserved for Scripture and devotional works, for texts used in educational settings, and, as I explored in chapter 2, for the work of established literary giants such as Milton. In addition to providing mediated access to published works that could not be read by touch, sighted assistants supported blind authors by reading aloud handwritten documents, from correspondence with prospective publishers to drafts of their own compositions.

Obliged, more often than not, to listen to text being read, some blind authors found the skill of reading by touch more useful to them in their creative work as a topic than a tool. This was certainly the case for landscape painter turned author W.W. Fenn. When he became blind in his early thirties, Fenn made a career change, writing essays and short stories, and, in time, a novel. Active in the 1870s and 1880s, he wrote on a wide range of topics, including his personal experience of acquired blindness. In an essay titled "Fingers versus Eyes," he shares a painfully bleak description of the experience of becoming blind, which he presents as a catastrophic disruption of a productive man's life. Though his own blindness was the catalyst for a successful writing career, Fenn asserts:

> Nothing, surely, can exceed the calamity of a hale strong man, in his prime and vigour, with all his schemes, hopes, and ambitions teeming with interest, and hourly yielding profitable fruits, to be suddenly brought to a stand-still, pulled up in his sturdy march through life, and placed perhaps at the disposition of a little child; to find every moment of his existence, every onward step he takes, every wish, trivial or important, no longer under his own control, but under that of his guide or helpmate [. . .]. ("Fingers versus Eyes" 452–53)

Identifying both the loss of productivity and reliance on others as tragic, Fenn does not hesitate to label blindness a "calamity." Understanding blindness as the cause of problems in need of solutions, Fenn was a champion of reading by touch, which he viewed as a way to foster blind people's sense of independence. Fenn also championed reading by touch as a way for blind people to manage social isolation and boredom. Notably, he recognizes reading by touch as a practice shaped by class status, believing isolation and boredom to be especially common among working-class blind people. While reading by touch is, Fenn asserts, a valuable form of mental occupation for all blind people, working-class blind people are, he feels, more likely to benefit from the acquisition of this skill because they are less likely to be read aloud to by sighted companions. Paraphrasing William Shakespeare, Fenn explains:

> if the sightless man be poor, his chances are very few and far between indeed of getting any one to read to him as a continuous source of pleasure and profit; and his feelings of isolation thus intensified, he must constantly be left for hours and hours together, 'to wear out his life in shapeless idleness,' unless he can read for himself. ("Fingers versus Eyes" 456–57)

A remedy for social losses related to blindness, reading by touch is, Fenn asserts, a source of solace for working-class blind people whose disability increases their chances of being alone. A raised-print book makes up for the absence, or illiteracy, of sighted companions:

> With no one perhaps to read to him, with nothing indeed around him that can reach his brain through his ear, he obviously feels about with his fingers for something to do. What, then, at such a moment so fitting to put before him as a book, which with his fingers he shall be able as readily to decipher as his more fortunate friends with their eyes? ("Fingers versus Eyes" 456)

The benefits of reading by touch are not, however, limited to working-class people. Fenn explains of a representative blind man:

> If he be rich even, and can afford the advantage of a regular attendant, secretary, amanuensis, guide, reader, whatever you call him, the sense of independence conferred by his ability to do this for himself would be an immense satisfaction, and go far to destroy the idea of being shut off by his calamity from habits common to the seeing. ("Fingers versus Eyes" 456)

His list of different titles for paid assistants gesturing in its own way toward extravagance, Fenn asserts that reading by touch enhances a blind person's life even in cases when he or she has both companionship and easy access to a sighted reader's services. Rewarded by "immense satisfaction" and a "sense of independence," even the most privileged blind people benefit, Fenn proposes, from reading books by touch instead of listening to them.

Interestingly, while reading by touch mattered to Fenn for what it made possible for other blind people—generating pleasure, promoting independence, and lessening the impacts of social isolation—Fenn dedicated his own leisure time to listening to books read aloud. In an autobiographical essay titled "My Own Story," Fenn shares that "being read to is the one main source of all my mental enjoyment" (17). Indeed, it is not clear that Fenn either owned or could read raised-print books. Referring to a collection of ink-print books, Fenn shares: "so long as I have my books, and by means of my faithful reader can hold companionship with the great and thoughtful minds of past and present times, and can take in by the ear all that most nearly touches the heart of man, I have no room for anything but gratitude that it is my sight and not my hearing of which I am deprived" ("My Own Story" 22). Using the passive voice, he describes "the pleasantest hour almost of the whole day" as the time at which "[t]he favourite book is opened, and I am read to as long as the light lasts" ("My Own Story" 17).

The unnamed sighted person doing that reading was, more often than not, his wife, Elizabeth, who married Fenn in 1867, soon after he became blind. In addition to enriching Fenn's leisure time by reading to him, Elizabeth played a key role in his professional life. Fenn explains, in the same autobiographical essay, how marrying secured him the assistance he needed to succeed as an author: "at once I had eyes and hands, pen and patience, put at my disposal, with an affectionate devotion not to be surpassed" ("My Own Story" 5). This mixed list—of body parts, a writing tool, and a personality trait—hints at the complexity of author-amanuensis relationships, which were shaped not only by gender convention but also by sensory difference, by one partner's blindness and the other partner's sight. In the Fenns' case, as in many other blind author-sighted amanuensis relationships, while the division of labor was determined by differences in sensory experience, the success of the partnership depended on the talents, interests, personalities, and compatibility of the participants. Appreciation for sighted people's assistance is a keynote not only of Fenn's autobiographical essays but also of the prefaces to three collections of stories and essays that he published. Take, for example, the preface to his 1885 collection *Woven in Darkness*, in which Fenn explains: "to those kindly and helpful hands which have assisted me in the actual writing as in the thousand and other wants hourly pressing in upon a blind man, I owe a debt of the deepest gratitude, one which can never be repaid" (*Woven in Darkness* vii). Bringing to mind Artman and Hall's frontispiece and the women depicted in it, Fenn acknowledges the central role Elizabeth plays in his literary success:

> There is one constant friend [. . .] whose devotion and help is so far beyond description or thanks, that I dare not attempt to render either. I can perhaps best hint at what I feel by slightly altering and adapting to the occasion a line or two from one of Wordsworth's sonnets: "The feather whence the pen was shaped," that traced these words and lines, "Dropped from an angel's wing,"—and I would reverently add, "into an angel's hand." (*Woven in Darkness* vii–viii)

Borrowing from William Wordsworth's "Walton's Book of Lives," a poem about Walton's authorial skill, Fenn glosses it to praise his wife's skills, to evoke the materiality of her work with pen and paper, and to identify her with an idealized femininity. Elizabeth, a helpmate in a companionate middle-class marriage, is an angel-amanuensis in the author's house, her support for Fenn's work inextricable from her support for him as a husband. Whereas Elizabeth, a "faithful reader" as well as a "patient scribe" assists Fenn both by reading aloud and taking dictation, Fenn reciprocates in his role as the person who secures a writer's income for their household ("My Own Story" 22, 14). Consistent with Schaffer's characterization of care as both given and received by people with disabilities, their relationship is, it seems, mutually beneficial and is also, as we will explore in the second half of this chapter, a real-world version of a type of relationship that fascinated writers of fiction.

Fenn's attention to how class status shaped blind people's experiences of reading by touch can be productively extended to the analysis of blind people's experiences of authorship. Neither Fenn's good fortune in his helpmate nor his literary success were shared by his working-class contemporary, the blind poet Edmund White. White was, however, like Fenn in that reading by touch was a theme in his writing but not a feature of his work life. White, whose poetry was a focus of chapter 1, lived in poverty and consequently relied on unpaid family members to help him prepare poems for publication, his two young daughters dividing between them the work done in Fenn's case by his wife. As noted in chapter 1, White, who lost his job as a railway guard when he lost his ability to see, wrote poetry not only to raise awareness of challenges faced by working-class blind people but also to "assist in providing the common necessaries of life for a young and numerous family" (*Blindness* viii). In the preface to his long poem *Blindness* (1856), White describes the difficulty of dictating poems to the same children he struggled to support:

> The composition of this little volume has [. . .] been to me a long, tedious, and protracted undertaking, having to instruct the writer, one of my daughters, who is only eleven years of age, how to spell almost every word as I dictated it, when it was afterwards corrected and copied by another of my daughters, thirteen years of age, in those hours that should have been devoted to rest, after the tedium of a long day's occupation. (ix)

One imagines these daughters at work, transcribing not only pages of poetry but also White's comments about their contributions, the younger child writing words about herself she cannot spell, the older correcting and copying drafts that describe the double duty she does working both outside the home and as her father's assistant. This preface also shares that one of the severest limitations White faced as a working-class blind poet was "the impossibility of appealing to works of reference" (ix). White authors poetry under difficult circumstances, doing work but also making work for others, his frustration with his reliance on his overtasked children markedly different from Fenn's pleasure in his wife's willing and capable assistance. White's experience consequently offers insight into the diversity of blind authors' and sighted amanuenses' relationships, reminding us of the existence of frustrations and pressures that did not, it seems, shape Fenn's career.

The working-class blind person, poet, and novelist Frances Browne faced challenges very similar to those faced by White.[5] Browne, who earned her first byline when she published a poem in a newspaper at age 25, used the money she earned in the first years of her literary career to educate her younger sister, Rebecca, to act as her amanuensis. Whereas Frances provided Rebecca with training, Rebecca assisted Frances in her work for over a decade, following Frances from their birthplace, in Stranorlar in Ireland, to Edinburgh, and then to London, where they lived and worked together. When Rebecca married and returned to Scotland, Frances made new arrangements. *Chambers's Journal* reported in 1861 that, following her sister's departure, Browne "had the assistance of a secretary for a few hours every day, her lengthened service to literature not yet enabling her to have one entirely at her command. In those hours she has written songs which have pleased many who little guessed under what circumstances they were dictated" ("Frances Browne" 282). The essayist's emphasis on limits placed on Browne's productivity by the cost of paying an amanuensis is noteworthy, as is the essayist's interest in the fact that readers of Browne's work were unlikely to suspect that her poems were authored by a person navigating challenges related to blindness. To put this differently, Browne's writing is, to this commentator's surprise, a product of her work with a sighted assistant but not a record of it.

Browne, like White, had a harder time than Fenn when it came to accessing the literary works of other authors. In a set of reflections shared with her editor, who in turn shared them in the preface to Browne's first volume of poetry, *The Star of Attéghéi* (1844), Browne explained she did not attend school as a child but instead gained an education by "listening attentively to my young brothers and sisters reading over the tasks required at the village school" (Editor's Preface x). The editor's preface, the closest thing we have to life writing by Browne, makes no mention of her learning to read by touch either as a child or as an adult. Instead, this mediated account shares how, while still a child, Browne developed different strategies for accessing written culture. Lacking the "power of reading," Browne explains how blindness

> obliged me to depend on the services of others; and as the condition of my family was such as did not admit of much leisure, my invention was early taxed to gain time for those who could read. I sometimes did the work assigned to them, or rendered them other little services [. . .]. The lighter kinds of reading were thus easily managed. (xvi)

Consistent with Fenn's portrait of a working-class blind person who cannot afford paid assistance, Browne had to work to secure access to text, especially when relying on people who, in addition to having limited time to read, were selective about what they read. As Browne explains:

> my young relatives were often unwilling to waste their breath and time with the drier, but more instructive, works which I latterly preferred. To tempt them to this, I used, by way of recompense, to relate to them long stories, and even novels, which perhaps they had formerly read but forgotten:—and thus my memory might be said to have earned supplies for itself. (xvi)

Using her storytelling skills to gain access to other authors' stories, Browne is not a passive recipient of her family's care but is instead an agent who labors, physically and intellectually, to secure familial support and, with it, the cultural access she desires. Exchanging chores as well as entertainment for her readers' services, Browne alerts us to the extent to which relationships between authors and assistants were defined by reciprocity as well as by blind authors' resourcefulness. Browne's circumstances also remind us that, when the blind and sighted partners of an author-amanuensis relationship were connected by a pre-existing bond, such as a familial bond, their work was very likely shaped by obligations, personal histories, and emotions not generated solely in the context of their work arrangements. Of course, people connected by familial or other forms of social bonds might also exchange money in the context of an author-amanuensis relationship. And, even in the case of a paid employer-employee relationship, initiated by, for example, an advertisement in a newspaper, both the blind author and the sighted assistant were in a position to give and receive emotional support.

Like Browne, the blind author Alice King accessed ink-print publications by listening to them. King, who made her living as a novelist and journalist, emphasized the importance of listening to sighted people read to her success. Sharing details of her life in *The Girl's Own Paper* in 1887, King explained: "I have learned how to write English fluently, partly through my parents, from my earliest days, reading out loud to me all the masterpieces of English literature. I have continued this practice of listening to well-written books all my life, and my ears have helped me in catching a good style of composition" ("Our Blind Contributor" 578). Supported in childhood by family members, as an adult King paid for secretarial help, though she, like Browne, faced difficulties securing the assistance she desired. At the outset of her career, she could not, for example, afford to pay assistants whose skill level suited her needs. She notes: "In the first years of my literary career I always wrote with an amanuensis. She was generally a girl from the village school, with a mind not too well instructed as to grammar and orthography" ("Our Blind Contributor" 578). Limited by her assistant's abilities, this in addition to limits on her ability to pay an assistant, King developed a pre-dictation process to speed their work together:

> I used to have to write out every sentence first thoroughly in my head, getting up thus, perhaps, half a chapter by heart, and considering well how each paragraph sounded, and how any specially long words were spelt; then I set to work with my amanuensis to get it all on to paper; and laborious the task often was for both her and myself. Here again, however, patience and perseverance stood me in good stead. ("Our Blind Contributor" 578)

In time, King found an even better solution to the challenges of working with an amanuensis. An early adopter of the typewriter, she was able, as she became more skilled at typing, to rely less on the services of sighted people. Preferring to use a machine than to collaborate with an inadequately skilled helper, King minimized both the amount of work she did with a paid secretary and her costs. As we will explore later in this chapter, typing, a skill that supported King in her work as a professional author, would also create new employment opportunities for blind people in the final decades of the century.

Taken as a group, these case studies of nineteenth-century blind authors, while neither homogenous nor comprehensive, reveal how little raised-print books featured in blind authors' work. Blind authors' relationships with amanuenses document instead the importance of blind people's creative management of challenging or unsatisfactory arrangements with sighted people. Importantly, blind authors' experiences of secretarial support alert us to assistants' reliance on authors for financial support in the form of a salary or, in the case of family members, a share in the household's earnings. Initiated by blind people, shaped by disability, reciprocity, gender, and class, these relationships offer insight into the different forms that both support and compensation for the provision of support can take. Notably, none of the case studies explored here touch on the possibility that blind authors might be deceived by their sighted assistants. That is, however, the possibility that energizes "Eyes that Saw not," a short story that allows us to contrast the lived experience of blind authors with their literary depiction.

"Eyes that Saw not": The Amanuensis as Coauthor

In fiction, as in the lives of real-world blind authors, author-amanuensis relationships are a productive context for the development and expression of ideas about blindness. Given the sighted majority's reverence both for blind authors such as John Milton and for mythical figures such as Ossian, we might expect sighted people's stories about blind authors to link sensory disability with heightened creative ability. "Eyes that Saw not," a 1902 short story co-authored by Bertrand W. Babcock and Winnifred Eaton, defies that expectation. Babcock and Eaton (who used the pen name Onoto Watanna) had been married for less than a year when their story appeared in *Harper's Magazine*. Though it explores connections between authorship and romantic love, it is not a thinly veiled depiction of their own collaboration. Instead, the story explores the role blindness plays in the life of John Swinnerton, a newspaper reporter whose loss of sight prompts him to abandon reporting to pursue a literary career. John works with a sighted assistant, Elizabeth, a member of his family's household who, in the course of the story, becomes his fiancée. Though "Eyes that Saw not" has, it seems, received little by way of critical attention, this story's depiction of blindness warrants our consideration, not least because it is a literary case study that can enrich our understanding of the limited role played by reading by touch in nineteenth-century blind authors' lives. In what follows, I argue that Babcock and Eaton's depiction of a sighted amanuensis's deception of the inept blind author she loves sensationalizes the experience of blindness, identifying blindness with inability in order to better understand the essential components not only of literary talent but also of successful literary collaboration.

At the start of the story, John has left New York City to return to his middle-class parents' home in the suggestively named Graytown. Soon after arriving, he begins to write fiction, work he aspired to when sighted but did not pursue. John does not perceive his acquired blindness in the same way the story's narrator does, namely as a "catastrophe" (31). He tells his mother: "My inability to see is a physical misfortune. It doesn't impair my ability to write, nor destroy my knowledge of life. Mother, I intend to devote my life to literary work" (31). His plan will devote Elizabeth's life to the same work, her affection for John prompting her to become his "sole co-worker and amanuensis" (32). Their working relationship is shaped by multiple power imbalances. Elizabeth, a young woman, an orphan, and a dependent on the Swinnerton family, has lived a sheltered life in Graytown whereas John, a doted-on only child, is a self-confident man who achieved success in the city. Blindness equalizes their positions, ending John's journalism career and returning him to the domestic sphere at the same time that it gifts Elizabeth an occupation as his secretary. Elizabeth who had, when John was a successful city reporter, "been passionately jealous of his work" (32), both takes dictation and reads aloud from the reporter's notebooks that serve as John's source material. She also acts as John's literary agent, traveling to the city with manuscripts on his behalf, enjoying a form of mobility that John has lost.

An effective newspaper reporter when sighted, once blind, John writes stories that are, to quote the story's narrator, "blundering" (32). These stories are repeatedly rejected by magazine editors—that is, until Elizabeth intervenes. When Elizabeth decides to assume, unbeknownst to John, a creative role in what he perceives as his solo literary career, she takes advantage of John's blindness, relying on his inability to read his own publications to hide her intervention. In control of what he reads, and also of what he publishes, Elizabeth manages to hide her authorial interference for several years before she is discovered. Importantly, Elizabeth is moved to act by generosity and pity, not by her own ambition. Lying to John spontaneously, telling him one of his stories has been accepted for publication, this after repeatedly delivering accurate news of its rejection by different magazines, she goes to her room to read the story over. She does so

> hoping against hope that she might be able to discover something in it that would make it sufficiently attractive. And as she read, the plot of the story grew into her consciousness, awakening in her all the power of the literary artist. She could almost hear John's rich voice, with its ringing enthusiasm, as he had glowingly told her the story. (33)

Painfully aware of his shortcomings as a writer but appreciative of his gifts as an observer and oral storyteller, she writes a new version of John's submission.

The collaborative nature of what she produces is emphasized by the materials she uses to write, "a quick nervous pencil and an old pad of John's" (33). The result, a much altered version of the original, is quickly accepted, becoming the first in a series of successful but secret rewrites that culminate in the publication of a novel published in John's name, a novel that John erroneously believes he dictated to Elizabeth but which Elizabeth has very thoroughly rewritten.

Dictation features centrally in the story's depiction of John's limitations. The narrator will, for example, emphasize the gap between John's spontaneous storytelling and his stilted dictation:

> His narrative to Elizabeth had been instinct with the charm of personal experience told in simple, direct, graphic language, and his assumption of the first person had led her to identify herself with the actor in the scene, as her imagination, warming at his words, had reproduced the experience to the smallest detail. But his dictation lacked every grace; all the strength and picturesque beauty of his narration were wanting. While he had been talking he was himself, natural, spontaneous; now he was somebody else, an author dictating a story. (32)

John's shortcomings alert Elizabeth to her own literary potential or, to use the narrator's term, her "latent power" (33). Spending hours listening to John and transcribing his words, Elizabeth learns how not to tell a story. John's failure is, in part, a failure to recognize where his skills lie: "As the time-chipped phrases of the daily newspaper fell from his lips, Elizabeth wondered that the fortunate possessor of such rich experiences, possessed by one, too, who was capable of forming such vivid impressions, could so miserably fail in their ultimate expression" (32). It is when he assumes an authorial identity, and specifically an identity associated with blind authors, dictating stories for Elizabeth to transcribe, that he disappoints. Consider the following description of John and Elizabeth at work: "as each grotesque experience was related to her she would thrill with the awakening instinct of creative power, but when John's blundering, bald-phrased dictation began she shuddered, and her artistic perceptions underwent crucifixion" (32). Clearly, there is little by way of narrative restraint in play in Babcock and Eaton's depiction of John's failings. Elizabeth's suffering is increased by her knowledge that the dictation she takes will never be shared with publishers, let alone with readers: "Hour after hour she took his dictation. She thought of those prisoners condemned to work forever at machines that merely registered their efforts—a round of endless labour with nothing but a dial face to show what might have been accomplished" (33). Scenes in which John dictates to Elizabeth evoke a conventionally gendered division of labor, with the blind man composing and the sighted woman transcribing, a division of labor experienced by Artman and Hall and exemplified by John Milton's oft-discussed working relationship with his daughters. But Babcock and Eaton's story does not depict a great man at work. Focused instead on that man's limitations, it positions the male collaborator as the female partner's muse, a source of inspiration for creative work that is far more successful than his.

As noted above, John does not understand blindness as a limit on his ability to write fiction. Indeed, he will tell Elizabeth when he returns to Graytown that "The light without has gone to feed the flame within," a statement the unsympathetic narrator notes he makes "melodramatically" (30). John does, however, delay proposing marriage to Elizabeth because of his disability. Following the publication of his novel, John tells Elizabeth: "A little while ago I was alone in the darkness, vainly groping toward the light. Now I have found it. Then I was only a blind man, without the right to hope. Now I am an author whom the world recognizes" (34). He describes his love as "the love of a strong, successful man, an author blind, but with insight into the human heart" (34). Like the conventional and clichéd language John uses to describe his blindness, the awkward and overly poetic phrasing of "an author blind" is noteworthy, as too is the phrasing of the "but" clause, which modifies his identity as a blind person by insisting on his possession of insight in lieu of literal sight.

Elizabeth, meanwhile, doing double duty as amanuensis by day and an author by night, perceives herself not as a creator so much as a collaborator:

> when she went to work on John's dictation, the passion of the writer possessed her, and she forgot that she had been walking the treadmill of letters. The instant acceptance and publication of most of the stories—*were they not John's as much as hers?*—whetted confidence in her ability and acted as a spur to her pen. (33–34; my emphasis)

Their separate strengths are unknowingly summarized by a reviewer who describes John as "the well-known short-story writer, who unites the observation of the reporter with the grace of the artist" (34). By having Elizabeth rewrite John's life experiences, with John supplying the content and Elizabeth that content's literary treatment, the story separates out elements of the creative process and also of a successful literary collaboration, assigning different components of literary success to different people. The problem is, of course, that John is unaware of the division of tasks and talents in which he participates; misled by Elizabeth to believe their shared literary success is his alone, he collaborates without having knowledge of doing so.

To secure as much control as possible over John's access to print, Elizabeth insists that "No one, not even his mother, must read his precious work to him but her who had shared his labors" (34). Elizabeth is repeatedly depicted delivering, but not reading, copies of their publications to John, her selective performance of the duties of a secretary to a blind person allowing her to keep her revision of John's submissions secret. Strangely, the story makes no mention of reading by touch as a practice, this despite John's identity as an educated middle-class man living in late-century North America. That John is barred from reading his own work by its publication in ink is emphasized by the story's references to John's hands. Take, for example, a passage describing Elizabeth's delivery of the magazine that contains the first short story she manages to get published. The narrator explains how, when the radically rewritten story is published, "she put the magazine, with the story printed over his name, into John's hands" (33). Similarly, readers learn that Elizabeth has succeeded in publishing a novel in John's name with the following phrase: "the day came when Elizabeth put the book into John's hand" (34). These passages emphasize the conspicuous absence of reading by touch in a privileged blind person's life. Making no mention of a widely publicized reality of blind people's lives, more interested in, for example, innovations in ocular surgery than those related to literacy, Babcock and Eaton engage raised-print culture at best indirectly, and likely unintentionally, evoking rather than representing it.

Both John's inability to read by touch and the story's surprising silence on this practice are especially evident in passages that describe John holding copies of publications that Elizabeth has delivered to him. Focalized through Elizabeth, as is the larger story, the following passage describes her observation of John a full hour after she hands a copy of their novel to him:

> she found him still alone with the book. He was rubbing it gently over his cheek, handling it as if it were a thing of life, to be touched reverently. He opened it, fingering with delicate affection the bold lines of print. "My book, Beth!" he said, almost in a whisper. (34)

John's extended and ardent touching of the book's cover and content is hard to ignore. "[F]ingering" the "bold lines" on a page, John resembles a blind person reading a book but, in contrast to a blind person who reads by touch, John's actions emphasize his lack of access to the book's inked text. Touching

Figure 11. "'MY BOOK BETH!,' HE CRIED," illustration by John Wolcott Adams. *Harper's Magazine* (June 1902). Author's collection.

a book, but not reading that book by touch, John is a blind author who cannot read and, what is more, cannot rely on his sighted assistant to read to him. A tragic representative of blindness, he is a writer who tries to contribute to an ink-print culture from which he is barred not only by blindness but by his sighted assistant's determination to keep his failure as a writer a secret. Of course, John's tragedy is significantly heightened by the fact that he has contributed far less to the literary world than he thinks.

Both the fervor of John's touching as well as the failure of his touch to reveal the book's content attracted the attention of John Wolcott Adams, the creator of two dramatic full-page illustrations for Babcock and Eaton's story for *Harper's Magazine*. Adams's first illustration depicts a shadowy domestic interior in which John sits with his eyes closed, the closed book pressed against his check; Elizabeth, standing in a second mass of shadow, watches him from behind. Captioned "'MY BOOK BETH!,' HE CRIED," the illustration emphasizes John's uninformative experience of touch (fig. 11). Dependent on Elizabeth but misled by her, he misunderstands himself as a literary success in a realm he cannot access without her help. This changes when John regains the ability to see following an eye surgery that he has kept secret from Elizabeth with the intention of delighting her with news of the restoration of his sight. As soon as Elizabeth realizes John can see, she insists he read his novel. Once again, Babcock and Eaton portray Elizabeth placing a book in John's hands: "She caught up his book and thrust it into his hands. 'Can you see well enough to read? There—do—just a few chapters—.' Her breath almost left her. His eyes strained as he turned the title-pages, and slowly, painfully, he began to read" (38). Telling him to read inked print she did not read aloud to him when he was blind, she insists the book is their shared creation, a product of collaboration: "Yours—and mine, John. You were my inspiration. You gave the life, the spark. I could not have written a line but for you. Your soul, which could not find expression through your medium, dear, entered into mine, and I—" (38). Here, Elizabeth represents herself as a conduit, indeed as a medium who channels or gives expression to the sentiments of another soul. John, in contrast, insists the novel he holds is a record of plagiarism, not a product of collaboration. Elizabeth is, he insists, "guilty of the most despicable, the meanest of thefts" (38).

Their confrontation is the subject of the story's second illustration (fig. 12). Adams's illustration of this scene features a more clearly defined parlor setting than his first illustration, the increased clarity of the depiction of the room's contents likely referencing the change in John's visual acuity. Elizabeth is present; her back turned to the viewer, she faces John. As with the first illustration, John is the central figure but this time his eyes are wide open and he is standing instead of sitting. He holds his right hand to his head and his left hand is clenched claw-like at his side, his fingers locked in place as though still gripping the novel that lies on the ground, having "dropped from his nerveless hands" (38). Babcock and Eaton's description of John's hands as "nerveless" (38), which Adams highlights when he takes this phrase as his caption, communicates the shock John feels but also implies a loss of confidence, of "nerve," this in addition to suggesting a loss of sensitivity in his hands, a possibility suggested by the illustration of John's forceful but ineffectual grip.

Figure 12. "THE BOOK DROPPED FROM HIS NERVELESS HANDS," illustration by John Wolcott Adams. *Harper's Magazine* (June 1902). Author's collection.

If John's sense of touch is compromised, his sense of sight is strong enough for him to continue reading. When Elizabeth leaves the room, John reads pages of dictation that Elizabeth has taken over their years working together and it isn't long before his unmediated access to text prompts an epiphany:

> His hands trembled violently as he turned page after page, and as he read, a great light, a light that was startling in its poignant clearness, dawned upon him. The crudities of his own work, the set, stupid, inane phraseology, the long, tedious duologues! And then, opposite, the delicate wit, the intangible art, the philosophy, the pathos! (38)

In a climactic scene that equates sight with insight and illumination with understanding, John realizes his limitations. Able both literally and metaphorically to see more clearly, he longs for Elizabeth: "One great feeling welled up and took full possession of him, a longing that was almost madness for the presence, the touch, the sympathy of her he had spurned" (38). The story ends with them apart, in different rooms, but with John calling desperately for Elizabeth, yelling her name with a "startled cry of fear and longing" (38). The final paragraph of the story is a single sentence that reads: "In her room she heard it, and was glad" (38). Thus, Elizabeth is forgiven by John, a development that encourages the reader to do the same and to understand her years-long deception as justified. It is an ending that emphasizes John's need for Elizabeth and not, as earlier stages in the story explore, what each of them gain through their connection.

In depicting a sighted person deceiving a blind person, "Eyes that Saw not" contributes to a larger pattern in Victorian literature: the deception of blind people by sighted people who try to hide painful realities from a blind friend or family member. Consider, for example, the plot of Collins's *Poor Miss Finch* (1872), a novel structured by the blind protagonist Lucilla Finch's inability to see that her lover Oscar Dubourg's complexion is blue, his skin discolored by silver nitrate, a treatment for epilepsy.[6] The sighted characters of the text, Oscar among them, conspire to hide this fact from Lucilla. Similarly, in Charles Dickens's *The Cricket on the Hearth* (1845), Bertha Plummer is misinformed by her father Caleb about basic facts of their life together, such as their poverty. Misled by him to believe their hostile and exploitative employer, Tackleton, is a generous benefactor, Bertha also lacks factual knowledge of their home. In direct contradiction to her reality, she lives "in an enchanted home of Caleb's furnishing, where scarcity and shabbiness were not, and trouble never entered" (56). Bertha is, in fact, defined by ignorance of her life circumstances; the phrase "The Blind Girl never knew" is repeated four times in the novel's opening description of the Plummers' home to assert, among other examples of her ignorance, "The Blind Girl never knew that iron was rusting, wood rotting, paper peeling off; the very size, and shape, and true proportion of the dwelling, withering away" (56).[7] Undeterred by the implausibility of this deception, which requires Bertha to be unable to sense her surroundings in non-visual ways, Dickens is unremitting in his characterization of Bertha as dependent on her sighted father for knowledge of her own life. A parent's deception of a blind child is also central to "The Prince of Illusion," a short story by John Luther Long published in 1900. Long's story is a painfully sentimental description of a single mother's efforts to convince her blind son that he is literally a prince living in a palace when he is, in truth, an ill and impoverished child living in an attic room. Eaton and Babcock participate in this trend, extending it to the blind author-sighted amanuensis relationship, a pairing in which blind authors might logically be expected to enjoy control over their working conditions and, similarly, to have accurate knowledge of literary works published in their name.

While neither Eaton nor Babcock had, it seems, personal experience of visual disability, they clearly understood its narrative potential. Eaton and Babcock portray John as untalented and unwitting in order to hypothesize about the potential of a creative collaboration between a disabled person and a nondisabled person, a collaboration in which only one collaborator, the nondisabled person, is a knowing participant. The depiction of a blind man's ineptitude and, relatedly, his vulnerability to a sighted person's deception allows Babcock and Eaton to explore a topic that was likely of more relevance to their lives than blindness, namely the different components that make a work of creative writing successful. In addition to dramatizing the value of combining lived experience with writerly instinct, their story explores the difference between, on the one hand, successful newspaper reporting and, on the other hand, the successful composition of novels and short stories. Blindness adds drama to their reflections on literary talent and literary collaboration. While they depict the interdependence of a blind and a sighted person as well as the complementarity of their abilities, they also identify visual disability with inability and vulnerability to deception, this in order to re-imagine the sighted secretary to a blind author as the true talent. If for no other reason, this story would be notable for the way that it characterizes dictation, a defining practice of blind authors, as an exercise in self-exposure. Fortunately, George du Maurier took a very different approach to the literary depiction of dictation and to imagining how blindness might shape an author-amanuensis relationship. The result is as surprising as it is radical.

The Blind Amanuensis: du Maurier's *The Martian*

Nineteenth-century literature's representation of relationships between blind authors and their amanuenses is both complicated and enriched by du Maurier's 1896 novel *The Martian*. An unusual and understudied exploration of visual disability, *The Martian*, which du Maurier wrote and illustrated, is shaped by du Maurier's personal experience of acquired blindness. Du Maurier, who became permanently blind in his left eye in his twenties, decades before writing this novel, described acquired blindness as "the most tragic event of my life" (Whiteley 21). Changes in du Maurier's visual acuity changed his plan for his life, prompting him to abandon a career as a painter to pursue a career as an illustrator, this in the hope of lessening the strain on his remaining eyesight. His experience of visual disability also featured in his decision to write fiction. In the last decade of his life, still anxious about his sight, du Maurier decreased the time he spent working on illustrations, opting instead to dictate a trio of novels to his wife, Emma.

While all three novels secured large readerships and critical attention, the first of the three, *Trilby* (1894), was a massive commercial success and secured du Maurier an international reputation as an author. *The Martian*, his third and final novel, was serialized in ten installments beginning in 1896 in *Harper's*, the same magazine that published "Eyes that Saw not" six years later. The novel's reception was influenced by du Maurier's death, which occurred in the course of its serialization.[8] Reviews of *The Martian* consequently did double duty as eulogies, with reviewers' jobs made easier by the fact that du Maurier had himself used this novel to reflect on his life and career. It is very likely that the novel's extended treatment of blindness reminded reviewers to consider how disability shaped du Maurier's work both as an illustrator and author. Writing for *Harper's* the year after du Maurier died, Henry James, who was a friend of du Maurier, proposed that visual disability may have facilitated du Maurier's development of an unusual level of visual perceptiveness. James shared:

> He saw, with a creative intensity, every facial and corporeal queerness, all the signs of temperament and character that abide in the composing and performing race—all the obesities and aquilinities, all the redundancies of hair and eye, the unmistakabilities of origin, complexion and accent. It seemed to me that he almost *saw* the voice, as he saw the features and limbs, and quite as if this had been but one of the subtler secrets of his impaired vision. (601)

In the same memorial essay, James suggests that du Maurier was, in fact, gifted with heightened visual acuity. James asserts, "His sight was beyond any other I had known, and, whatever it had lost, what it had kept was surprising. [. . .] He had, in a word, not half, but double or quadruple the optical reach of other people" (599). Referencing du Maurier's visual disability in order to insist on his "optical reach," James evokes a compensatory model of acquired disability, imagining his friend as mysteriously gifted by "the subtler secrets" of "impaired vision."

As with "Eyes that Saw not," some plot summary is a useful preamble to the detailed discussion of this novel. *The Martian* is a fictional biography of Barty Josselin purportedly authored by Robert Maurice, one of Barty's oldest friends, not long after Barty's death. Notably, in the novel's opening pages, Maurice thanks "Mr. du Maurier" (4) for his work as the book's editor and illustrator. The first chapters of the novel are dedicated to Barty's privileged childhood in Paris, the first of many parallels between Barty's and du Maurier's lives. The novel turns next to Barty's adventures as a young artist in training and to the sudden disruption of his training by partial blindness. Continuing to parallel his creator closely, Barty, shocked by the sudden loss of sight in his left eye, searches for a medical cure or, at the very least, assurance from oculists that he will not lose sight in his right eye. Detailing stages in du Maurier's own pursuit of a cure for his partial blindness, these sections of the novel depict Barty traveling Europe and enduring months of ineffectual treatments that include the ingestion of mercury and the use of leeches behind his ears.

Barty, a once carefree person, does what he can to resign himself to partial blindness. When, however, he discovers the natural blind spot in his right eye, he mistakes it for a sign that he is losing his remaining vision. It is here that Barty's and du Maurier's stories diverge. Barty plans to commit suicide, writing suicide notes and preparing a glass of cyanide. Fortunately, Barty loses consciousness before he can proceed and, when he wakes up, both the suicide notes and the cyanide are gone. He finds in their place a letter written in his own handwriting. Addressed to him, it explains his suicide was prevented by the letter's author: Martia, a disembodied spirit who has traveled to Earth from Mars in a meteor shower and who is able, now she is on Earth, to inhabit the bodies and minds of humans. Showing Martia's possession of a surprisingly practical personality, the letter explains the science behind the blind spot in sighted people's eyes, assures Barty that a blind spot is not an indication of impending blindness, and advises him to eat a good breakfast and get on with his life. It ends with a postscript instructing Barty to "Always leave something to write with by your bedside at night" (265), this so that Martia can continue to write to him.

Barty takes Martia's advice: he puts away any thought of suicide and gets married. Soon after the birth of his first child, Barty and Martia's unusual correspondence evolves into an author-amanuensis relationship. Whereas Barty previously transcribed letters to himself, Martia calls on him for help realizing her literary ambitions, dictating, over a series of nights, a novel titled *Sardonyx*, sharing it telepathically with Barty who transcribes it while he sleeps. Though little is said about its contents, Barty's wife, the book's first reader, describes it as "one of the most beautiful and important books ever written" (366). Published, at Martia's request, in Barty's name, it quickly becomes a bestseller. Barty continues to personate Martia, transcribing then publishing additional novels, presenting them as his work in the literary marketplace. They include *Motes in a Moonbeam* and *Interstellar Harmonics*, which are, like *Sardonyx*, critically acclaimed. His novels become so popular with audiences that they are "translated into almost every language under the sun" (368). Maurice, the narrator, offers little information about these novels' style, settings, and plotlines. He does, however, allude to their immense cultural significance, noting that they "have had as wide and far-reaching an influence on modern thought as the *Origin of Species*" (370).

Becoming very rich and very famous, Barty learns that visual disability is fully compatible with happiness. That said, Barty's ability to see with one eye is important to Martia and their collaboration. Unable to see what he writes as he writes it, Barty reads what he has written once he wakes up so that, somewhat confusingly, Martia can read her drafts through him and make changes to them. If the novel is coy about the content of Martia's novels, it is very clear about the circumstances of their transcription. Before they begin their work together, Martia gives Barty a set of detailed directions. An adept manager of her amanuensis, Martia tells Barty (in a note he writes to himself while sleeping) how to organize the manuscript. She instructs him: "Only write on one side of a page, leaving a margin and plenty of space between the lines, and let it be in copybooks, so that the page on the left-hand side be left for additions and corrections from my [. . .] notes [. . .]; you'll soon get into the way of it" (361–62). A pragmatic discussion of the mechanics of a writing process supported by an amanuensis, this is not what one might logically expect from a disembodied alien presence whose goal is to impart the wisdom of a highly evolved Martian culture to an Earth audience.

Du Maurier's portrait of a visually disabled, male amanuensis who enjoys a public reputation as a successful author engages a range of Victorian-era ideas about blind authorship and the author-amanuensis relationship. Though Barty's partial blindness mirrors du Maurier's own experience of blindness, Barty's entry into an author-amanuensis relationship with an extraterrestrial very obviously differentiates his experience from du Maurier's arrangements with his wife, Emma. Part of what is achieved by du Maurier's fictionalization of his own experience of disability is a rethinking of the gendered pairing of a blind author who is male with a sighted assistant who is female. Given how large Milton's shadow loomed in popular thought about blindness, and how centrally his work with his daughters featured in accounts of his career as a blind poet, it is not surprising that Milton makes a cameo appearance

Figure 13. "DOES SHE *KNOW* YOU'RE VERY FOND OF HER?" George du Maurier. *The Martian* (1896). Author's collection.

in du Maurier's novel. Briefly described in the letterpress, Milton appears in an illustration that features a painting of the poet at work on *Paradise Lost*, a popular topic with late eighteenth- and nineteenth-century European painters interested in the blind poet's relationship with the daughters who took his dictation (fig. 13). Below the painting, in the gallery in which it hangs, Barty and a woman, who, incidentally, would like to marry him, sit on a bench. Positioning the partially blind Barty below Milton and placing his sighted female admirer below Milton's female scribe, the illustration accurately foreshadows Barty's imminent transfer of his energies from painting to writing. What it does not make clear is that it will be Barty, the visually disabled man, who will take dictation from a female author. Thus, du Maurier gestures toward the figure of a celebrated blind author, compensated by creativity and supported by a gendered division of labor, only to rewrite the standard story, recasting the visually disabled man not as an inspired creator but as a capable and well-compensated assistant.

Similarly notable is the way in which *The Martian* promotes a perception of blindness as enabling, not by way of gifting an author figure with compensatory inspiration or superhuman talent, but instead by better suiting a person to secretarial work. Barty takes Martia's telepathic dictation in the dark, with his eyes closed, while sleeping, a trio of circumstances that intensify his experience of visual disability, from blindness in one eye to a total lack of vision. In a reversal of expectations, Barty's loss of visual acuity is inconsequential, if not, in fact, helpful, in transforming him into a skilled scribe: a wholly passive and thus highly effective conduit for the communication of an advanced being's creative work to an earthly audience. Perhaps du Maurier's decision to write a novel about a blind amanuensis instead of a blind author might strike some readers as unfortunate, as a demotion of sorts. After all, his blind protagonist is portrayed not as a creative genius but as a passive but capable amanuensis, mechanically and accurately transcribing another being's words and ideas. Given that the stereotype of the gifted blind poet, whose tragic blindness is divinely compensated by literary inspiration, is an image that both romanticizes and catastrophizes blindness, du Maurier's portrait of a partially blind man taking dictation, hour after hour, can, however, be positively perceived as an affirmative portrait of a blind worker who is depended upon rather than dependent, reliable rather than reliant. Attentive to both the biology of vision and the mechanics of transcription, du Maurier reimagines the role of disability in the author-amanuensis relationship, decoupling the ability to write from the ability to see, linking disability not to creativity but to productivity and also, and not inconsequentially, to happiness.

The Typewriter's Blind Operators

A bildungsroman about an alien and a blind amanuensis that challenges not only gender conventions but expectations about sensory difference and ability, du Maurier's novel has, unsurprisingly, attracted critical attention. Catherine Golden has pointed out valuable connections between the novel's representation of writing and the automatic writing practices of late-Victorian spiritualists who claimed to transcribe spirit messages while in a trance state. Genie Babb has argued convincingly that Barty, who she usefully terms an "unwitting amanuensis" (10), is a prosthesis, a kind of writing machine used by the bodiless Martia. I would like to propose an additional context for consideration: blind people's early adoption of the technology of the typewriter.

As historian and theorist of writing technology Friedrich Kittler points out, the advent of both the typewriter and the telegraph challenged the conventional understanding of writing as simultaneous with, and inextricable from, reading.[9] Interested in how operators of early typewriters could not read the text they were typing as they typed it, this regardless of their visual acuity, Kittler understands the typewriter's history in terms of a necessarily nonvisual experience of writing. Importantly, Barty uses a pencil, not a typewriter, but like all members of the first generation of typists, both sighted and blind, Barty does not see what he writes as he is writing and, what is more, he does not need to see in order to write. The history of the typewriter and, more narrowly, its use by blind people, is, as such, a useful context for the analysis of a novel whose plot disentangles and distances both reading and seeing from writing.

Notably, du Maurier's depiction of a blind amanuensis is contemporaneous with the historical emergence of a new category of clerical workers: blind secretaries whose skilled use of typewriters enabled them to take dictation for a living. Consider, for example, how, in 1898, only a year after the publication of *The Martian*, a typewriting office staffed by "three blind operators" opened for business in Edgbaston ("A Typewriting Office"). The opening of this office was, it seems, a development of interest to many blind people, one that Henry J. Wilson, the editor of a periodical titled *The Blind*, was pleased to announce in his magazine's inaugural issue. In the same issue, contributors, including Henry Stainsby, the Secretary for Birmingham's General Institution for the Blind, promoted typewriting as an occupation well-suited to blind people. Stainsby, who proposed typing was a skill "by which the more intelligent, educated, and refined, may be enabled to earn their living" (18), shared detailed information regarding the advantages of different models of typewriters, the typing speed of blind operators (between 80 and 120 words a minute), and the value of aggressively advertising typewriting offices staffed by blind operators to the general public. Notably *The Blind* described how some blind operators used typewriters to take dictation from wax cylinders, pairing use of a typewriter with use of a phonograph. It is a real-world scenario that makes du Maurier's portrait of a partially blind man dutifully transcribing the words spoken by a disembodied voice far less outlandish than it might otherwise seem.

While the typewriter made careers for blind amanuenses possible, as already noted above, blind authors were among the earliest adopters of the typewriter. Both Alfred Hirst, the activist whose essays are explored in chapter 2, and Alice King, whose career was discussed earlier in this chapter, used typewriters. They also very energetically encouraged other blind people to do the same. In his 1897 essay "My Dark World," Hirst described what the use of a typewriter had made possible for him: "I often write for four or five hours a day without the slightest hitch. I conduct a very extensive correspondence, chiefly dealing with blind affairs, and, of course, I am writing this article upon it" ("My Dark World" 14). Hirst observed of his typewriter that "[w]ith the single exception of Braille it is the greatest blessing that has come to me since I entered this dark world" ("My Dark World" 14). King, Hirst's contemporary, described her typewriter as a "wonderful and beautiful machine" ("Our Blind Contributor" 578). She explains of typewriting: "I resolved, the moment I heard of it, that I would learn it and make it useful in my literary work" ("Our Blind Contributor" 578). Modifying her typewriter by, for example, adding carved letters to the keys, King did what she resolved:

> Now I can write with the type-writer quicker than most people with the pen, and it is one of the blessings and comforts of my life. There is now no need for elaborate preparation beforehand when I write, for my thoughts flash in a moment from my brain on to the key-board. ("Our Blind Contributor" 578)

No longer reliant on a sighted amanuensis to take dictation, King enjoys a new method of transcription that has both freed her from working with an assistant and radically improved her experience of composition.

While understandably interested in the typewriter's special value for blind authors, King promoted its wider adoption by blind people. In her essay "A Few Words about Blindness," King proposed that the typewriter is "likely to open a new gate in the world's vast workshop for the blind to enter in at. [. . .] With the outlay of about twenty guineas to buy a type-writer, a blind man can become a clerk who writes more distinctly and swiftly than the readiest scribe that ever put pen to paper" (194). Hirst struck a similar note when, having explained that he writes for "an hour at a stretch without committing a single fault," he asks: "Is it any wonder [. . .] that [. . .] I strongly advocate that every child in our blind elementary schools should be turned out an expert typist? It is a liberal education in itself, and imparts a sense of independence, which is a priceless boon" ("My Dark World" 14). King and Hirst's optimism was shared by schools, charities, and activist organizations whose records indicate that they invested in training in typewriting in the hope of securing paid work for the underemployed graduates of specialized schools for blind students. The addition of typing classes to school curriculums is well-

Figure 14. "Typewriting for the Blind (A scene at the Normal School)," *The Quiver*, July 1899. Author's collection.

represented by developments at the Royal Normal College for the Blind. An 1899 essay in *The Quiver* included a photograph of twenty-five of the school's students, both girls and young women, each of them seated at a typewriter with an additional six machines displayed in the foreground (fig. 14). While it is difficult to determine whether any of these students found work as typists, *The Temple Magazine* reported in 1901 that "the ordinary type-writer has [. . .] opened up new paths of usefulness to blind workers, as it can be readily mastered by them with even less instruction than is necessary in the case of those who possess their eyesight" (Hammerton 342). Here again is the suggestion that freedom from sight is an advantage, supporting a person's success in clerical tasks.

Of course, typewriters produce written text that can not be read by touch, neither during that text's creation nor once it is complete. Consequently, while skill in typewriting could lessen blind authors' work with sighted assistants, it did not put an end to that work. Blind authors, including King and Hirst, continued to turn to sighted assistants to share the text they had typed with them by reading it aloud. Blind amanuenses were similarly supported in the work they did by sighted proofreaders. Notably, this was not the case for people who employed tools that generated tactile text, tools developed for and by blind people in the course of the nineteenth century. The next chapter will explore blind people's experimentation with, for example, thick and consequently tangible ink; stamps that pierced through paper, leaving a roughened surface; and writing systems that used knots in twine to represent different letters of the alphabet. That chapter will also explore the steady growth in the course of the century of the popularity of braille, a raised script with the unique advantage that it could be used not only to print books but also to handwrite a single copy of a document such as a letter, memorandum, or draft. In what follows, I demonstrate how the ability to write tactile text made different kinds of reading experiences available to blind people, notable among them the opportunity to conduct a private correspondence with other blind people.

Four

On Letter Writing

Boarding an express train in Paris in the 1880s, the blind author and activist Maurice de La Sizeranne took a seat, opened his valise, and began to sort through his mail. The editor of three braille magazines and founder of the world's first braille library, La Sizeranne made notes on letters he had received while his sighted secretary relaxed with a Jules Verne novel. A passenger who shared their carriage was surprised enough by this scene to comment aloud. Watching La Sizeranne use a braille slate and stylus, he addressed the secretary, asking "He *writes*?" (xiv) before adding, "He must be unhappy enough! What can he do?" (xiv). Pausing in his work, La Sizeranne explained that it was not necessary to speak about him in his presence, "as it would be with a chimpanzee, a well-trained dog, or a child under age" (xv). He then gave, for his fellow passenger's benefit, an impromptu lecture "on the physical, intellectual, and social conditions of a man without sight" (xv). Stirred by this encounter, La Sizeranne did not return to his correspondence; he began instead to make plans to write a book about the abilities of blind people, including the ability to write letters.

This chapter extends *By Touch Alone*'s scope to include handwritten letters. In it, I explore different methods blind people used to write letters, both letters that can be read by touch, such as letters written in braille, and letters that cannot be read by touch, such as those written in ink. I turn next to letters authored by the blind activist Elizabeth Gilbert, including letters she wrote using a now obsolete embossing machine. I also engage the literary record, offering a new reading of Wilkie Collins's *Poor Miss Finch* (1872), a novel that uses its protagonist's handwritten correspondence to chart her changing experience of blindness. I argue that, both in reality and in fiction, nineteenth-century blind people's letter-writing methods reflect the tension between, on the one hand, blind people's desire for self-expression, social connection, and privacy and, on the other hand, sighted observers' investment in letter writing as a normalizing practice, as a way, in other words, to minimize differences between blind and sighted people. By focusing on the "how" of blind people's letter writing, I hope to demonstrate that blind people's use of tools such as styluses and slates changed more than the materiality of handwritten letters. It initiated a non-visual culture of correspondence, one that rejected ocularcentric investment in penmanship in order to prioritize private communication by and between blind people.

"The readiest way of correspondence": Braille Letters

The history of blind people's writing methods reflects the fact that blind people's relationship to writing differed from that of sighted people in at least two ways: blind people's relationship to literacy was of a far shorter duration and, critically, their history of literacy had a very different trajectory than that of the sighted majority. In contrast to sighted people's history of reading and writing, in which the production and circulation of handwritten text predated the production of text with a printing press by millennia, handwriting was not the earliest phase of raised-print culture. Reversing the timeline of ink-print culture, the first books made for blind people's use were not handwritten but were embossed with a press. This might be the reason for a significant imbalance in the investment of both energy and funding in, on the one hand, reading materials and, on the other hand, tools and methods for writing. It is possible that the relative neglect of blind people's writing skills at a time of significant optimism about and investment in reading by touch reflects a societal perception of blind people as consumers rather than creators of written culture. The imbalance between investment in reading and investment in writing might also reflect the tenacity of a belief that blind people should just dictate their letters and accept the lack of independence and privacy as an inevitability of blindness. More certain is the fact that, by considering the different writing methods blind people employed, both methods that produced text that could be read by touch and methods whose results were inaccessible to touch, we can better appreciate the lived experiences of literate blind people and the material realities that shaped those experiences.

Braille, the first of a series of writing methods employed by nineteenth-century blind people explored in this chapter, is noteworthy not only for its continued importance in contemporary blind readers' lives but also for the debates it inspired. As the Introduction of this book outlines, the rise of braille to its present-day status as a near universal choice for raised-print reading and writing was a fitful and slow process in Britain and the United States. Though very positively received in France when introduced by Louis Braille to the students and teachers of the Institut National des Jeunes Aveugles (INJA) in Paris in 1824, it took decades for braille to gain comparable levels of acceptance among Anglo-American educators. Skeptics objected to the use of braille for writing letters on the same grounds that they objected to its use for the publication of books. They argued that braille isolated blind people: the use of a script that could not be read by sighted people without special training distanced blind people from the sighted majority, differentiating them from sighted people, including members of their own families. Advocates for braille rejected this assessment, arguing instead that braille helped blind people connect with other people, both blind and sighted, in no small part because braille could be easily written with inexpensive tools.

Whereas Roman-letter scripts were produced exclusively with a printing press, braille could be handwritten with a stylus and a hinged slate, this in addition to being embossed with a press or, in the final quarter of the century, typed with a brailler. Using the same method as our own era's raised-print writers, nineteenth-century people handwrote braille by placing a sheet of paper into the slate and pushing the tip of the stylus into holes that correspond to the six dots that make up a braille cell. Writers repeat the process, dot by dot and cell by cell, creating impressions on the paper that represent different letters, numbers, or punctuation marks. Braille writers transcribe their messages in reverse, from right to left, on the back side of the sheet of paper; when the paper is removed from the slate and turned over, raised dots made with the stylus can be read, from left to right, by touch.

Nineteenth-century advocates for braille's wider adoption emphasized the speed and ease with which students could learn this way of writing. Essayist and sighted American educator Edward E. Allen noted that "[b]eginners usually take to this kind of writing as ducks take to water, and spend much of their free time in practicing it" (322). Robert Meldrum, an educator and blind person, shared a similarly positive account of this method. Describing how students at the Edinburgh School for the Blind responded to their first lessons in braille, he wrote:

> [they] enter upon the study of it with a zest previously unknown. This is particularly the case when set to writing it. It then becomes 'not a task but as it were the joy of their life,' and morning, noon and night, it would form their untiring occupation, provided the necessary paper (stiff cartridge) were but supplied in sufficient quantity. (90–91)

La Sizeranne, whose expert use of a stylus and slate brought braille to a sighted traveler's attention, also commented on beginners' experiences. He explained that: "blind children learn to read, and especially to write, in less time and with less effort than those who see, owing to the logical simplicity of the Braille system" (114). More than a substitute for sighted people's use of pen and ink, braille is, for these commentators, a writing method with unique advantages.

Even non-expert observers recognized the value of braille as a script that could be written with ease. Consider the case of Sir Francis Bond Head, a sighted person, colonial administrator and travel writer who learned about braille when he traveled to Paris in 1851. After visiting INJA, he published a detailed description of a student's use of a stylus and slate, which he refers to as an awl and groove:

> [a] blind boy was required to write down before me, from the dictation of his blind professor a long sentence. With a common awl, not only kept in line, but within narrow limits, by a brass groove, which the writer had the power to lower at the termination of each line, the little fellow very rapidly poked holes tallying with the letters he wished to represent. (239)

Head was struck by the difference between this child's experience of writing and that of nonblind children. He explains:

> There was no twisting of his head sideways—no contortion of face—no lifting up of his right heel—no screwing up of his mouth—no turning his tongue from beneath the nose towards one ear, and then towards the other, in sympathy with the tails of crooked letters, which, in great pain and difficulty, in ordinary writing, the schoolboy may be seen successively endeavouring to transcribe. On the contrary, as the little fellow punched his holes he sat on his stool as upright as a cobbler hammering at the sole of a shoe. (239)

A disciplined and admirably ergonomic method of writing, braille is, for Head, well suited to the abilities and bodies of children, whether sighted or blind. In contrast to a nonblind child, whose body is contorted from head to heel by the effort of handwriting, the blind child keeps an upright posture, producing text easily and efficiently. Indeed, for Head, the child's movements are so orderly and productive that the child brings to mind a craftsman at work.

While the ease with which a blind child could write text more than justified the wide adoption of braille, its usefulness for correspondence made the case even more compelling. As a contributor to *The Times* noted, in an era when family groups were increasingly dispersed by urbanization and emigration, braille answered blind people's need for an "easy means of holding written communication with others" ("Literature For the Blind," 3 Jan. 1870). While an essayist for *All the Year Round* promoted braille as an "admirably logical and ingenious" system for "intercommunication between the blind," other commentators recognized it as a useful method of written communication between blind and sighted people ("Blind Guy Fawkes" 257). In *The Education and the Employment of the Blind*, the blind activist Thomas Armitage proposed in regard to schools for blind students that braille "furnishes to the pupils the readiest way of correspondence, both with their blind friends and seeing parents" (11). Armitage, head of the British and Foreign Blind Association, a group that investigated the advantages of different script systems before ultimately championing braille, added regarding the sighted parents of blind children that they, "if of average intelligence, can learn the system in a very short time, and can then correspond directly with their children—no small advantage when children are at school or away from home" (11).

Braille's appeal was only increased by blind people's ability to read and reread letters in braille, both those they wrote and those they received. Edward Allen shared the following reflection from Florence Hawk, one of his blind students: "I have the great pleasure of receiving letters from my family and my friends, which I can read myself. It is much pleasanter for me to read my own letters than to have others read them to me. I can read them when I choose, and as many times as I wish" (325). Allen adds that the use of braille for blind people's letter writing "insures their perfect privacy of correspondence, for it makes them independent of any one to read or write their letters" (326). Robert Meldrum contrasted the experience of receiving letters written in braille with that of receiving letters written in ink. He asserted that "the objection to all intangible systems of writing is the need for a third person to *read* the communication; to a blind person especially this destroys the charm of it" (103). Meldrum turned to other commentators to buttress his assessment of braille, sharing, for example, the following statement by educator Gilbert Macculloch: "As a system of writing for the blind it has hitherto been unrivalled, not only from the ease and despatch with which it is managed, but also and chiefly from its being such that the blind writer can immediately and with perfect facility, decipher what he has written" (104–5). Printed with a press but also written by hand, used for the publication of books as well as private forms of writing, braille provided the first generations of literate blind people with a combination of convenience and privacy in their letter writing that other scripts could not match.

Notably, the privacy that braille secured for blind people was perceived by some sighted educators as a problem. In his 1847 collection *A Blind Man's Offering*, the American commentator and blind person Benjamin Bowen shared a dramatic account of two students who sent each other love notes by "pricking the letters with a sharp-pointed pencil, so that by the touch on the opposite side of the page, the words could be read" (63). Braille is not named in Bowen's account of this blind couple but the writing they exchanged has obvious commonalities with it. They include its legibility by touch and its indecipherability for sighted people who had not made the effort to learn a script designed by and for blind people. While Bowen's story might well be apocryphal—his book pairs social commentary with fiction and poetry—his account of the use of a pencil point to write tactile text offers an exemplification in miniature of actions that blind people took to adapt the writing tools and methods of sighted people to their own needs and preferences. It signals their desire for self-expression, social connection, and privacy as well as their determination to both produce and consume handwritten documents.

The opportunity to write letters using private methods was, in the assessment of some blind activists, a human right. In his 1891 essay "Types for the Blind," Lorance Carter insisted that blind people needed a means of unmediated, unmonitored correspondence. He also rejected the characterization of blind people as unusually or inappropriately desirous of privacy:

> Why should the blind be called a 'secretive race'? Are they to be debarred from receiving private letters? Debarred from communicating with their friends? Debarred from taking notes, and keeping their accounts? Debarred, in short, from what every seeing man, woman, and child has by natural right, because a few managers and teachers of schools for the blind cannot take the trouble to adapt themselves to the wants of the pupils committed to their care? (53)

Advocates of braille, such as Carter, were fully aware of its value as a method of writing that secured users a level of privacy in their correspondence comparable to that enjoyed by sighted people. Of course, as advocates also knew, the utility of handwriting braille extended beyond letter writing. As Allen reminded his sighted readership, the ability to write braille enriched a blind person's life in a range of ways. Quoting an unnamed admirer of Louis Braille, Allen shared how, with knowledge of braille, a blind person "could keep his own accounts, correspond with all those acquainted with his alphabet, preserve his impressions and his inspirations, and transmit them to his fellows. Immense advantages these, the mere mention of which cannot but make every one of you comprehend the resulting benefits" (329).

Skepticism about braille among sighted educators in the United States and the United Kingdom impeded more than the private exchange of letters: it limited the teaching of writing as a skill in schools for blind students. In a letter written to the directors of Boston's Perkins School for the Blind in 1882, the British activist and educator Thomas Armitage urged his American colleagues to follow the example of European schools and adopt braille. Arguing for change, he hoped that "in a few years it will be considered as disgraceful for a blind school not to teach writing as it is now in the case of a school where the pupils can see" (*The Education* 213). Literacy for blind people must, activists insisted, encompass both reading and writing. Allen complained: "it is idle to dwell upon the use of writing as a factor in education. It is enough to bear in mind that if fingerless children were so numerous as to form a class, toe-writing or mouth-writing would be systematically taught in their schools" (321). Messages about the importance of writing to blind people were amplified by the periodical press. *All the Year Round* reported in 1876 that it is not "sufficient that blind children should be taught to read; they must be taught to write—not quite so easy an operation" ("Blind Guy Fawkes" 257). Half a century after the invention of braille, the teaching of writing to blind people was not, in fact, an inherently difficult operation: it was only made so by the reluctance of sighted educators to embrace a raised-print script that was as well-suited to writing by touch as it was to reading by touch.

"A common current hand": Inked Letters

While the invention of braille broadened the definition of handwriting to include text written with tools other than a pen or pencil, braille's invention did not preclude nineteenth-century blind people from using a pen or pencil to write autograph letters (letters handwritten and signed by their author). Some blind people retained this skill after becoming blind; others learned to write with a pen or pencil without past experience of sight. While the results were impressive in the sense that blind writers succeeded in handwriting documents that sighted people could read, the fact that blind writers could not read what they had written was far from ideal. A celebrity example offers us insight into both this practice and its reception. When Charles Dickens visited Laura Bridgman, a deaf-blind student at the Perkins School in

Boston, he took close note of her handwriting. Interested not only in the legibility but also the appearance of Bridgman's penmanship, Dickens was intrigued enough to request a second demonstration of her skills:

> I turned over the leaves of her Diary, and found it written in a fair legible square hand, and expressed in terms which were quite intelligible without any explanation. On my saying that I should like to see her write again, the teacher who sat beside her, bade her, in their language, sign her name upon a slip of paper, twice or thrice. In doing so, I observed that she kept her left hand always touching, and following up, her right, in which, of course, she held the pen. No line was indicated by any contrivance, but she wrote straight and freely. (50)[1]

Notably, Dickens finds written language a point of connection between himself and Bridgman, this in contrast to non-written forms of communication, which require the help of a mediator who communicates with Bridgman in what Dickens terms "their language." Of course, in Bridgman's case, mediation is also a feature of her relationship to her own writing. Dickens can read Bridgman's diary without assistance but Bridgman cannot: she relies on a sighted assistant to share text she wrote with her.[2]

Whereas Bridgman guided her own hand as she wrote, some blind writers used a guide to help them position lines of text on a page. In 1872, the blind activist W.H. Levy estimated that he had personally experimented with "more than sixty different inventions for enabling the blind to write" (128). Not satisfied with this selection, Levy developed an appliance of his own, a writing-card to guide the blind writer's pencil. He marketed this device to other blind people as "the most efficient contrivance for pencil-writing" (129). Selling the card for five shillings, Levy explained how it "has been the means of enabling hundreds of persons to correspond with their friends, who would otherwise have been cut off from that inestimable privilege" (129). Decades earlier, in 1837, the sighted inventor and printer James Gall marketed a handwriting guide he called the typhlograph, a reference to the Greek root "typhlo," meaning "blind." He proposed that his guide enabled users who could not see to "write a common current hand, as small and as elegant in its form as that used by those who see" (15). Gall was especially pleased with "[t] he elegance of the writing" (16) produced by users of his guide, handwriting which, he explained, "may be formed in the most beautiful manner" and "with great ease and precision" (16). He added that "[a] great variety in the style of writing may be obtained by a different formation of the Typhlograph. It may either be sloped or horizontal, thin or broad" (18). Encouraging blind people to both normalize and personalize their handwriting, Gall hoped users would develop a style of penmanship that conformed to that of sighted people in the sense that it was not only visually pleasing but unique to each writer, their penmanship as distinctive as their personalities. Blind people could not see the "elegance" or "variety" of their handwriting but they could, Gall proposes, rest assured that their handwriting met mainstream culture's visual expectations, both conforming to the "common" hand of sighted people and having a satisfactory degree of individuality.

While a typhlograph may have allowed blind users to emulate the penmanship of sighted people, it was of little use to a blind person who wanted to read what they had written. Some blind users of pens, unable to review their own writing, worried that they might inadvertently mail a blank sheet of paper, having dipped their pen in an empty ink well, or, conversely, that they might send a letter marred by too much ink, by finger prints, smudges, or the splutters of a pen's nib. Thomas Bull, a blind person, referenced the challenges of writing with ink when he described a letter he had received from another blind man. The letter, "written in pencil, by his own hand," asks Bull for information about how best to use a pen: "Your letter is written in ink; I should very much like to know if you have any apparatus for the purpose, or how you can tell when the pen is empty" (212). A sighted commentator suggested that the problem of inked text's intangibility could be solved by sprinkling sand over "characters boldly written with viscid ink on common writing-paper" ("Instruction of the Blind" 523). The ever-inventive Gall took things a step farther; he proposed that blind people handwrite letters with a steel point on a sheet of blackened paper placed facedown on blank paper, writing the same script with the same movements of their hands as sighted people but "without the inconvenience of using a fluid ink" (19). Gall hoped that the blind writer, by avoiding the use of ink, "need never be afraid of laboring in vain" (19). Of course, this method would not make the text legible to its author. Thomas Lucas, a sighted teacher and the creator of a namesake script that resembled shorthand, hoped to find a way for blind people to handwrite a tangible version of the Roman-letter alphabet. Lucas proposed that blind people could write with a stylus on very thin sheets of lead instead of paper. An 1838 report explained that: "Mr. Lucas has succeeded in having some words written on [. . .] leaden sheets in order to prove that this kind of writing is possible" (Carton 55). The report's author was, however, far from optimistic about this method; he concluded that "for practical purposes it is utterly useless" (Carton 55).

Lucas's well-intentioned but impractical proposal offers us insight into the partial participation of blind people in correspondence in the nineteenth century. Whereas braille both challenged established definitions of handwriting and diversified the material qualities of letters, writing with a pencil or pen was more than inconvenient for blind writers: it imposed an incomplete or divided experience of literacy on blind writers. It allowed blind people written self-expression but it did not secure for them either unmediated access to what they had themselves written or opportunities for private communication with other people, including blind people. As the next section proposes, writing with stamps, a method that produced text that was both tangible and visible, was more practical than the substitution of lead for paper but not without drawbacks of its own.

"Without any loss of privacy": Stamped Letters

Writing letters with stamps was slow but it was also simple. Nineteenth-century blind people's stamps did not use ink; they were, instead, studded with pins in the shape of different letters. When applied to the reverse side of a sheet of paper, the pins punctured the paper, creating small perforations that could be read by touch as well as sight. Regarding this method, *Household Words* contributor Henry Morley observed in 1859,

> the great advantage of the plan lies in the fact that it is blind writing in raised letters legible by the blind [. . .] the letter writer can himself, without any loss of privacy, run not an eye but a finger over what he has written, and make any addition or correction before sending it away. (323)

Gall gave stamps a similarly positive review; he noted that, once acquainted with this method, blind people "are able to write a long letter upon a sheet of paper, to write the address by the same means, and when they have finished, they can read with their finger all that they have written" (Gall 13). Alexander Barnhill reported in 1875 that "[s]uch letters are frequently sent to a distance, and even pass through the Post-Office, addressed with the pin-point letter perforations as correctly as if written by a pencil or pen" (37). The circulation of stamped letters through the postal system suggests the extent to which letters written with this method conformed to ocularcentric norms of correspondence. Though written with pins instead of pens, the addresses on stamped letters were, it seems, fully legible to sighted postal workers.[3]

In his book *Blind People: Their Works and Ways* (1867), B.G. Johns described how a letter written with stamps helped a blind child stay in touch with his family while he was away at school. Johns, who was committed to teaching writing to his students, was equally committed to the use of Alston's script, a Roman-letter script which he believed would help blind people integrate into sighted culture. Here is Johns's description of a student's first letter: "When once a boy has learned to read a chapter of 'Robinson Crusoe' in Alston's type (the Roman letter), he is very soon able to write home and tell of his accomplishments" (17). He goes on to explain:

> The process is a slow one, as every letter has to be separately stamped down and held in its place till its next neighbor is introduced, that not a grain of precious space be wasted; but at last, duly reversed and in good order, appear the pleasant words, 'MY DEAR FATHER.' (18)

Notably, Johns shares these three words in an inked imitation of pinpricked writing. An engraving embedded between lines of regular inked print, the special treatment of these words gave sighted readers a sense of the appearance of this form of writing. Eager to raise awareness of how writing with stamps facilitated contact between people who are separated not only by distance but also by sensory difference, Johns emphasized the pinpricked letter's socially unifying effects:

> proud enough, we may well imagine, is Sam Trotter, the village blacksmith, when he gets his first letter from 'our blind Johnny in London;' it goes the round of the whole community, and in spite of some grievous lapses in orthography, is fairly worn out at last with continual handling, unless locked up by the good wife as too precious a document for the perusal of ordinary mortals. Their wonder will be doubled when Johnny comes home next year at the Midsummer holidays, and reads off his own epistle with the tips of his fingers. (18–19)

This letter, which fosters family ties and cultivates connection between blind and sighted people, is, for Johns, a model product of blind correspondence. Notable for how it downplays distinctions between touch and sight, Johns's account of Johnny's letter minimizes differences between blind people and sighted people by minimizing differences between the kinds of letters they write and read. Notably, the circulation of the stamped letter in the village naturalizes or normalizes raised-print text, an example of which is read and reread by sighted people. What is more, sighted people's repeated touching of the letter resembles reading by touch, bringing the reading practices of sighted people into temporary alignment with those of blind people. That said, the slow wearing away of the pinpricks that results from this touching enacts a subtle but problematic dissolution of difference; "continual handling" makes Johnny's letter increasingly indistinguishable from text written by and for sighted people and thus makes it less legible to a blind reader. Wearing down distinctions between a letter written with stamps and a letter written in ink, Johns's anecdote celebrates both the integration of blind people into sighted communities and the similitude of blind and sighted writing practices.

It is worth noting that some sighted people acquired samples of stamped writing that were not addressed to them. John Alston, a teacher and the creator of the raised-print script that Johns championed, recorded how, following a public demonstration of a student's use of stamps, "most of the company were proud to possess themselves of specimens of so novel and useful a mode of communication" (66). Samples of stamped writing were similarly gifted to sighted visitors to schools for blind students as souvenirs. Gilbert Macculloch, Principal of the Edinburgh School for the Blind, reported of student Robert Edgar, whose life is discussed in chapter 2, that:

> A favorite occupation of his spare hours was selecting, and printing in *pin-type*, appropriate texts of Scripture, to be presented to various classes of persons, as opportunity offered. And not unfrequently Christian ladies of our acquaintance, when engaged in supplying articles for sale at Bazaars, in aid of benevolent or charitable objects in town or country, were glad to provide themselves with texts of Edgar's printing, and to have them tastefully set in fancy borderings for the purpose. (28)

Easy to read by sight yet visually unusual, poignant but also cheering, stamped messages written by blind people appealed to sighted people both for their novelty and for their materialization of progress in the arena of blind people's literacy.[4]

That said, not everyone perceived the use of stamps for writing as a positive development. Some commentators complained that the process was slow and tiring, in part because stamping, like braille, required users to write in reverse on the back surface of a sheet of paper. In 1891, Lorance Carter, quoted above, complained about the inefficiency of this method. He explained that "it is possible, by the aid of a clumsy and expensive apparatus, for a blind person slowly to stamp out, letter by letter, a short exercise in similar characters, although an hour's hard and painstaking labour would scarcely cover two foolscap pages with the matter that could have been written on one page of note-paper" (54). Thomas Anderson, a teacher of blind students, was similarly critical. Arguing that writing in this way is a "routine of 'toil and trouble'" (75), he aligned writing with stamps with disablement rather than ability. Take, for example, how, when describing a blind person writing stamps, he draws attention to the uncertainty of that person's movements by noting how "the letter D is groped for" (75). Indeed, Anderson went so far as to suggest that stamping is not really writing. He explained: "I do not see how a process so slow, tiresome, and perplexing, as this must be, can, in fairness, be called 'writing,' as in all Mr. Gall's publications it is. [. . .]. Acquirements, as well as doings, should be called by their right names" (61). Distancing the use of stamps and handwriting, he scoffs regarding a stamped document that "we are soberly told of this as constituting 'writing!'" (75). Anderson's point was echoed decades later, in 1870, when the blind activist Thomas Armitage suggested that "[t]his plan ought rather to be called printing than writing; it requires great practice, and is at the best very slow and imperfect" (McHenry 12).

Opposition to stamped writing is a surprising point of connection between Anderson and Armitage, two men who would have agreed on very little. Anderson, a sighted person, was a proponent of oral forms of education and was very skeptical about investment in blind people's ability to read and write; Armitage, a blind person, was an energetic champion of blind people's literacy. Yet they both identify the use of stamps by blind people as something other than writing, as more akin to printing. In doing so, they distance text produced with stamps by blind people from the handwriting of sighted people. Their common claim, that the term "writing" cannot be applied to the task of creating a letter with stamps, effectively sidelined this writing method: both sighted and blind people produce letters, both use tools to produce their letters, but blind people who use stamps do not "write" letters. Though both commentators resist the broadening of the definition of handwriting to include text made with stamps, they do so for different reasons. Anderson understood writing by blind people as a gimmick, a way to fundraise for schools, whereas Armitage promoted the widespread use of braille, a more efficient, not to mention more affordable, method of writing.

Whether they used stamps, a stylus and slate, or pen and ink, blind people were handwriting documents and their choices both broadened the definition of handwriting and changed the material qualities of letters. The coexistence of writing methods as markedly different as braille and stamping is indicative of the difficulty of developing effective methods of writing that were suited to the needs of a newly literate group. It is also indicative of the enduring challenge that blind people's writing methods posed to conventional definitions of handwriting. Investment in the look, versus the legibility by touch, of handwritten text was only one of a number of ways in which ocularcentric values influenced blind people's experiences of private writing. The nineteenth-century reception of blind people's writing methods by sighted commentators reveals that the tangibility of documents and their consequent legibility to touch came, for some observers, at a perceived cost: the individuality of blind people's handwriting. Letters written in braille or with stamps standardized the visual appearance of blind people's writing; like text from a press, tangible forms of writing did not differ from author to author, from hand to hand. By engaging the life of Elizabeth Gilbert, a prolific writer of letters who mastered different writing methods, we can learn how sighted people's values shaped blind people's letter writing, with sighted people's preferences promoting, for example, the production of autograph letters even in cases when more efficient and accommodating methods were, quite literally, at hand. We can also better appreciate the experiences of nineteenth-century blind people who employed multiple writing methods, alternating between them in the course of their lives or even in the course of a day.

Elizabeth Gilbert's Letters

Frances Martin's 1887 biography of Elizabeth Gilbert identifies letter-writing to improve the lives of working-class blind people as the defining action of Gilbert's life.[5] Though Gilbert is largely forgotten today, both her identity as the daughter of an Anglican bishop and her work as a philanthropist made her one of her era's most socially prominent blind people. Founder of London's Association for the General Welfare of the Blind, Gilbert wrote many letters on behalf of the Association, whose mandate was to provide vocational training and paid work to blind men and women. While many of her letters dealt with the manufacturing and sale of mats, brushes, and brooms, Gilbert was by no means oblivious to the importance of literacy in blind people's lives. Indeed, to use her own words, she believed that "the power of writing in some tangible form, with the greatest possible ease and rapidity" was a matter of "highest importance to the blind" (149). Interested in not just the social but also the cognitive benefits of writing, Gilbert proposed that "the mind of many a blind person remains far below the degree of cultivation and maturity to which it might attain, simply from want of being able to

Figure 15. Frontispiece to *Elizabeth Gilbert and Her Work for the Blind* (1891). Author's collection.

emboss its thoughts upon paper" (149). Eager for improvements to the status quo, she added: "Some one, I know not who, says: use the pen to prevent the mind from staggering about; and this help should certainly be placed by some means or other within the reach of the blind generally" (149).

Given how central letter writing was to Gilbert's activism, it is fitting that the frontispiece to her biography includes a copy of her signature (fig. 15). This frontispiece pairs her signature with a painting of her by William Boxall. A half-length portrait depicting Gilbert in her early twenties, it shows her pale face and neck against a dark background. Her dark straight hair is parted in the center and worn down; her head and shoulders are turned to the right. She is dressed in a flowy cape and her eyes are covered by a pair of dark glasses. While the portrait is noteworthy for its very loose and unfinished quality—it could, in fact, be described as blurry—the same cannot be said for the signature: written in crisp cursive writing, reproduced in dark ink, this signature has solidity as well as flair. The words "Elizabeth Gilbert" lean, as per convention, slightly to the right while both the capitalized E and G include decorative loops, their descending portions dipping below the level of the other letters. Like the portrait, this signature is for sighted people's consumption. Created with the tools of sighted culture and shaped by that culture's conventions, it offers sighted people a means to satisfy a visual form of curiosity. They might even choose to study Gilbert's signature for visual clues about her personality.

While Martin does not comment on what Gilbert's signature might reveal, she has a great deal to say about Gilbert's use of a pen. Gilbert learned to write with a pen, in what Martin calls "the ordinary way" (9), at an early age. A governess taught her to write alongside her sighted sisters; to assist Gilbert, the governess devised a bespoke writing guide that used lengths of thread which Gilbert used to position her writing on the page. Gilbert became skilled at this method but found writing with ink frustrating. Martin describes Gilbert's use of a pen to write as, for example, "slow and laborious" (73). Martin also notes that this method obliged Gilbert to rely on sighted family members; she explains that, for Gilbert, "[r]eading and writing depended largely on the time that others could give her" (73). Gilbert could write letters with ink without assistance but she depended on sighted people to read them for her before she mailed them. Writing in ink thus imposed significant limits not only on Gilbert's independence but also on her privacy. As Martin explains "Such writing had to be looked over in case a word should be unintelligible, and she could therefore have no private correspondents" (73).

Both privacy and independence were similarly unavailable to Gilbert in the case of letters she dictated, a method she employed throughout her life. Fortunately, Gilbert gained a third and, for her, a better option for writing letters when she acquired a new writing tool: a Foucault frame. A keyed machine that produced text that could be read by touch as well as sight, the frame was introduced to London from Paris in 1851 by its inventor, Pierre-François-Victor Foucault. Foucault's machine embossed sheets of paper with Roman-alphabet letters, the shape of each letter formed by raised dots. Foucault, a mechanic and blind person, demonstrated its operation at the Great Exhibition of 1851.[6] An illustration from that event, titled "FOUCAULT'S PRINTING KEY FRAME, BY WHICH THE BLIND MAY WRITE," shows a man using the frame. His back to the viewer, he stands at the machine, which sits on a bench with four legs. His left hand touches the keys, which are arranged in

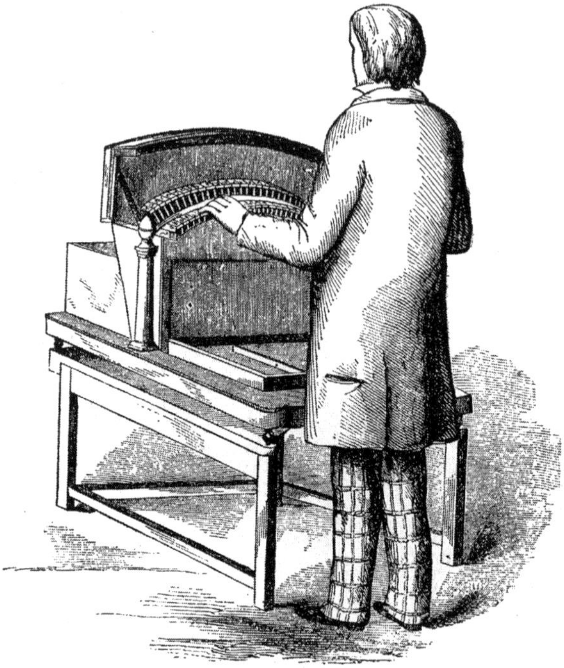

Figure 16. "FOUCAULT'S PRINTING KEY FRAME, BY WHICH THE BLIND MAY WRITE." *Leading American Inventors* (1912). Author's collection.

two parallel arcs (fig. 16). These keys are at waist height and the machine is large, wider than its operator's shoulders.

The fact that the Foucault frame required significant skill as well as physical effort to operate likely accounts for its limited adoption and obsolescence by century's end. Gilbert, who met Foucault during his visit to London, became a proficient user of his invention. While letters written with the frame resemble letters written with stamps in that they can be read both by sight and by touch, writing with the frame was far more efficient than writing with stamps. At least this was the case when the frame was operated by a practiced user such as Gilbert. The ability to write a raised-print letter, one that she or a blind recipient could read by touch, transformed Gilbert's experience of correspondence. As Martin explains regarding the frame, Gilbert "found that it made her independent of supervision and assistance. She could write and address a letter herself; and here at last she stood in one respect on equal footing with those around her" (76–77).

Gilbert used her frame to extend her social network, making new friends, including Isabella Law, a blind woman with whom she had a long friendship that was, Martin explains, "inaugurated over the Foucault frame" (77). Gilbert also used it to write to her family members, noting at the start of a letter she wrote after a period of illness to her father, a sighted person, that she "had long settled that my first letter with the frame should be" written to him (212). Thankful to be able to operate the frame again, she compares the process of letter writing to machine knitting, telling her father: "most thankful I am to be able to be at the 'stocking making' again, though very likely I shall not make a very good workwoman" (212–13). The frame was also Gilbert's go-to tool for business letters. Gilbert used it, for example, to correspond with W.H. Levy, the blind manager of her Association, named above as the inventor of a writing guide. Using a complicated keyed machine to write letters, doing so several decades before the popularization of the typewriter among sighted people, blind people such as Gilbert broadened the category of the personal letter to include letters written with something other than a pencil or pen.

Notably, though she was an adept user of her frame, Gilbert continued to write some of her letters with a pencil or pen. In 1856, she chose, for example, to write an autograph letter to Queen Victoria to request royal support for the Association's work. That Gilbert opted to write with a pen a letter that she could have written more easily and efficiently, not to mention independently, with her frame, is revealing.[7] What did she gain by writing in ink, a method that made her reliant on sighted people? It is possible that Gilbert, having observed the reactions of recipients of letters she wrote with a pen in her youth, believed that letters written in ink had particular utility in helping her achieve her goals as an activist. She was, after all, well aware that the people she wanted to help were blind but that the people she hoped to influence were sighted. Autograph letters, written in her own hand and signed by her, were, Gilbert knew, highly valued by sighted recipients. A representative reply to a letter in ink that she wrote as a young person shares the unnamed recipient's delight in having received an "autograph of such affecting interest" (67). Her ability to write a letter that a sighted person could read, and that she could not read, had, it seems, a powerful effect on sighted people. Prioritizing the sighted majority's preferences and conventions over her own convenience and independence, Gilbert's penned letters made literally visible both her blindness and her willingness to work hard to conform to the norms of sighted culture.

Whatever reason prompted her to use a pen to write to the Queen, Gilbert's inked appeal secured the result she had hoped for. Martin shares that

Gilbert's letter secured a gift of fifty pounds from the Royal Treasury, the first in what turned out to be a series of royal donations to Gilbert's Association. Curiously, and arguably unnecessarily, Martin also shares that a draft of Gilbert's letter to the Queen contained numerous spelling errors. Martin reproduces that draft, explaining that: "Bessie's autograph letters are rarely free from defects; and the letter here copied may have been discarded when it was found on supervision to contain *admition* for admission, *Concert* for Consort, and one or two other trifling inaccuracies" (107). It seems that Gilbert's decision to write with a pen made her not only dependent on sighted people's assistance but also vulnerable to their scrutiny: to their identification, to borrow from Martin, of "defects" and "inaccuracies." Following the letter-writing etiquette of the sighted majority, trying to conform to societal standards of written communication, Gilbert falls short. Of course, her penned letters' perceived shortcomings are side effects of what we can think of as an imposed form of partial illiteracy—her inability to read her own writing. Of course, the non-standard orthography that Martin views as evidence of inadequacy can also be understood as a measure of the importance of oral forms of communication to Gilbert and, relatedly, of limits on blind people's access to raised-print text.[8]

If some of Gilbert's letters were notable for their inaccuracies, others were, for Martin at least, remarkable for their flawlessness. In the late 1850s, when the rapidly increasing needs of her Association obliged Gilbert to devote entire days to letter writing, Gilbert opted to author multiple letters at the same time. Working beside her two sisters, who acted as amanuenses, Gilbert could, Martin claims, "emboss a letter upon her Foucault frame and dictate two others at the same time; always without mistake or omission" (154). A claim of extreme ability, Martin's description of the creation of three faultless, concurrently-authored letters is reminiscent of Hirst's account of a man who could read two raised-print books at the same time, an anecdote discussed in chapter 2. Irrespective of the truth of Martin's claim, Gilbert's letters offer significant insight into both material realities and social dimensions of blind people's letter-writing culture. An autograph letter to petition the Queen, a tactile letter keyed with a machine to connect with a blind friend, a dictated letter written by a sister's hand for everyday business: Gilbert moved between different modes of letter writing, tolerating different levels of privacy and independence in pursuit of self-expression, connection, and social influence. In their variety, if in nothing else, her letters signal the complexity of blind people's letter-writing lives in the second half of the nineteenth century.

Penmanship and *Poor Miss Finch*

Like historical accounts, literary representations of nineteenth-century blind people's letter writing explore how their correspondence was shaped by both material obstacles and cultural conventions. Though far more likely to depict a blind person dictating a letter than handwriting one, sighted authors were interested in the challenges and pleasures of writing by touch. Some portraits of blind people writing letters, such as Edward Bulwer-Lytton's depiction of the Nydia writing on a wax tablet, are, as I proposed in the Introduction, curiously proleptic. Others reveal a troubling preoccupation with connections between blindness and suicide, a topic explored by David Bolt in relation to twentieth-century literature.[9] It would be fair to say that a worrying number of nineteenth-century authors engage blind people's ability to write letters only in order to generate a written record of the anguish that led to their deaths.

That is the case for the anonymous short story "A Blind Man's Love," which appeared in *Harper's New Monthly Magazine* in 1857. The story features excerpts from a lengthy suicide note written in ink. The letter is discovered at the scene of its blind author's death by a nonblind woman. She read the letter, noting how changes in its author's penmanship chart changes in the intensity of his emotions. The letter's most passionate passages are, in fact, illegible. The deceased man's handwriting becomes "undecipherable" (338) when he writes about the unrequited love that motivated him to take his life. The narrator explains how, in this section of the note,

> [t]he letters ran one against the other, words strove with words, and phrases interlocked like carriages in a narrow street; it was in truth an alphabetic confusion that would have driven desperate a decipherer of Egyptian hieroglyphics, or a student of a celebrated Boston lawyer's chirography. (338)

Even when the blind man's words cannot be read, his penmanship communicates his desperation, making the intensity of his emotions visible to the sighted reader.

A novel with the same title as this short story offers a less sensational depiction of the role writing plays in a blind man's life. Published in 1895, Laurence John's *A Blind Man's Love* explores the experience of acquired blindness by telling the story of Sir Giles Attwood, an aristocrat who learns braille soon after becoming blind in midlife. Giles learns to read braille not only quickly but easily; as the narrator explains, "as his touch was sensitive and his memory excellent, he soon took great pleasure in it" (104). Reading aloud from a braille edition of Charles Dickens's *Bleak House* at home or, similarly, from a braille Bible at church, Giles retains his connection to written culture. He also writes braille, resuming a position of cultural influence in his community that he lost hold of temporarily when he first became blind. Using braille notes, he gives, for example, public lectures on his experiences as both a world traveler and amateur photographer. Notably, before Giles becomes blind, his future wife, a sighted person, studies braille, using a stylus and slate to make copies of books that she donates to a library for blind readers. Normalizing the writing of braille by both blind and sighted people, John's novel promotes the wide adoption of a writing system that supports blind people's wellbeing by supporting their participation in the cultural life of their community.

The literary text that is the focus of this section, Wilkie Collins's novel *Poor Miss Finch: A Domestic Story*, makes no mention of braille writing but has a great deal to say about both a blind woman's penmanship and her correspondence. Given that the novel was published in 1872 and is, moreover, set in the same era, it is somewhat surprising that the only option the novel's blind protagonist has for writing is pen and ink. Though Collins leaves unmentioned other methods a blind person might use to write in the second half of the nineteenth century, his novel is nonetheless progressive in its portrayal of a blind person's letter-writing life and, indeed, of blindness generally. As I noted in the Introduction, Collins's unconventional approach to blindness has attracted the attention of critics who have explored connections the novel makes between, on the one hand, blindness, and on the other, a wide range of topics including the conventions of melodrama, the depiction of epilepsy, and the construction of racial difference.[10] In what follows, I add to knowledge of the novel by examining Collins's depiction of his blind protagonist's penmanship. As I hope to demonstrate, *Poor Miss Finch* uses changes in Lucilla's handwriting to track changes in both her relationship to blindness and her perception of the value of vision.

In a dedicatory preface, Collins noted how his beliefs shaped the unconventional nature of his novel's treatment of blindness. He explains, "I subscribe to the article of belief which declares, that the conditions of human happiness are independent of bodily affliction, and that it is even possible for bodily affliction itself to take its place among the ingredients of happiness" (xl). Narrated by Madame Pratolungo, Lucilla's comically self-assured paid companion, the novel explores this possibility by contrasting Lucilla's years of experience of blindness with a brief period of sightedness following cataract surgery. Lucilla, who is the novel's only blind character, is motivated to seek a surgical cure for blindness by her love for Oscar Dubourg, a man whose body is also non-normative. Oscar, who lives with epilepsy, manages his condition by taking a medication that turns his skin blue, a fact he hides from Lucilla during their courtship because, though blind, she has a dread of dark colors. Lucilla wants to see the man she loves but the success of her surgery, performed by the oculist Herr Grosse, threatens Oscar with exposure. In an attempt to buy time, Oscar's identical twin, Nugent, impersonates him. Lucilla, able to see for the first time in her memory, is confused by her lack of attraction to the man she thinks is Oscar. To try to make sense of her disappointment, she writes both day and night in a journal. Initially eager to experience sight, Lucilla discovers that the ability to see comes at the cost of the rich sensory life she enjoyed while blind. Fortunately, within weeks of her surgery, Lucilla becomes blind again and is reunited with Oscar. She forgives his deception and accepts his blue complexion; they marry, have children, and live a happy life together. Her blindness restored to her, Lucilla's fate confirms Collins's thesis that disability can be an ingredient of happiness rather than an obstacle to it.

Early in the novel, readers learn that Lucilla, a modern, middle-class blind person, can read by touch, but Lucilla is never depicted reading raised print. Collins chooses instead to punctuate his convoluted plot with scenes of letter writing. Lucilla dictates some of her letters but, like real-world blind people, she does so at the cost of her privacy. What is more, those who assist her by taking dictation from her repeatedly coattail her letters, adding postscripts to her letters without her knowledge. Writing with a pen gives her more privacy and independence but is a comparatively tedious process. The first letter Lucilla writes in the course of the novel reveals the strength of her desire for independence. When Lucilla decides to write to Oscar soon after their first meeting, Pratolungo offers to write for her but, she explains, Lucilla "jealously declined to let me hold the pen" (60). Rejecting the offer of help, Lucilla insists: "My first note to him must be all written by me" (60). She tells Pratolungo: "I can write—in my own roundabout way. It's long and tiresome; but still I can do it. Come and see" (60). Recalling Martin's use of the phrase "slow and laborious" (75) to describe Gilbert's real-world experience of writing with a pen, Lucilla works hard to conform to sighted norms of letter writing.

In another connection to Gilbert, writing letters with ink exposes Lucilla to sighted people's scrutiny. Pratolungo observes how, "[g]uiding the pen in her right hand with the fingers of her left hand, she wrote slowly, in large childish letters, these words:—'DEAR MR OSCAR'" (61). Here and elsewhere, Pratolungo draws attention to how Lucilla's blindness quite literally shapes her words. When she receives a letter from Lucilla at a later point in the novel, she imagines Lucilla writing it, "feeling her way over the paper, in her large childish characters" (106). Whereas Pratolungo focuses on Lucilla's inferior penmanship, Lucilla ends her letter to Pratolungo on a positive note, declaring "This is the longest letter I have ever written" (107), this in regard to a letter of just over one hundred words. Persevering in a practice she finds "tiresome," Lucilla creates documents that are fully legible to sighted people but that differ from those of a similarly educated nonblind person in both appearance and length.

Lucilla's experience of letter writing is shaped by her blindness but also by her short-lived fascination with seeing. Of particular importance to Lucilla is a letter she writes to Herr Grosse to ask him to operate on her eyes. Its serious subject matter justifies the effort she invests in writing it. As she tells Pratolungo: "Writing is long, long work for *me*. But this was a letter I felt bound to write myself, if I could. Can you guess who I am corresponding with? It is done, my dear! I have written to Herr Grosse!" (217). Notably, both Lucilla's medium and her message express her willingness to conform to ocularcentric norms: writing with ink, creating a document that can only be read by sight, Lucilla seeks a medical cure for her own blindness. What is more, the opportunity to improve her handwriting is, it turns out, no small part of what motivates her to seek sight. Early in her healing process, soon after the removal of her bandages, Lucilla asks Grosse: "May I try if I can write? [. . .] I do so want to see if I can write with my eyes instead of my finger" (302). Grosse refuses this request but Lucilla, impatient to participate more fully in ink-print culture, decides to teach herself to write by sight. Pratolungo explains:

> Conscious that her handwriting—thus far, painfully and incompletely guided by her sense of touch—must present itself in sadly unfavourable contrast to the handwriting of other women who could see, she persisted in petitioning Grosse to permit her to learn 'to write with her eyes instead of her finger,' until she fairly wearied out the worthy German's power of resistance. (322)

Using the words "painfully" and "incompletely" to describe Lucilla's experience of writing with ink by touch, Pratalungo observes Lucilla's progress as a newly sighted writer closely. She discovers how, "Little by little, using her eyes for a longer and longer time on each succeeding day, [Lucilla] mastered the serious difficulty of teaching herself to write by sight instead of by touch" (322). Like a child learning to write for the first time, Lucilla works in stages, writing "lines in copybooks" (322) before graduating to taking dictation. Determined to conform to sighted people's standards of penmanship, Lucilla, once proud of her ability to write by touch, is embarrassed by the visual appearance of her handwriting. After her surgery, she refuses, for example, to let the man she believes is Oscar see it: "He tried hard to prevail on me to let him see my writing. I refused. It is improving as fast as it can; but it is not good enough yet" (333).

That being said, writing with ink is far easier for Lucilla after her surgery than it was before; indeed, Lucilla finds writing by sight so easy that she writes at all hours of the day and night. When blind, Lucilla wrote concise letters but, once sighted, she becomes an enthusiastic diarist. A "private record of the events of the day" (342), her journal allows her to refine her penmanship in private and is, moreover, a record of her life that she can, for the first time, read without assistance. Lucilla is so dedicated to her journal that her life after surgery is surprisingly deskbound. One might expect an educated middle-class person who has recently acquired sight and who is recuperating at a seaside resort to be eager to visit an art gallery, or study the coastline, or sample the visual richness of street life but Lucilla prefers to devote herself to writing. Indeed, Lucilla begins writing at such an early point in her recuperation from surgery that her journal records the earliest phases of her adaptation to sight. Take, for example, the following entry:

> We have a cat and a dog in the house. Would it be credited, if I was telling it to the world instead of telling it to my Journal, that I actually mistook one for the other to-day?—after seeing so well, too, as I do now, and being able to write with so few false strokes in making my letters! It is nevertheless true that I did mistake the two animals. (333)

Lucilla compares the progress she has made in refining her penmanship, now notable for the rarity of "false strokes," with her still limited visual knowledge of her environment.

Lucilla writes in her journal so compulsively and avidly that writing returns her to blindness. Her journal entries provide Collins with a compelling way to trace the decline in Lucilla's visual acuity, a development Lucilla is slower to perceive than the novel's readers. In a representative entry, made at 1 o'clock in the morning, she writes: "My eyes are beginning to ache; and, strange to say, I have hardly been able to see the last two or three lines I have written. They look as if the ink was fading from them" (363). When she begins to write again at 6 o'clock in the morning, she looks at the sea out her window and notes "[t]he mist this morning is the thickest mist I have yet seen here" (366). Soon after, she complains that "[t]he mist is stealing in [. . .]. It gets between me and my paper, and obliges me to bend down close over the page to see what I am about" (366). When her maid explains later that there had not been any mist that day, Lucilla takes up her journal to record her realization: "The idea struck me for the first time that the dimness which I had attributed to the mist, was, in plain truth, the dimness in my own eyes" (372). Aware that she has "fatigued" her eyes with writing but unable to resist the temptation to write, she continues to make entries in her journal until, overwhelmed with emotion when she learns the man she believes to be Oscar plans to leave town, she declares: "I must drop the pen, and try if I can think. My eyes completely fail me. I can write no more" (373). And yet Lucilla continues to try to write, adding a few final sentences to the journal. As Pratolungo explains, "Except a word or two, here and there, it is impossible any longer to decipher the writing" (374). Pratolungo, ever attentive to the appearance of Lucilla's handwriting, adds: "The last lines of the Journal are, as writing, actually inferior to her worst penmanship when she was blind" (374).

When Lucilla loses the ability to see, her journal loses its value as both a workbook and means for self-expression. It also loses its status as a private record. Relinquished by Lucilla, the journal passes to Pratolungo who incorporates its contents, word for word, into her narration of the novel. Transcribed and repurposed into four chapters, the first of which is titled "The Story of Lucilla: told by Herself," Lucilla's journal enriches the novel with a second narratorial perspective. Notably, Lucilla has the power of narration, of telling her own story, only for the portion of her life when she is sighted. With the exception of a handful of handwritten letters, in her life as a blind person, both before her surgery and after its failure, Lucilla's story is told by others. Sight is thus identified by Collins with the ability to write one's own life, be it in the pages of a private journal or as chapters in a sensation novel.

Notably, even in the case of chapters that share the contents of her journal, Lucilla's handwriting is subject to a sighted person's judgement. Pratolungo intersperses her transcription of the journal with editorial comments that reflect the tenacity of her fascination with the appearance of Lucilla's handwriting. Take, for example, a passage in which Lucilla expresses measured satisfaction with her penmanship, using the phrase "backward child" to do so: "How has my writing got on for the last week? I am becoming a little better satisfied. Less like the hand of a backward child than it was. I shall be able to write as well as other ladies do when I am Oscar's wife" (323). But Pratolungo adds a bracketed corrective:

> "[*Note.*—She is easily satisfied, poor dear. Her improved handwriting is sadly crooked. Some of the letters embrace each other at close quarters like dear friends; and some start asunder like bitter enemies. This is not to reflect on Lucilla—but to excuse myself, if I make any mistakes in transcribing the Journal. Now let her go on.—P.]" (323)

Identifying Lucilla's writing while blind as immature and effortful, and her writing while sighted as awkward, irregular, or illegible, Pratolungo is an unlikeable and unimaginative representative of ocularcentrism. Unrelenting in her judgment of a blind person's penmanship, her commentary functions as a counterpoint to the novel's largely progressive portrait of blindness.

Handwriting, both a learned skill and a cultural practice associated with the expression of a writer's identity and personality, functions, in Lucilla's case, primarily as a measure of changes in her visual acuity. It has, in other words, a diagnostic quality. Though Pratolungo is fascinated by the appearance of Lucilla's handwritten letters, it is not a handwritten letter but a dictated letter, the last that Lucilla authors in the course of the novel, that alerts Pratolungo that Lucilla's blindness has returned. Pratolungo explains:

> Before I had read a word, the sight of the writing struck a sudden chill through me. The body of the note was written by the hand of a stranger! And the signature at the end was traced in the large straggling childish characters which I remembered so well, when Lucilla had written her first letter to Oscar in the days when she was blind! (410)

Lucilla, determined when she is sighted to improve the visual appearance of her handwriting, is, once blind, no longer concerned with meeting ocularcentric standards; she signs the dictated letter in "large straggling childish characters" (410). By adding the word "straggling" to her habitual description of Lucilla's handwriting as both large and childish, Pratolungo references the irregular appearance of Lucilla's writing as well as the slow pace at which she writes. Once again, Lucilla's writing makes her blindness visible.

While Pratolungo thinks of the return of Lucilla's blindness as tragic,

Lucilla feels otherwise. She insists: "Don't cry about my blindness [. . .]. The days when I had my sight have been the unhappiest days of my life" (412). She reiterates this message when she is reunited with Oscar, announcing that "My blindness is my blessing" (417). These words fill Pratolungo with "horror" (417) but Lucilla explains: "You *will* persist in thinking that my happiness depends on my sight [. . .]. Try to understand me, and you won't talk of my loss—you will talk of my gain" (418). Disabused of her hopes regarding sightedness, now actively rejecting societal investment in the ability to see, Lucilla celebrates the return of the richness of her non-visual sensory life. And so does the novel. As I have suggested, Collins gives handwriting center stage in this dramatic story of blindness and temporarily acquired sight, using both Lucilla's penmanship and her desire to normalize her handwriting to energize his own critique of ocularcentrism. Writing in ink, which speeds Lucilla's return to blindness, produces a compelling record of her unhappiness with sight. Whether they occur at times of blindness or sightedness, scenes of Lucilla handwriting in Collins's novel buttress a message most obviously communicated by the failure of a medical cure to secure Lucilla happiness: just as the ability to see is not a necessary component of a happy and satisfying life, sight is not required for either literacy or letter writing.

Before leaving this novel, it is perhaps worth acknowledging that the publication of *Poor Miss Finch* involved Collins himself in an exchange of letters with blind people. At least he claimed that was the case. In a note Collins added to the preface of a new edition of the novel, in November 1872, he reported that:

> The German oculist—'Herr Grosse'—has impressed himself so strongly as a real personage on the minds of some of my readers afflicted with blindness, or suffering from diseases of the eye, that I have received several written applications requesting me to communicate his present address to patients desirous of consulting him! Sincerely appreciating the testimony thus rendered to the truth of this little study of character, I have been obliged to acknowledge to my correspondents—and I may as well repeat it here—that Herr Grosse has no (individual) living prototype. (xl)

This anecdote normalizes blind people's experiences of literacy, recognizing real-world blind people as both readers of contemporary fiction and writers of letters. Collins, clearly flattered by these readers' responses, seems surprisingly untroubled by the fact that blind people who write to him are would-be patients in search of a medical cure. A key message of Lucilla's story, that the medical cure of blindness is not necessary for happiness, had, it seems, been lost on a portion of his readership for whom the message had special relevance. Collins's response seems to mark a limit to the unconventionality of his thinking about visual disability. One might well wonder what portion of the letters Collins received from "readers afflicted with blindness" were written with a Foucault frame, with stamps, or even in braille, methods that Collins did not make available to his protagonist. Had he done so, *Poor Miss Finch* would have been a very different novel, one in which penmanship played a lesser part.

Opting Out

A brief reflection on the letter writing of Henry Fawcett serves as a postscript to this chapter's exploration of both real and fictional accounts of nineteenth-century blind people's letter writing. Fawcett, a contemporary of both Elizabeth Gilbert and Wilkie Collins, was one of nineteenth-century Britain's most accomplished and respected blind people.[11] After becoming blind in early adulthood, in 1858, Fawcett studied political economy at Cambridge, where he was appointed Professor of Political Economy in 1863. Elected to Parliament for the first time in 1865, Fawcett was so effective as a statesman that, in 1880, he had cause to hope he would be invited to join the Cabinet of William Gladstone's second premiership. Fawcett was, however, passed over by Gladstone and it is likely that his work with sighted assistants was a factor in Gladstone's decision. As Fawcett's biographer Leslie Stephen explains, "A member of the Cabinet has to see many confidential papers, and there would be a difficulty in admitting one who would have to use other eyes for reading them" (410). Given that Fawcett's inability to read the contents of a Cabinet member's mailbag limited his advancement, it is arguably ironic that Gladstone decided to appoint Fawcett to the role of Postmaster General, a position which put him at the head of Britain's extensive and innovative postal network until his death at the age of fifty-one.

But what of letters written by Fawcett? According to Stephen, Fawcett was able to write letters with ink after becoming blind but preferred to dictate them. Stephen, who was a close friend of Fawcett, shares the following regarding how Fawcett's relationship to letters evolved in the course of his life as a blind person: "He tried for some time to continue writing with his own hand, and I have seen an autograph letter of his dated in 1860. He found the practice irksome, however, as is, I believe, the general experience of men who lose their sight, and soon confined himself to dictation" (55–56). Stephen's choice of the word "irksome" recalls both Martin's description of Gilbert's experiences writing with a pen and Collins's fictional depiction of Lucilla Finch. By examining a celebrated portrait of Fawcett, as well as engaging both nineteenth-century and twenty-first-century people's interest in his letters, we can learn more about Fawcett's experiences of letter writing.[12]

Painted in 1872, Ford Madox Brown's double portrait of Fawcett and his wife Millicent Garrett Fawcett has a letter at its center (fig. 17). In the painting, Millicent, who was a respected political reformer in her own right, perches on the arm of a chair in which Henry sits. Both are dressed in autumnal-colored clothing. He wears an academic gown and holds a mortarboard; a gold pin ornaments his cravat. She wears a wine-colored bodice and ruffled skirt; her hair is arranged in a braided chignon. Seated higher than her husband, Millicent has one arm wrapped around Henry's shoulders. Her right hand, which rests on his shoulder, holds a pen. Henry's eyes are closed; he is not wearing the wire-framed glasses he wears in studio photographs taken of him throughout his adult life. Millicent looks at his face, the line of her gaze guiding the viewer's gaze first to her husband's eyes and then, past him, to the pen that she holds. With his left hand, Henry grasps Millicent's left hand, specifically her thumb. With the fingers of the same hand, she holds the top edge of a letter, not yet folded, which she presents to him. He points to the letter with the extended index finger of his right hand, the paleness of his hand against the dark background of his clothing drawing attention to his gesture and, in turn, to the letter. His mouth open, his finger pointing at a blank section of the page, Fawcett appears to be proposing the addition of a postscript.

This letter is central not only to the canvas but to the painting's messages about blindness. Henry's finger, very near to but not touching the letter's surface, brings to mind the action of reading by touch but, as the pen in Millicent's hand reminds viewers, the surface of the letter is inked, not embossed. Whereas Henry's gesture indicates that he is thinking about the letter, Millicent's attention is on her husband. Her mouth is closed whereas his is open; he speaks while she listens. It looks very much like a scene of dictation, an accomplished male scholar dictating a letter to his wife, except that the letter in this painting is their shared composition. Three lines of the letter's handwritten, inked text are visible: the first reads "Your Obed. Servants," the next M. Fawcett, and the final Henry Fawcett. Separated by the flourish of a line drawn below Millicent's signature, both partners' names are written in the same ink by the same hand: Millicent's hand. Depicting the blind husband

Figure 17. Henry Fawcett and Dame Millicent Fawcett; double portrait by Ford Madox Brown (1872). © National Portrait Gallery, London.

and the sighted wife as co-authors of a letter, the painting celebrates their joint authorship of political essays and, more broadly, their many collaborations as social reformers.

Brown's laudatory portrait, which celebrates letter writing as important to a blind person's life, does not downplay the fact that Fawcett's relationship to written correspondence is mediated by sighted people. The painting acknowledges that Fawcett does not handwrite or even sign letters that bear his name but there is nothing about this painting that figures his difference from cultural norms as a crisis or tragedy. Wearing his academic gown, depicted in a private space before he re-enters the public sphere, Fawcett does not need to hold a pen to author a letter any more than he needs to hold a pen to be recognized for his academic and political achievements. He enjoys self-expression, social connection, and social influence regardless of who does the work of writing. He has no attachment to handwriting and, it seems, no desire or need for privacy beyond what he enjoys as a partner in a collaborative and equitable marriage.

If Fawcett cared little about handwriting, his lack of investment was not shared by his sighted admirers. Indeed, the fact that Fawcett dictated the vast majority of the letters he wrote in the course of his adulthood did not discourage sighted people from wondering what his handwriting looked like. Consider, for example, the evidence of a letter that Millicent Garrett Fawcett authored in 1902, almost two decades after Fawcett died. Her letter replies to the letter of an unnamed correspondent who had reached out to her regarding her late husband's handwriting. It reads:

> Dear Sir, I am afraid you will be disappointed to hear that this letter, now returned, was not written by my husband but by his secretary Mr. F. J. Dryhurst—now of the Home Office. It may interest you to have this little photograph which I am sending you. It was taken about 1868 at Brighton, yours very truly, M.G. Fawcett. (Letter by MGF dated Oct. 16th, 1902; offered for sale by Blackwell's Rare Books, 2023).

The bearer of bad news, Millicent Garrett Fawcett is sorry to inform her correspondent that he is not in possession of a sample of her late husband's handwriting. Returning the letter that her husband dictated, she adds a second enclosure: a photograph.[13] A consolation prize, this offering speaks to the visual basis of sighted people's interest in famous people's handwriting. Her late husband's image will, Millicent hopes, speak to her husband's character in ways that a letter he dictated to his secretary cannot.

Lest we be tempted to think the desire to own a sample of the handwriting of a blind statesman is a whim of centuries past, a letter advertised for sale online in 2023 offers a corrective. The letter's content is quite everyday; in it, Fawcett asks his friend and former teacher Henry James Maine about a date in Trinity College's administrative calendar. The seller, who understandably has little to say about the letter's mundane content, opted to advertise it for sale under the following heading: "An Original Handwritten Letter Signed by Economist Henry Fawcett to Sir Henry James Maine / Henry Fawcett SIGNED" (Letter by HF, dated 24 March, 1883; offered for sale online by AbeBooks in 2023). One wonders if the buyer of this letter would be disappointed to discover that Fawcett had abandoned writing with a pen decades prior to dictating this note.

Fawcett's dictated letters are, of course, as much a part of the history of blind people's correspondence as Elizabeth Gilbert's autograph letters. When he prioritized self-expression and convenience over privacy, authoring letters but not bothering to handwrite them or sign them, Fawcett made a choice that was as progressive as Gilbert's decision to master the intricacies of a Foucault frame. While histories of visual disability tend to celebrate innovation and achievement, emphasizing the invention of new tools or the mastery of new skills, the history of blind people's literacy needs to reserve space for a spectrum of forms of self-determination. These include the choice to not learn how to write with pen, or a stylus and slate, or a frame or, as was also the case with Fawcett, to not learn how to read by touch. The history of disability is enriched by the diversity of blind people's experiences and choices related to literacy, including the choice to delegate the tasks of reading or writing letters to sighted people. Privileged to have the help of both his wife and professional secretaries; able to secure influence, self-expression, and social connection through letters he dictated; more interested in communication than in privacy, Fawcett contributed to a non-visual culture of letter writing by leaving the task of putting ink on paper to other hands.

Whereas this chapter has explored blind people's experiences of writing letters, and to a lesser extent, literary depictions of those experiences, the next chapter will explore nineteenth-century blind people's encounters with non-textual objects, from scientific specimens in natural history museums to works of art in galleries. It will propose that blind people's experiences of their era's educational entertainments were shaped by sighted people's growing recognition of the information gathering potential of the sense of touch.

Five

Beyond the Book

The first four chapters of *By Touch Alone* have examined blindness, touch, literacy, and literature in nineteenth-century Anglo-American culture. While each chapter has explored a different facet of the history of blind people's literacy, all four have elucidated this book's principal claim: that the ability and opportunity to read by touch changed the lived experience of blindness, in part by changing perceptions of blindness and blind people. Analyzing the experiences of blind people as diverse as Alice King, a successful author who typed her own manuscripts, and William Hawkes, a man arrested for reading aloud on Waterloo Bridge, each chapter has explored contributions blind people made to the development of raised-print culture: an inkless, tactile alternative to the print culture of the nonblind majority. Accounts left by members of the first generation of blind people to read by touch indicate that reading by touch made a profound difference to the lives of blind people; the poet Jane Crosby, the inventor William Moon, and the activist Alfred Hirst are just some of the individuals whose experiences of education, leisure, spirituality, and social engagement were transformed by reading by touch.

In addition to exploring the experiences and opinions of blind people who learned to read by touch, the preceding chapters also featured the writing of visually disabled people who did not learn to read by touch, such as George du Maurier and W.W. Fenn. While the prevalence of literacy among blind people at different points in the century is, unfortunately, difficult to assess, what is certain is that blind people's lives were shaped by the proliferation of reading by touch regardless of whether they read using this method. Because reading by touch changed perceptions of blind people by challenging conventional identifications of blindness with tragedy, dependency, and social isolation, this innovation's effects were very broadly felt.

The work and opinions of sighted commentators such as Harriet Martineau and creative writers such as Wilkie Collins also demonstrate the breadth of this innovation's reach. As raised-print books and the skills required to read them proliferated, sighted people were more likely to perceive and depict blind people enjoying independence, social influence, and a rich sensory life. That being said, negative stereotypes about blindness and blind people endured and they shaped both the experience and the reception of reading by touch. What is more, as the challenging lives of nineteenth-century street readers demonstrate, the ability to read by touch did not transform the nonblind majority's thinking to such a degree that blind people were able to secure the kinds of paid employment or social influence they sought. There were, in other words, real-world limits to the transformative and equalizing effects of reading by touch.

As preceding chapters have argued, while the most notable changes brought about by reading by touch were changes to blind people's lives and to ideas about blindness, blind people's entry into literacy had a secondary set of effects. It prompted both blind and sighted people to think in new ways about bookmaking, printing, and alphabets; it was a catalyst for exploration of new possibilities for the inscription, whether by hand or machine, of language. Whereas the publication and circulation of inkless books broadened definitions of the book, the production of raised-print materials, from primers to books to weekly magazines, required the development and refinement of new methods and machines. What is more, the emergence of a new kind of reader, one who did not need to see in order to read, changed the physiology of reading, transforming the relationship between books and human bodies.

Additional topics of importance to the first four chapters of this book include nineteenth-century blind people's perception of acquired blindness as an enriching experience, as both a biological and cultural identity defined by gain rather than loss. Another notable thread is blind people's desire to be recognized as creators, rather than consumers, of culture. This thread connects real-world figures such as Elizabeth Gilbert and Edmund White to fictional characters such as du Maurier's Barty Josselin. A less positive connection between history and literature that surfaces in the first four chapters of this book is the historical tendency of sighted people to approach blind people and their ways of being with suspicion—with suspicion about, for example, the validity of their claims to be literate or even of their claim to be blind. Unsurprisingly, where this study has found points of connection, it has also discovered profound differences. The extent to which both class and gender shaped and differentiated nineteenth-century experiences of blindness, including the experience of reading by touch, has been a recurring theme.

Also of note is the diversity of blind people's experiences of sensory difference and, by extension, their experience of literacy. "Blind" was a capacious if not a nebulous label in the nineteenth century and people's lived experiences of blindness varied drastically. The difference between, for example, the experience of lifelong blindness and the experience of the sudden acquisition of blindness as the result of violence, accident, or disease would be difficult to overstate. Reading by touch changed the lived experience of blindness but that experience was, both before and after the advent of reading by touch, a remarkably diverse one. That being said, reading by touch was a skill that blind people with very different identities and histories of disability had in common. What is more, the work of improving raised-print culture—through activism, innovation, experimentation, and debate—was a common cause that brought blind people from different backgrounds together. Literacy was, in short, both a prompt and a means for blind people to connect with one another in the course of the nineteenth century.

My goal for this, the final chapter of the book, is the same goal that has guided my work in preceding chapters: to add to existing knowledge of the entry of blind people into literacy by creating a balanced study that, while it is attentive to the perspective of the sighted majority, is guided by and gives priority to the perspectives of blind people. Accordingly, in what follows, I engage the life writing of nineteenth-century blind people but, in this instance, I break with a pattern of previous chapters. Shifting my focus away from the reading of raised-print books, I explore blind people's participation in their era's educational entertainments. I argue that blind people's experiences of hands-on learning in museums and galleries was shaped by changes in both blind and nonblind people's perception of the power of touch, changes that can be traced to the spread of reading by touch.

The work of B.G. Johns, a sighted educator of blind students whose opinions have been engaged throughout this book, provides a useful preamble. The richness of touch's contributions to the cognitive lives of blind people was a theme of Johns's book *Blind People: Their Works and Ways* (1867). Exploring the importance of this historically underappreciated sense to the life of a representative blind child, Johns understands touch as a highly effective substitute for sight:

> To the seeing, touch is an auxiliary, but to the blind boy it is the primary sense of all. By it he knows his own clothes, and almost all the property that he possesses—his tools, box, bed, hat, fiddle, cupboard, seat in chapel, school-room, and workshop; by it he reads his chapter

> in St. John or in Robinson Crusoe; he plays chess or dominoes; works a sum in Long Division, or writes a letter home to his mother which she can read by eyes, and he with his fingers. (10–11)

A "servant-of-all-work" (10), touch is invaluable to reading but also to other aspects of life. Adding to this already long list, Johns notes that touch supports a blind child's study of unfamiliar objects. He explains: "by touch he *sees* any curiosity, such as a lamp from the Pyramids, or a scrap of mineral, which you describe to him, and which, having once handled, he always speaks of as having been seen" (11). Johns's substitution of "*sees*" for "feels" drives his point home: touch is sight for this representative blind child. The sense of hearing also has a role to play but that role is a lesser one. Learning by touching, the boy listens to a description of what he handles, touch and talk combining to generate knowledge.

Attentive to touch's status as "the primary sense," interested in forms of material culture other than a raised-print *Robinson Crusoe*, this chapter extends *By Touch Alone*'s exploration of the history of blindness to include nineteenth-century blind people's touching of non-textual objects such as machinery, natural history specimens, and works of art. It begins with an analysis of an anonymous blind essayist's account of his experiences touching machines and manufactured objects in the halls of London's International Exhibition of 1862. It turns next to museums and to blind people's experiences studying, as well as curating, natural history collections. A third space explored in this chapter is the art gallery. I examine non-visual, hands-on encounters blind visitors had with works of art, including, surprisingly, oil paintings. In regards to all three spaces, I propose that reading by touch had an unanticipated but welcome consequence: it licensed blind people's handling of a wide range of exhibited objects. Put differently, following the advent and proliferation of reading by touch, nineteenth-century blind people's participation in their era's educational offerings changed. Invited by sighted people to employ their sense of touch in cultural settings that privileged visual forms of knowledge and pleasure, nineteenth-century blind people secured access to valued collections, the handling of which deepened their knowledge of both material culture and the affordances of touch.

At the Exhibition

Exhibitions such as London's celebrated Great Exhibition of 1851 or Chicago's World's Fair of 1893 were era-defining events. Attracting crowds who were eager to view the contents of long rows of glass cases and marvel at elaborate wall-mounted displays, nineteenth-century exhibitions might seem to have had limited appeal for blind visitors. Yet, as with so many facets of the history of visual disability, firsthand accounts tell a different story. "How a Blind Man saw the International Exhibition," an anonymous, autobiographical essay, is one of several records that challenge conventional understandings of the nineteenth-century exhibition as appealing primarily, if not exclusively, to the sense of sight. By following this essayist's lead through the halls of London's International Exhibition of 1862, we get a better sense not only of the sensory richness of nineteenth-century exhibitions but also of the role sensory difference played in blind visitors' experiences.[1]

Published in January 1863 in *Temple Bar* magazine, "How a Blind Man saw the International Exhibition" shares an account of that event that differs markedly from those of sighted visitors. Engaging experiences of the heard, the smelt and, most significantly, the felt, the essayist describes a multitude of sounds, from "a deafening clatter of foreign voices" (228), to the noise made by a fellow visitor's "creaky boot" (234), to "the rustle of silks" (235) worn by women visitors. He also recalls "the smell of hot oil" (233) in the machinery section and the feeling of a "vibration under-foot" (233) when he stood on the halls' wooden walkways. The essayist explains that, like Johns's representative blind student, he acquired knowledge of the objects on display through both touch and talk. As he moved through different areas of the Exhibition, exhibitors offered to describe their displays for his benefit. He notes, for example, the surprising readiness of sighted people to facilitate his exploration of the Industrial Annex, explaining: "I was greatly assisted in my endeavours by the kindness and civility I met with from the intelligent men who had charge of this part of the building" (233). In relation to Britain's achievements in the design of machinery, he adds, "I now realize to myself, in a manner impossible before, the fact that I was brought in contact for the first time with that special branch of the industry of the present age" (233). The contact he experienced was literal as well as figurative. Encouraged to touch the machinery, the essayist had to overcome understandable anxiety. Regarding machines in motion, he writes:

> I could not divest myself of the idea [. . .] that by merely resting my hand for a moment upon one of the straps which served to connect the machinery with the motive-power, I rendered myself liable to be caught up and torn to pieces by one revolution of the wheels. Fortu-

> nately for me, however, there were many who were both able and willing to prevent such a catastrophe; and what with studying attentively such as were still, and listening to the explanations so kindly given relative to those that were at work, I managed to gain a pretty clear insight into the marvels with which the place abounded. (233–34)

Rewarded for his courage in touching machines, accommodated by sighted exhibitors, the essayist is able to develop new knowledge of the Exhibition's extensive industrial displays.

In other areas of the building, including the International Halls, the essayist found his appetite for knowledge similarly accommodated. To take one example, he shares an account of his visit to the Japanese court, a cluttered display area. An engraving from the *Illustrated London News* for September 20, 1862 of this popular portion of the Exhibition shows sighted visitors looking at a miscellany of imported objects that are either arranged in glass display cases or hung high beyond their reach at the back of the stalls. Experiencing this space in a non-visual way, the blind essayist recalls how:

> owing to the civility of one of the stall-keepers, I was enabled to form a very correct estimate of the habits and general mode of life of this people. He put himself to infinite trouble, reaching down various interesting objects for my inspection, bringing them near to me that I might feel them. (232)

The objects the essayist handled included decorative items, weapons, and a waterproof raincoat that he describes as "strong, and remarkably light" (232). Glad to have had this opportunity, an accommodation offered to him because of his blindness, the essayist adds regarding the exhibitor: "These and many more curiosities he put before me with evident pleasure, taking care so to explain each object that they became well impressed upon my mind" (232). As was the case in the machinery halls, the essayist secures knowledge by handling objects that sighted visitors only view. Here and elsewhere, the essayist delivers on the promise of his essay's irreverent title, explaining "How a Blind Man saw" the Exhibition. As his title signals, he shares his experiences in full knowledge of his sighted contemporaries' understanding of nineteenth-century exhibitions as narrowly visual spectacles in which participants learn by looking.

The essayist feels so well informed by his hands-on exploration of objects displayed in the International Halls that he contrasts a day at the Exhibition with the reading of a "whole library" of books. Arguing for the supremacy of exhibitions over libraries as educational tools, he proposes that:

> the articles exhibited were arranged with such care and judgment, that one left them with a much better idea of their resources, present condition, and future prospects, than could be gained by reading a whole library of volumes devoted to them, filled, as such works are in general, with dry details and crabbed statistics, which latter, we all know, may be made to prove any thing the writer wishes to be credited. (232)

A skeptical consumer of published information, the essayist rejects book learning in favor of the object lesson, a mode of instruction that paired a teacher's spoken commentary on the significance and attributes of an object with a student's physical examination of it. Theorized by Swiss teacher Johann Pestalozzi and promoted in Britain by nineteenth-century educational reformers such as Elizabeth Mayo and Robert Owen, the object lesson became a fixture in schools for sighted children.[2] Educators who adopted this method believed that the multisensory nature of this style of learning increased student engagement and improved students' recall of facts. Given the emphasis on senses other than sight, it's unsurprising that object lessons also became a fixture of specialized schools for blind students that opened throughout Britain and the United States in the course of the nineteenth century. In the halls of the International Exhibition of 1862, both the sighted exhibitors' accommodations and the blind essayist's assertion that his learning is enriched by the hands-on study of objects reflect the rise of the object lesson as an educational practice. Notably, in the context of the Exhibition, the blind visitor is granted permission to touch objects in ways that sighted visitors are not. Touch, of value to many people's educational lives, is recognized by exhibitors as uniquely valuable for a blind visitor.

Of course, a blind man's remarks on the role that libraries of books play, or fail to play, in his education have special resonance in the second half of the nineteenth century. By 1862, the development and expansion of a canon of raised-print books for English-speaking blind readers was well underway but it was still a work in progress. The essayist, who hopes for both more rapid progress and a richer set of raised-print offerings, shared his frustration with his nonblind readers. Disappointed by a display of items designed for blind people's use, "a collection of objects" that includes samples of new embossed alphabets, tangible maps, and an array of writing tools, he explains:

> In the department devoted to educational works and appliances I discovered, after careful search, a collection of objects intended to illustrate the numerous inventions devised by the ingenuity of man for elevating the condition of the blind, and promoting, as far as possible, their general welfare. Of course these things had peculiar claims upon my notice; and I occupied a considerable time in examining them, hoping to discover among them the germ of some process which might be made available for bringing within the reach of this class a collection of books more varied in character, and better adapted to their wants, than those which are at present in use. In this hope I was disappointed. (231–32)

Pleasantly surprised by spontaneous, one-on-one interactions with accommodating exhibitors, the essayist is let down by a planned gesture of inclusivity: the inclusion of specialized teaching apparatus and books for blind readers in the Exhibition's celebration of British innovation. Though eager to examine this display, the essayist is disappointed by what it documents. What a sighted person might view as evidence of progress, is, for the essayist, evidence of problems with the development of raised-print culture. Though not noted in any detail by the essayist, these problems include, as previous chapters have explored, resource-wasting rivalries between different raised-print scripts and the tendency of charitable institutions to prioritize the printing of religious material.

Of course, a display of inventions for "elevating the condition of the blind" was not created exclusively for blind visitors. Like coverage in the periodical press and public displays of reading by touch, exhibitions were an opportunity for sighted people to learn about developments in the realm of blind people's literacy. When the sighted author of *A Guide to the International Exhibition* visited this display, he gave it a far better review than the blind essayist:

> The small court in the north-east corner of the Educational Department is entirely devoted to the illustration of methods employed in teaching the blind. Here will be found specimens of all kinds of embossed or raised type, of writing and ciphering frames, of musical notation, and of maps in relief. A very beautiful embossed globe used in the School for the Indigent Blind adorns the centre of this recess, while specimens of the work done in various blind asylums are displayed on the walls and on the screens. (Pardon 98)

The dedication of even a "small court" in the corner of the Exhibition's Education Department is, like this guidebook's account of it, evidence of the sighted majority's interest in the development of a print culture created by and for blind people. The celebrated Great Exhibition of 1851 had included a similar display; the same was true of Chicago's World Fair of 1893. These displays educated sighted observers about blind people's literacy, alerting them to how centrally touch featured in developments related to reading and writing. Exhibits of this kind also raised awareness of the role touch played in nineteenth-century blind people's study of mathematics, music, astronomy, and geography. More than theoretical, having real-world and immediate effects, this category of display influenced how blind visitors were both perceived and accommodated. To put this differently, the touching by blind people of objects on display at the International Exhibition was by no means unrelated to the display in the small court in a corner of the Educational Department.

Consider, for instance, the way in which the blind essayist's experience of the International Exhibition as a surprisingly accommodating cultural space exemplifies the optimism of Harriet Martineau's 1854 essay on "Blindness" for *Household Words*, which I quoted in the Introduction to this book. As I noted there, nineteenth-century press coverage of reading by touch suggests that blind people's literacy changed sighted people's perceptions not only of blindness and blind people but also of the place of touch in a hierarchically-organized human sensorium. In her essay, Martineau announced that "The blind can now read—a good many of them—and all will, by and by" (424). Prompted by this development to reconsider the information-gathering potential of touch, Martineau goes on to propose that blind people's sense of touch has acquired new utility in an era of raised-print books:

> Their nice sense of touch, which used to be little more than an empty marvel to us, we have now learned to make use of in unbarring the door which shut them out from literature. We now print books for them, in a type which they feel, instead of see; an embossed type which they learn to run over with their fingers with great readiness. (424–25)

Formerly an "empty marvel," touch gains usefulness—or, more accurately, is newly recognized as useful—as a result of the invention of reading by touch. Of course, Martineau's decision to credit the sighted majority with the development of raised-print culture is regrettable; the same is true of her understanding of haptic ability as an inevitable offshoot of blindness rather than a product of effort and education.[3] Yet her optimism and her excitement were likely an encouragement to other sighted people to reconsider the value of touch and to contemplate ways in which touch might support blind people's cultural inclusion.

Like Martineau, the blind author W.W. Fenn reflected on the utility of touch in his writing about blindness but, unlike Martineau, he believed that touch was a sense that benefited from training. Fenn asserted that:

> [t]he fingers of the intelligent and skilful blind can be trained to afford very fair compensation for sight and [. . .] may be made to light up a darkened world. The power of fingers to convey intelligence to the brain is only one degree less, it would seem, that that of the eyes, but the power must be developed in the right manner. ("The Welfare" 478)

B.G. Johns, quoted above, shared Fenn's assessment of haptic sensitivity as a learned skill. "It is," Johns explains, "only by dint of long experience, and after an infinite series of mistakes—of many of which he is unconscious—that the blind boy manages to see with his fingers" (*Blind People* 39–40). The idea that touch could be educated and, moreover, that it needed to be educated, also shaped the thinking of nonblind author Charles Baker. Baker proposed in 1859, that "[i]f a seeing person would cultivate his sense of feeling to the same extent as the blind, his perceptions of touch would be as delicate as those of the blind man" (*English Cyclopaedia* 209).

Comments about the training of touch suggest that reading by touch shaped sighted people's perception of this oft-underestimated sense's information-gathering potential. As knowledge about the literacy of blind people spread, optimism about the complexity and utility of touch followed close behind. Alerting the sighted majority to the role of touch in education but also to the extent to which touch might itself be educated, reading by touch made touch seem more refined, complex, and useful. A traditionally low-ranked sense, touch gained respect. When sighted exhibitors offered up valuable and fragile objects to the touch of blind visitors, they signaled their appreciation of the power of touch to teach. More than an example of accommodation, their actions are a measure of a heightened appreciation of tactile experience. It is in this sense that the sighted majority's perception of touch as a sophisticated and refined sense allowed blind people to participate more fully in educational entertainments.

It is perhaps worth emphasizing that the anonymous author of this essay was not the only blind person to attend nineteenth-century exhibitions. Six years after the Great Exhibition of 1851, B.G. Johns remarked regarding students of the Blind School in St George's Fields that "[m]any of them [. . .] visited the Great Exhibition, and were delighted with the wonders of the place, of which they still talk" (*Land of Silence* 122). In reference to the 1862 International Exhibition, the author of an 1866 obituary published in the *Wakefield Journal and Examiner* noted of the obituary's subject, a young blind person named Henry Brown, that "I was indebted to his clear explanations for much of the pleasure I derived from the late exhibition, especially in the scientific departments, as improvements in telegraphy, etc." (qtd. in Levy 301). The *Temple Bar* essayist is thus remarkable not because he was the only blind person to attend exhibitions but instead because he published a detailed account of his experience.

It might also be worth noting that the *Temple Bar* essayist decided to publish an account of the International Exhibition because he felt that "what I have to say will interest many, and tend to throw some light upon the manner in which the blind are impressed with the outer world in which they live and move,—a subject on which at present much ignorance prevails" (227). Yet, at least one reader of the essay questioned its author's claim to be a blind person. A reviewer for the *Daily Southern Cross*, a New Zealand paper, shared the following:

> 'How a Blind Man Saw the Exhibition,' is a very interesting paper, and only wants the undoubted stamp of truth to render it still more so. We confess we have experienced some doubts about the author's blindness at times as we read. Be this however as it may, the descriptions are highly ingenious, and, if not by a blind man, argue a great power of throwing the mind into an imaginary situation in no common degre [sic]. ("English Magazines" 3)

Though fascinated by what the essay shares, this reviewer questions its blind author's claim to be blind. The reviewer's doubts bring to mind the sighted majority's suspicion of street readers, who were, as chapter 1 explored, not infrequently suspected of misrepresenting themselves as blind. We have an opportunity to respond differently, not with skepticism about the Exhibition-going essayist's disability but with attention to what his experiences can teach us about the nineteenth-century history of blindness.

In the Museum

If growing public awareness of reading by touch played a role in enriching blind people's participation in nineteenth-century educational entertainments, so too did the efforts of blind activists. Whereas invitations to touch objects displayed in the semi-commercial space of the International Exhibition seem to have been extended spontaneously, blind people had to work hard to secure similar opportunities in the context of the public museum. Elizabeth Gilbert, the blind activist whose letters were explored in chapter 4, took matters into her own hands when she took a stuffed crocodile to a tea-party. The crocodile was, it seems, a welcome addition to the gathering of blind working-class women; Gilbert noted in a diary entry for 1858 that "the women were delighted with it" (Martin 171). Gilbert was the founder of London's Association for Promoting the General Welfare of the Blind, an organization that employed working-class blind people, providing them with training and supplies to make, among other items, brooms and mats that were sold in the Association's store on Euston Road. Gilbert hoped to supplement the Association's support of working-class blind people's wellbeing by opening a small museum on the Association's second floor. Her goal was to create a natural history collection in which "every specimen could be handled" (Martin 166). As her biographer Frances Martin explained, "She found that the perceptive faculties which take the place of sight suffer from want of due cultivation, and she wished to remedy this by enabling the blind to obtain information about natural objects" (Martin 166). What Gilbert wanted for blind people was, in short, a museum of their own: a bespoke collection that blind people could use to learn not only about the natural world but also about the affordances of their own sense of touch.

Gilbert took inspiration from existing initiatives. In an 1858 essay about the education of blind people, Gilbert shared that she was "delighted to find that Monsieur K., the blind director of the institution at Breslau, has succeeded in obtaining permission for his pupils to *feel* the specimens of natural history contained in the Museum of that city" (Martin 146). She adds, "How glad I should be to hear of such permission being given in England" (Martin 146). She also noted that efforts were underway in the UK in a fledgling way: "I think, as I have heard Mr. D. Littledale, a blind gentleman say, that in schools there ought to be classes formed for the special object of exercising the touch. He himself has begun to form a Museum of objects with this view for the York School" (Martin 146). Closer to home, Gilbert visited Chichester Museum, located in the town where she lived, to learn more about the preparation of specimens from its sighted managers. Her diary shares: "Went to Museum to ask the cost of stuffing birds and about collections of eggs, and the order of arranging birds. Settled with E. that she should ask Mr.—to shoot some birds, and with Mr. H that he should tell Smith the bird stuffer to come to me next Wednesday" (Martin 166).

Taking a hands-on approach to the making of her museum, Gilbert collaborated closely with W.H. Levy, the blind manager of the Association for Promoting the General Welfare of the Blind. A fellow activist, Levy shared her frustration with blind people's inability to access collections in what he termed "ordinary museums" (Levy 142). When the sighted journalist Henry Morley visited the Association's workshop in 1859, Levy shared plans for the addition of a museum to its already crowded rooms. In his essay "At Work in the Dark," Morley encouraged readers to donate specimens to this initiative. He explained:

> All substances of which the chief characteristics can be learned through the sense of touch, would be fit contributions to a Museum for the Blind. Stuffed beasts and birds, preserved insects, and vegetable productions, shells, specimens of various grains, minerals, and manufactured articles,—nothing would be inappropriate that can be delicately handled without injury. (323)

Morley doesn't specify if the injuries to be avoided are to the articles or their examiners; his focus is on what "can be learned through the sense of touch" (323). He adds:

> Persons who are making collections in any department of physical science open to the intelligence of the blind, and who have specimens which they do not want, would do good by sending them as contributions to this projected museum. Mr. Levy will know what to do with them. (323)

Two years later, in 1861, when author Dinah Craik visited the Association, Levy took her to the second floor of the Association to see the now-open museum. After her visit, Craik echoed Morley in urging the public to support the Association by donating to the museum. She explained:

> any collector of objects of science, fossils, minerals, stuffed animals, and the like—not subject to injury by handling—may give entertain-

> ment and information to many an intelligent mind, to whom otherwise the wonderful works of God in nature must for ever remain unknown. (6)

She adds, regarding the Association's modest, one-room museum: "The delight his little museum affords is, Mr. Levy told us, something quite incredible" (6).

Unfortunately, less than a decade later, the museum on Euston Road had closed. In his 1872 book *Blindness and the Blind*, Levy explained: "The managers of the Association [. . .] were compelled to relinquish the museum for want of space, but they would be only too happy to have it in their power to reorganize the plan" (143). It seems that the room that housed this early example of what would be referred to today as a touch collection was needed for making and storing the household items whose sale kept the Association's doors open. Levy, regretting the loss, called on mainstream museums to accommodate blind people. He wrote: "we cannot help expressing surprise that no provision should be made for the blind in connection with the national and local museums of the country. Surely thirty thousand human beings are not the less to be cared for, because they have the misfortune of being blind" (142). Levy had, like Gilbert, considered the problem of the inaccessibility of public museums closely:

> it has been supposed that articles displayed in ordinary museums are of no use to persons without sight; this idea is altogether an error, for all stuffed objects, models, shells and specimens, connected with mineralogy, botany, etc. etc., may be examined by the blind with great advantage. No doubt the fear of injury to articles from being handled, has had something to do with the neglect of the blind in this matter, but we would venture to suggest that an official connected with the museum should be allowed to accompany blind visitors to afford information, and to see that no objects were examined that would suffer from being felt. (142–43)

Levy included living specimens in his plans: he proposed that botanical gardens open their collections to blind people's examination by touch, noting that "Many rare plants may be examined without injury at botanical gardens and the pleasure derived from the varied perfumes will be an additional source of enjoyment" (35).

Similar arguments were made by the activist Alexander Barnhill. Writing in 1875, Barnhill affirmed the educational potential of touch and argued for improved access to public museums. Of blind students, he wrote:

> personal examination, with explanations, would be so helpful in giving them an intelligent knowledge of the objects. But as parents might not have access to many articles that it would be important that their children should come to know and handle, such as stuffed animals, skins, shells, models, statuary, precious stones, &c., which are usually to be seen in museums, and give much information to visitors, it would be of great use if such collections, or portions of them, were made available to the blind, where they might handle the objects under proper inspection. (40)

He added that, "If objections were made to the blind touching them or inspecting them as frequently as might be necessary, then there would be a clear call to have a museum for the blind in large towns, where they might have access to examine such articles" (40). Like Gilbert and Levy, Barnhill paired argument with action. He created a small bespoke museum for blind visitors in Glasgow. He was particularly eager to accommodate working-class people with this initiative. As he explained, "[t]he blind who cannot receive the advantage of [. . .] higher education should surely have the privilege of examining such objects, and thus share in the benefit which such a valuable means of information gives" (41). The managers of schools for blind students agreed with Barnhill's assessment of the value of touch collections. In 1896, a writer for the *Dundee Courier* reported regarding British schools for blind students that, "A well-stocked museum of models of animals and natural objects is attached to each school, and when lessons in natural history are given the models greatly aid in conveying a correct idea of the object to the pupil's mind" ("About the blind").[4]

While the development of small, specialized collections was an important achievement of blind activists and educators, the most enduring legacy of their efforts was the influence they had on mainstream museums. Whereas, as the first section in this chapter demonstrated, the presence of a blind attendee at the International Exhibition of 1862 occasioned a series of spontaneous acts of accommodation, museums were a different matter. Slower, it seems, than temporary exhibitions to welcome and accommodate blind visitors, museums prioritized preservation over accommodation. As scholars such as Fiona Candlin and Constance Classen have demonstrated, for more than two centuries, both blind and sighted visitors' experiences of museums have been shaped by an "anti-touch" ethos.[5] To have blind visitors' needs and desires recognized, activists needed to overcome an entrenched (though, at the time, relatively new) precept of museum culture.

The first decades of the twentieth century witnessed the success of blind activists' decades-old efforts to secure access to the collections of public museums. Evidence of the influence of the efforts of Gilbert, Levy, and like-minded contemporaries can, for example, be found in a 1913 account of blind visitors' experiences at the Sunderland Museum in England's Northeast. Developing an early iteration of today's touch tour, the museum's director, J.A. Charlton Deas, welcomed groups of blind adults and children to explore objects in the museum's collection over the course of a series of weekly visits. Photographs of these visits show children and adults touching, among other things, taxidermy animals, marble busts of famous men, a Buddhist statue, and a human skeleton. They also show clay models of the museum's holdings made by child visitors. Whereas these models, created five weeks after the children's visit, suggested the lasting educational value of this initiative, letters from adult visitors expressed their deep appreciation for the Sunderland Museum's accommodations. Mr. Walker, a blind teacher of blind students, shared an especially powerful response: "Our people are simply astounded with the way they have been treated on the various visits. This may seem odd to you, but to me it is quite explicable. We are mainly accustomed to be treated as if we were something less than human beings" (93). Another blind visitor, Mr. Ramsay, wrote to the museum to share a reflection on a particularly memorable encounter:

> The lecture on the human skeleton was a rare treat. On first putting our hands on the bones it set up uncanny and creepy feelings, but we became quite familiar with the skeleton. It brought to our minds a quotation from the Psalmist, David— 'I will praise Thee, O God, for I am fearfully and wonderfully made.' The advantages of this method should be carefully studied by everyone interested in the blind. (96)

Making connections between their reading of a Psalm and the museum's specimen, referencing reading but moving beyond the book, blind visitors clearly valued opportunities for experiential forms of learning in museum spaces.

Letters like these made it easy for Charlton Deas to offer advice on touch tours to his fellow museum professionals. In the final moments of a lecture he gave in 1913, Charlton Deas made a compelling pitch for the accommodation of blind visitors:

> I can honestly say that I have never shown or explained any of the possessions of our institutions to a more eager, appreciative, and grate-

> ful class of people. Should you feel induced—as I hope you will—to try similar experiments in your various museums, all your trouble, and all the kindness of those who assist you, will be rewarded by the most sincere and profound gratitude, and this will be followed by convincing evidences of the usefulness of the effort. (97)

The rewards of accommodation, of making a museum accessible to blind visitors, were not, it seems, limited to the visitors; they were shared by sighted staff. Inspired by Charlton Deas's work, curators at the American Museum of Natural History (AMNH) in New York instituted a progressive and ambitious program of their own. In a 1914 report, staff member Agnes Laidlaw Vaughan described the AMNH's efforts to accommodate and engage blind visitors. She explained how, for example, "specimens were taken out of the cases for examination, and where this was not possible, [. . .] the visitors were taken to the storage study collections" (39). In addition to welcoming blind people, the museum loaned specimens to schools for blind students. Vaughan assured AMNH stakeholders that these items would be handled with care: "The material is selected outside of its interest value with regard to form, use and durability under use, although the care exercised by the teachers is effective in keeping the objects intact" (40). A photograph taken at the museum in 1914 shows two boys examining a taxidermy hippopotamus; a girl sits on a stool beside them, a small model of a hippopotamus, which she feels with both hands, resting on her lap (fig. 18). Students demonstrated the knowledge they had acquired through their hands-on examination of the museum's collections in compositions they shared with AMNH staff. One student's essay began: "Would you like to know what an idea the camel impressed upon my mind? His head is small in proportion to the rest of his body, his legs are long and its feet are flat" (40).

Thoroughly convinced of the value of her museum's efforts, Vaughan proposed that, for blind students,

> [t]he visit to the Museum means more than an hour's instruction, more than the mere viewing of new objects, it means a change of environment, a stimulation of intellectual expression, the appreciation of the socializing forces which go to produce public institutions for the distribution of knowledge and the betterment of life. (41)

Notably, the AMNH's outreach extended beyond school programming. Placing notices in raised-print magazines and developing a mailing list of

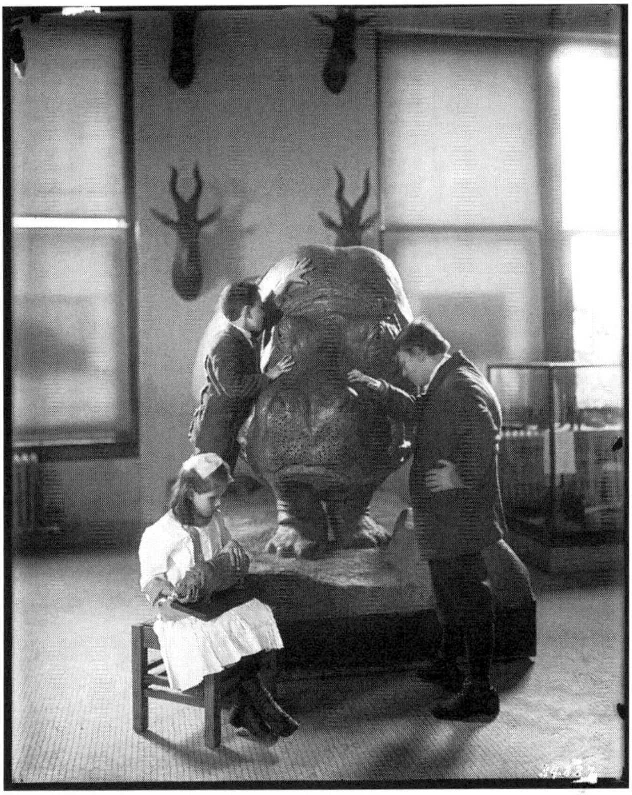

Figure 18. "Blind children studying the hippopotamus" (1914). American Museum of Natural History Library.

blind people living in and near New York City, staff hoped to welcome large numbers of adult visitors. They surveyed blind people to identify topics of special interest to them and, what is more, they offered funding to cover the cost of transportation to the museum for both blind adults and sighted guides. These accommodations were remarkably progressive, more than realizing nineteenth-century blind activists' hopes.

It's worth noting that Vaughan's report, published in the *American Museum Journal*, documents connections between reading by touch and museum going. Consider, for example, a photograph of four children, two girls and two boys, gathered around a taxidermy specimen of a stag (fig. 19). The girls feel the fur-covered back of the deer; both boys hold an antler in one hand and use their free hands to touch the deer's body. All four children seem intensely engaged by the experience. The photograph is captioned: "A

Figure 19. "A New Experience for Sightless Children," *The American Museum Journal* (January 1914). Author's collection.

NEW EXPERIENCE FOR SIGHTLESS CHILDREN: The American Museum furnishes an instructor for classes of blind children who are allowed to 'see' with their hands the many interesting animals they read and talk about" (42). In 1913, the ability of blind children to read by touch is no longer newsworthy; it is instead their presence in a museum, studying its exhibits, that is the "new experience" of note.

The opening up in the early twentieth century of public museums to blind visitors likely diminished the importance of bespoke natural history collections made for and by blind people. The opening up of public museums did not, however, put an end to an important subset of museums created by blind people, some of which continue to operate today. Prioritizing the educational history of blind people, these museums collect and display artifacts such as early writing tools, embossed globes, and specimens of raised print. In 1886, the *Daily News* reported that, in Paris, "A Museum for the Blind was opened;" established by Dr. Guilbeau, a teacher and blind person, it "contains specimens of nearly all the objects invented for a long course of years for schools [. . .] for sightless pupils" ("Museum for the Blind" 6). This museum was named for Valentin Haüy, the French creator of the world's first raised-print book for blind people. The Musée Valentin Haüy continues to operate today, welcoming visitors interested in the history of reading by touch. Museums at the American Printing House for the Blind in Kentucky, Illinois, and at the Perkins School for the Blind in Boston, Massachusetts, have comparable collections of the English-language history of blind people's education. Permanent versions of the temporary display in the Education Section of the International Exhibition in 1862, these museums realize yet another goal that guided Elizabeth Gilbert's activism. As her biographer explained:

> she proposed to form a department for the exhibition of inventions in aid of the blind. These were to be arranged without reference to the 'sighted,' and in such a manner that the blind could easily examine and compare them. An exhibition of this kind was opened in Paris in October 1886, but the idea originated in the fertile brain of Bessie Gilbert. (Martin 166)

It might be more accurate to say that the idea originated with a community of blind people who wished to see investment in reading by touch matched by investment in non-textual routes to knowledge.

In the Gallery

While natural history specimens featured centrally in blind people's experiences of museum collections, museums did not limit their touchable offerings to taxidermy animals, fossilized shells, and human skeletons. The Sunderland Museum, for example, made the arguably surprising decision to invite blind visitors to touch oil paintings from their Fine Arts collection. This decision allowed blind visitors to handle a form of visual art whose tactility is rarely considered, let alone explored, by sighted people. Indeed, the very first event that the Sunderland staff designed for blind visitors featured visual art. The tour began with a description of the gallery space; visitors then handled relevant materials. In addition to painted and unpainted canvases, "an artist's palette, brushes, and paint tubes were handed to each individual to feel and examine closely" (Charlton Deas 87). Moving on to works of art, specifically to "glazed" (87) paintings, visitors were encouraged to feel the surface of canvases with their fingers. Charlton Deas explained that, "[a]fter the subject of a picture had been described, the positions of the important features were indicated by guiding the first finger of the person's hands over the outlines, and in this way the relative location and size of the principal points were made clear" (88). The detailed questions participants asked about the paintings led Charlton Deas to conclude that "a good deal more of the description of the picture had been absorbed than one had at first dared to hope" (88). His arguably radical decision to include paintings in the Sunderland Museum's touch collection is a measure of his commitment to making the full range of his museum's holdings available to blind visitors.

The writing of W.W. Fenn shares a blind person's perspective on the study of visual art. A blind author whose experiences working with an amanuensis were featured in chapter 3, Fenn was, prior to becoming blind, a successful landscape painter. In prefaces to collections he published, Fenn lamented the loss of his career as a painter but he also emphasized that blindness had not lessened his love of visual art. In an 1878 essay titled "My Own Story," Fenn explains that his understanding of visual art was not diminished by acquired blindness: "I by no means abstain from visiting exhibitions because I cannot see" (7). He adds, "Nay, I have gone so far as to write notices of pictures, and I flatter myself I have sometimes managed to see and understand as much of what I have been writing about as some critics and observers do who have their eyes" (7). Publishing reviews of art shows he attended, commenting on paintings that he was unable to see, Fenn insisted not only on his unaltered pleasure in art but also on his undiminished knowledge of it. Importantly, when he explains that "pictures on the easel or on walls are not found beyond my comprehension" (11), Fenn acknowledges the importance of conversation to his experience of art. Comparing his experiences as a blind person with those he had while sighted, he notes: "talk about [art] and all matters naturally relating to the world of art I can listen to and take part in with no less amount of satisfaction than of yore" (7).

Like the blind visitors in the art gallery at the Sunderland Museum, Fenn's sense of touch shapes his experience of art. He explains:

> The picture on the easel from a well-remembered hand has but to be sketched out upon my palm, or my forefinger guided deftly over the composition and arrangement upon the canvas itself, with a *viva-voce* description of subject, colour, light, shade and detail, and lo, with what I knew before, I have an image in my mind's eye vivid enough to give me infinite pleasure. ("My Own Story" 6–7)

Supported by memory and imagination, either feeling the dried paint on a canvas or presenting his hand as a substitute canvas, Fenn uses touch to access artworks he can no longer see. Finding in touch and the mental images it produces a substitute for sight, appreciating the contribution made by what we now refer to as audio description, Fenn refutes the notion that acquired blindness excludes people from art appreciation. Eager to demonstrate not only the equivalence of blind and sighted experiences of art but also the common humanity of blind and sighted people, Fenn thrives in the role of blind art lover.

We can gain an even deeper sense of blind people's experience of art by re-engaging "How a Blind Man saw the International Exhibition." Whereas the anonymous essayist was accommodated in both the Industrial Annex and International Halls, he felt markedly less welcome in areas of the Exhibition devoted to visual art. His own lack of interest in touching works of sculpture was, admittedly, a contributing factor. His sense of touch, useful for learning about machines or imported goods, proves of significantly less value when applied to sculpture. Commenting on statues displayed throughout the Exhibition's halls, the essayist remarks:

> I must at once confess that, were I desirous of presenting a blind person with a correct idea of the human face and figure, I should never think of showing him a statue with that object, for the simple reason that he would not understand it [. . .] I go up to a [statue] having been previously informed of all that is meant to be portrayed; and what is presented to the touch? A cold, dead, smooth, monotonous surface. (231)

Touch does not serve him well, it seems, when the object being touched is a marble sculpture representing a human body. Challenging the expectation that three-dimensional works of art will be both accessible and interesting to blind people, the essayist explores the limits of touch's ability to stand in for vision. Touch is not, he explains, the same as vision; a statue that looks like a living person does not feel like flesh. Touching a representational work of sculpture, is not, it seems, as valuable or pleasurable or informative as touching a Japanese raincoat, or, we might add, a well-prepared skeleton.

But what of the paintings on display at the International Exhibition? Again, the anonymous essayist encountered obstacles. He explains: "It was my custom, after being nearly deafened by the constant din ever audible in the machinery annex, to turn for relief towards the picture-galleries" (234). As he moved through these galleries, nothing was offered up to his touch nor was he engaged in conversation by other people. He explains that he tried to listen to the talk of other visitors about the art, this in order to learn about the works on display, but he was not able to gather much from what he heard. Indeed, instead of learning about the art on display, he overhears, in muttered tones, remarks about his presence in the gallery. He reports hearing the following responses to his presence: "'Lor'! I wonder what he's come here for?' or, 'What good can he be doing here? he can't see the pictures?' to which some one would reply, 'Lor', no! Can't you see he's blind?'" (234). The sociability and accommodation that the essayist experienced in the Industrial Annex and International Halls did not, it seems, extend to the art galleries. Indeed, in this space, the blind man is made to feel unwelcome, a blind interloper in a space dedicated to visual experience. No longer a consumer of spectacles, he is, not unlike the paintings hung on the walls, both a spectacle for sighted people's consumption and a topic of their conversation. In the case of the International Exhibition, when the object of a blind person's interest is a painting, accommodation is, it seems, nowhere to be found.

The blind essayist's experiences in the picture galleries at the International Exhibition are made more troubling by the fact that blindness was exhibited on the walls of those galleries. Notable among a handful of paintings on display that engaged the experience of blindness was Michael Frederick Halliday's 1858 painting "The Blind Basket-Maker with his First Child," a standout entry in the section of the Exhibition dedicated to British painters (fig. 20). Given that this painting explores, and indeed celebrates, the role of touch in a blind person's life, it seems especially unfortunate that the essayist was not alerted to its presence. By offering here, more than a century and half too late, a description of Halliday's painting, a description the anonymous essayist might have found interesting, I hope to return us to a core concern of this chapter: the relationship between the ability to read by touch and the status of touch in the hierarchy of human senses.

The setting of Halliday's painting is a corner of a modest but cheerful cottage workshop. A blind man, the basket-maker of the painting's title, stands with the stone wall of the cottage behind him and a tiled floor beneath his feet. A small decorative basket sits half-made on the bench behind him. Neatly dressed and groomed, conventionally handsome, he pauses in his work to embrace his wife, who holds their sleeping baby in her arms. A portrait of a blind man as worker, husband, and father, not as a blind beggar or blind poet, this painting is a notable exception to conventional patterns of repre-

Figure 20. "The Blind Basket-Maker with his First Child" (1858) by Michael Frederick Halliday. Private Collection.

sentation for blind men. While the painting extols the pleasures of vision through its very colorful and detailed depiction of the basket-maker and his family, there are no signs in it of sorrow or distress about the basket-maker's blindness. Instead, the painting documents the blind man's full and satisfying sensorial life. While both a violin resting on the window ledge and a bird in a cage on the workshop's wall bring sound into the painting, the pleasures of touch are foregrounded—most obviously by the embracing family, but also by a cat who rubs against the basket-maker's legs, its own eyes closed like the basket-maker's.

The painting can, in fact, be described as a multifaceted celebration of touch and its potential—economic, educational, sexual, familial, and emotional. Though there are no books in this painting, reading by touch matters centrally to Halliday's depiction of blindness. Recalling the importance of the depiction of hands and their positioning in Ford Madox Brown's portrait of Henry and Millicent Fawcett, Halliday's painting also features the hands of a blind husband and his sighted wife. Specifically, in Halliday's painting, the wife cradles their baby with her left hand while she uses her right hand to hold and guide her husband's right hand, moving it so that his extended fingers hover just above their child's face. This positioning of a human hand is not one that visual culture associates with the touching of a baby's face; this hand is positioned, instead, like the hand of a reader of an embossed book. Consider, for example, a widely circulated lithograph of Oliver Caswell and Laura Bridgman, two American deaf-blind students who were painted by Alanson Fisher in the 1840s (fig. 21). The lithograph shows Bridgman teaching Caswell, the younger of the two, how to read by touch. Her right hand rests on top of his right hand; his index finger is extended to touch the embossed script on the page of an open book of raised-print, which she holds. The positioning of hands in Halliday's painting of the blind basket-maker and his wife is remarkably similar to the positioning of hands in Fisher's celebrated and widely circulated double portrait of two blind readers.

I would like to suggest that Halliday's painting references, and indeed celebrates, reading by touch. It does so less explicitly but no less powerfully than Fisher's painting. The unusually horizontal position of the basket-maker's hand subtly but necessarily evokes reading by touch; the man depicted in it is a father and worker, but he is also, for Halliday, a reader. The face of his infant child becomes, through Halliday's careful positioning of his hand, a text to be read in a familial scene of blind education. The workshop doesn't contain a single book but, when Halliday, a sighted person in mid-nineteenth-century Britain, portrays a blind man, he portrays a blind reader. This painting does

Figure 21. “Oliver Caswell and Laura Bridgman reading embossed letters from a book,” lithograph by W. Sharp after A. Fisher (1844). Source: Wellcome Collection. This engraving shows two young people standing shoulder to shoulder. Caswell, whose eyes are closed, reads a raised-print book with the index finger of his right hand. The book is held open by Bridgman, whose eyes are covered by a band of dark fabric. Her right hand guides Caswell’s right hand as he reads. They stand at a table near a window. The table holds a large bound book, which is closed, as well as a pencil and sheets of paper. The image’s pairing of reading by touch with writing by touch is emphasized by the inclusion of each sitters’ signature beneath their portrait.

more than document nineteenth-century interest in the reading experiences of blind people: it records newfound optimism about the potential of touch to lessen the distance, real and perceived, between sighted and blind people.

A Coda

My goal for this chapter, as for the larger book, has been to deepen our understanding of nineteenth-century blind people's lives by exploring the history of reading by touch. As I noted at the start of this chapter, while only a portion of Anglo-American blind people learned how to read by touch, this practice had culture-wide effects; blind people did not need to be able to read by touch to experience these effects. What is more, many sighted people's perceptions were changed by this innovation, their ideas about blindness becoming, in many cases, more progressive. But, as this book has demonstrated, reading by touch was not a cure-all for attitudinal and material barriers to blind people's cultural and economic participation. Indeed, the perception of blindness as a tragic state, defined by deprivation and dependency, persists today as do other barriers to education and employment that past generations of blind people faced. I undertook the research shared here with the goal of countering ableist ways of thinking about blindness, both past and present. I hope my work supports not only progressive thinking about blindness but also progressive action.

As I noted in the Introduction, the study of the history of reading by touch has present-day relevance for a community of readers with important decisions to make about their reading lives. Barriers to access to written culture and indeed, to written information generally, remain a reality in many blind people's lives. On a more positive note, both technological innovation and blind readers' preferences continue to shape blind people's experiences of literacy. The practices and values that inform blind people's experiences of reading today are no more static, no more fixed, than they were two centuries ago. The importance of braille education and of the publication of braille books, for example, is debated anew in our own moment. In recent decades, resources have been redirected away from the publication of braille books toward the development and provision of digital tools, tools which include refreshable braille technology but in which screen readers, which use sound instead of tactile surfaces to communicate information, feature centrally. Of course, improving access to audio books, whose popularity with both blind and sighted readers has increased immensely in recent years, has also changed blind people's reading lives. While investment in digital and audio-based access might portend the obsolescence of braille books, experimentation with new forms of access to written information builds on and extends previous generations' achievements, which include, among other things, the adoption and adaption of the Roman-letter alphabet, of the printing press, and of writing tools for blind people's use. While obsolescence can be perceived in terms of loss, the abandonment by users of scripts such as Moon's and, similarly, of tools such as the Foucault frame reflects the changing preferences, and circumstances, of blind people.

While I have very frequently engaged sighted people's opinions and observations throughout this study, I have tried to prioritize blind people's perspectives. By bringing attention to the lives and writing of, for example, Alice King, Edmund White, Alfred Hirst, and Elizabeth Gilbert, I have, I hope, contributed to an effort initiated by leading scholars in the field of Anglo-American blindness studies. They include Mary Klages, Martha Stoddard Holmes, and Heather Tilley. Published statements about blindness authored by blind people are, unfortunately, radically outnumbered by those of sighted people, yet firsthand accounts of blindness in nineteenth-century Anglo-American culture reward those who search for them. From the unnamed street reader interviewed by Henry Mayhew, who read aloud until he was hoarse; to Robert Edgar, who delighted in quizzing fellow students about the books they shared; to W.W. Fenn, who wrote at length about reading by touch but did not himself practice this skill: records left by blind people document the diversity of blind people's experiences in the first century of reading by touch.

Given the importance of blind people's perspectives to the history of blindness and to this book, I am unwilling to let Halliday's *The Blind Basket-Maker and his First Child*, a sighted person's creation, be the final record of blind people's literacy explored in this study. I would like to offer instead a closing reflection on a tiny but compelling record of the early history of reading by touch. In a nineteenth-century raised-print book, in the middle of the reverse side of a page of Roman-letter script, a blind reader left their mark: two capital letters, written with a pin, an M followed by an E. Placed at the center of the page, not in its margins, the inscription, pricked out dot-by-dot with a pin, embellishes a copy of Adolph Bernhard Marx's *The Universal School of Music*, a textbook published by the American Printing House for the Blind in 1877. The added letters, written in reverse on the front of the page, run in the opposite direction of the book's text. Legible by touch, pricked out in a Roman-letter script that is similar to the one used in the book, this handwritten message would be legible to a blind reader who had the skills

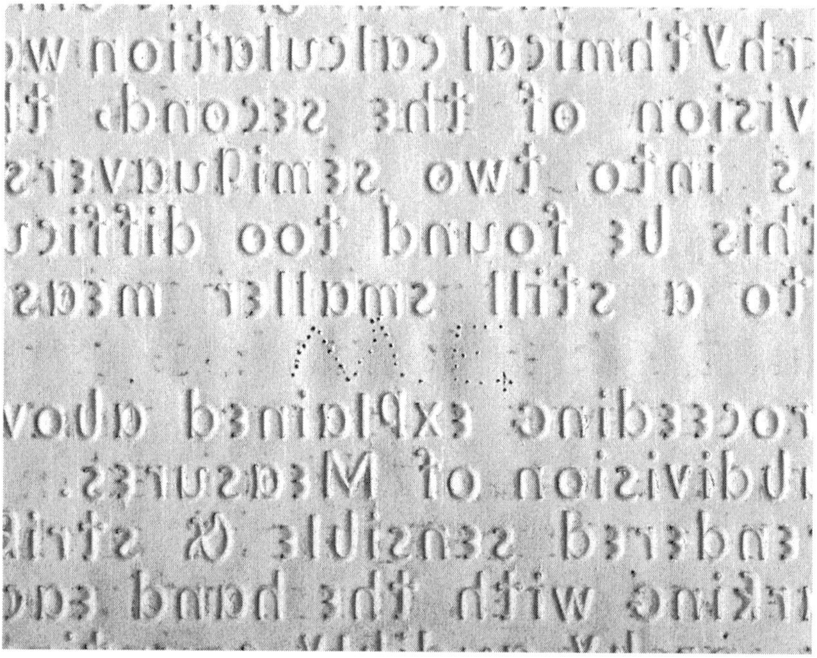

Figure 22. A detail from Adolph Bernhard Marx's *The Universal School of Music* (1877), part of the Michael Zinman Collection of Printing for the Blind. The Library Company of Philadelphia.

required to read the book that houses it. It would also be visible as well as legible to a sighted person. Whereas a sighted reader can see this inscription on the front side of the page, the inscription's raised perforations are on the back of the page, meaning a blind reader would have to discover it by accident or, alternately, know where to search for it. Notably, the inscription includes a tiny ornamental flourish: the lower leftmost dot of the E is embellished by four dots arranged around a central dot like the points of a compass (fig. 22).

Created by a now unknown maker, this inscription was featured in artist Teresa Jaynes's *Common Touch: The Art of the Senses in the History of the Blind*, an innovative exhibition held in 2016 at the Library Company of Philadelphia, where Jaynes was an artist-in-residence. Jaynes's exhibition, an exploration of the history of blind people's education and cultural contributions, paired her own original artwork with nineteenth-century artifacts from the Michael Zinman Collection of Printing for the Blind, to which the inscribed copy of *The Universal School of Music* belongs. Both a reflection on and an experiment in accessibility, Jaynes's exhibition featured tactile elements, audio experiences, and, remarkably, a scent narrative, which visitors accessed by inhaling different fragrances released in a programmed sequence from a wall-mounted cone. As Jaynes explained regarding *Common Touch*, "Sight does not dominate here. The senses of touch, hearing, and smell all play a role" (*Common Touch* 46).

Jaynes exhibited the inscribed "ME" with the pages of the book that contains it opened to the word ME, the page positioned so the added "ME" rather than the raised print of the book can be read. The ME was highlighted for sighted visitors to the exhibition by a cardboard circle that framed it, resting on the open page. Unfortunately, the book and its pinpricked inscription were displayed in a glass case. Obliged to protect a rare and fragile book, part of a library collection, Jaynes made a different surface available for touching. Beside the glass-cased book, she installed a life-size model of an owl. Titled "Gift #1," it was one of six multisensory artworks she created for the exhibition. Notably, the form of the owl was not covered in feathers but in slips of paper that share the words of nineteenth-century blind authors in three different raised-print scripts. A three-dimensional exploration of themes I have explored in this book, "Gift #1" references, among other topics, the role of natural specimens in blind people's education, the coexistence and rivalry of different scripts, and the insights of blind authors regarding sensory experience.

Though smaller than any of the installations that surrounded it, less charismatic and less tactile, the inscribed "ME" in the glass case was, for me, *Common Touch*'s most compelling offering. Like many artifacts of the history of blind people's education, it is an enigmatic object. The identity of the creator of the pinpricked "ME" is, after all, only one of many things we don't know about it. We don't know if the letters represent a person's initials or if the inscription spells out a two-letter word, the pronoun "me." We don't know what motivated its maker to add it to the book. In an interview about *Common Touch*, Jaynes proposes that the "ME" might be a "pinprick doodle by a student" (*Common Touch* 38), a phrase that suggests the inscription was made in an absentminded moment. I appreciate Jaynes's interpretation of this artifact for the way in which it normalizes reading by touch, recognizing boredom or restlessness as part of blind readers' lives. There are, however, other interpretative options at hand. We could, for example, interpret the addition of the word "ME" to a page of raised print as a very deliberate and conscious choice. Made by a creator who punctured the surface of the page, dot by dot, adding to a published book but not annotating it, this addition has a mischievous if not rebellious quality. Shaped by blindness, made by touch, it might be interpreted as a small-scale work of graffiti, a tactile tag. Like graffiti, it records its creator's presence as well as that creator's willingness to break the rules. Written between the lines, legible to touch only on the reverse side of the raised-print page, it feels assertive and oppositional. Re-purposing a portion of a publication as a writing surface, its maker claimed space in an institutionally created and owned textbook. Whether made consciously or absentmindedly, the "ME" literally marks a blind person's transition from the act of reading to the act of writing: from consuming to creating.

For all these reasons, this tiny inscription exemplifies the richness of the history of reading by touch of which it is a part. Easy to read but hard to interpret, it is a prompt for us to handle the history of blind people's literacy with care and to seek that history not only in raised-print books but in traces of their use. A message stored in the material culture of blindness, it directs us toward many of the issues this book has engaged: the history of education, differences between the senses of sight and touch, experimentation with tactile writing methods, and the obsolescence of Roman-letter script systems. It guides us to read the history of non-visual forms of literacy as just one facet of the history of a non-normative way of being: of being blind. It encourages us to remember that every member of the first generation of blind people to learn to read was an individual: a "ME." Perhaps most importantly, the inscription reminds us that the most valuable information we can access about the first generations of people to read by touch will come, not from what has been written about them, but from what was written by them.

Notes

Introduction

1. To learn more about Thomas Lucas and his work, consult Mills. To learn more about exhibits at schools for students with sensory disabilities, consult Bergen.

2. To learn more about the poetry and life of Jane Frances Crosby, consult Cohen.

3. To learn more about the Free Circulating Library for the Blind in Philadelphia, which specialized in books printed in Moon script, consult the *Report of the Pennsylvania Home Teaching Society and Free Circulating Library for the Blind*, published in 1904.

4. Writing in 1913, Henry J. Wilson noted that the NLB had a collection of "17,000 volumes (16,000 in Braille and 1,000 in Moon)" (8). For a Victorian-era history of the first years of the NLB, consult Leach.

5. Many nineteenth-century commentators offered estimates of the numbers of people who could read by touch at different times in the century in the US or the UK. For example, an 1876 report in *The Times* asserted that not fewer than 5,000 blind persons could read Moon's script; the same report shared that 100,000 volumes in Moon script were in circulation at that time ("The Blind"). For information about historical definitions of blindness, consult my essay: "Blindness: Creating and Consuming a Nonvisual Culture." Regarding the number of blind people living in the US and the UK in the nineteenth century, Charles Baker shares in his entry under "Blind" for *Chambers's Encyclopaedia* that US census records for 1880 recorded a blind population of 48,928 people and that the 1881 census records for England and Wales enumerated 22,832 blind people (224).

6. For a detailed discussion of visual depictions of blind readers, consult Tilley's "Portraying Blindness: Nineteenth-Century Images of Tactile Reading."

7. The impact of surgical cures on the representation of blindness in literary works by sighted authors is a focus of Tilley's *Blindness and Writing: From Wordsworth to Gissing*.

8. Blind activist and author W.H. Levy shared his opinions on the affordances of touch in his book *Blindness and the Blind* (1872). Levy shared the story of a girl

who "having lost the power of reading with her fingers, found, when in the act of kissing her embossed Bible, that she could read with her lips" (58). Levy added that he "tried this experiment with perfect success" (58). He objected, however, to the circulation of stories about blind people's ability to sense colors by touch. He wrote: "Telling colours with the fingers is a fallacy, which has become widely spread through the deception of interested persons. All that touch can do is distinguish between surfaces; it cannot feel rays of light; as colour is a combination of rays [. . .] touch cannot deal with it" (59). On the history of the education of blind people, consult Baker, Illingworth, and Jones ("Education").

9. Altick initiated not only the study of literacy in the nineteenth century but also debates about how literacy should be both defined and measured. What, for example, are the benefits and limits of relying on marriage registrars, school inspectors' reports, or census records to measure literacy levels? In 2016, Rosalind Crone authored a detailed overview of several decades of debate, summarizing the contributions of key figures, such as Philip Gardner, David Vincent, and David Mitch. Crone's exploration of questions that continue to shape this field begins with a helpfully straightforward definition of literacy. She asserts, "Literacy comprises two skills: the ability to read and the ability to write." As *By Touch Alone* will demonstrate, in the context of blind people's education, fewer blind people had access to writing skills than to reading skills. Thus, for the purposes of this study, I measure literacy as the ability to read raised print by touch (and not the ability to both read and write by touch). I explore the ability to write by touch in chapter 4.

10. Influential commentators on the nineteenth-century history of literacy include Vincent, Rose, and Flint. For an important example of work that engages the history of visual disability and literacy, consult Bourrier's "Reading Laura Bridgman: Literacy and Disability in Dickens's *American Notes*." Consult also Oliphant.

11. A letter sent on September 11, 1839 records Queen Victoria's donation of 400 pounds toward "the printing of the Bible in raised Type for the use of the Blind throughout the Kingdom" (Alston, *Statements* 41).

12. On June 9, 1879, *The Times* printed a portion of a letter from Thomas Hughes, author of *Tom Brown's School Days* (1857), to students of Worcester College for the Blind. In it, he grants them permission to emboss his novel and offers to donate a guinea to the costs ("'Tom Brown' For the Blind," 13). Tilley's essay "The Sentimental Touch: Dickens' *Old Curiosity Shop* and the Feeling Reader" shares a detailed analysis of the cultural significance of Dickens's presentation of 250 copies of a raised-print edition of *The Old Curiosity Shop* to blind students in America.

13. Wilson commented on the size of a braille version of *Dombey and Son* in a paper he gave at the Royal Society of Arts and published in its journal. He observed: "Few public libraries would be willing to give the necessary space required" to store raised-print books (413).

14. Details of this competition, including the awarding of a gold medal prize to a script proposed by Dr. Edmund Fry, are shared by William Taylor in a "Report on the various modes of Printing for the use of the Blind."

15. Armitage regretted how in the first decades of reading by touch: "the blind

had to learn to read by the character which happened to be in favour at the institution where they received their education, and on leaving they found that, if they were to obtain the benefit of the few books that had been embossed, they had to learn two or three fresh systems, and perhaps discard altogether the one which it had taken them years to acquire" (*Education* 37).

16. For a different reading of the student's encounter with this portrait, consult my essay "'So that the sense of touch may supply the want of sight.'" For more information on the history of tactile images created for blind people's use, consult Eriksson.

17. For information about the life of William Moon, both his personal life and his professional life, consult Rutherfurd.

18. In my essay "'So that the sense of touch may supply the want of sight,'" I explore the opposition of some sighted commentators to so called arbitrary scripts. B.G Johns, in his essay "Blind People" described arbitrary systems as "semibarbarous" (465), "mysterious" (464), and "half-barbarous looking" (464). In 1910, historian W.H. Illingworth observed that: "so lately as 1884, a superintendent of one of the best schools for the blind in the kingdom, when pressed to introduce the Braille system, exclaimed: 'What! that barbarous and heathen system of reading? Never! It had not the smallest resemblance to ordinary print! How are we teachers to learn it?'" (145).

19. For more on blindness, reading, and the nineteenth-century reevaluation of the sense of touch, consult my essay "'So that the sense of touch may supply the want of sight.'"

20. On mailing raised-print books, consult Fryer.

21. For a focused discussion of how reading by touch inspired concern about the transmission of contagious disease, consult my essay "Between the Sheets: Contagion, Touch, and Text."

22. For more on attitudes toward blindness and blind people in Western culture, consult Barasch.

23. For an important discussion of reading by touch and Dickens's account of meeting Laura Bridgman, consult Bourrier's "Reading Laura Bridgman."

24. For a discussion of these three texts and their similarities, consult Carpenter's "Blinding the Hero." For important discussions of disability in *Jane Eyre*, including a reading of the novel by David Bolt, consult *The Madwoman and the Blindman: Jane Eyre, Discourse, Disability*, co-edited by David Bolt, Julia Miele Rodas and Elizabeth J. Donaldson.

25. The depiction of blindness in *Poor Miss Finch* has been explored by Tilley (*Blindness and Writing*), Sparks, O'Farrell, and Holmes ("Bolder").

26. Consult chapter 4 for more information on blind characters who author suicide notes.

27. To learn more about so-called "toga plays" and specifically about James Pain's nineteenth-century pyrodrama of *The Last Days of Pompeii*, consult Mayer.

28. For a compelling reading of *Romola* as one of a series of literary re-imaginings by women authors of Milton's relationship with his daughters, consult Nardo.

Chapter One

1. The London Society for Teaching the Blind to Read was founded in 1839 by Thomas Lucas, a sighted person and the creator of a namesake raised-print script. For more information about its history, consult Pritchard.

2. Mayhew shares an interview with a "'Farm-Yard' Player," who he describes as "half-blind" (3:161) in Volume 3 of *London Labour and the London Poor*. The same section features interviews with, among other blind street performers, a "Blind Performer on the Bells" and a "Blind Female Violin Player."

3. For an insightful discussion of Mayhew's interview with a blind seller of bootlaces that engages both Mayhew's practice and street begging, consult chapter 5 of Holmes's *Fictions of Affliction: Physical Disability in Victorian Culture*.

4. James Hatley Frere was a sighted British person who developed a tactile script system for blind people's use in the late 1830s. His system, which was phonetic, combined circular shapes and lines to represent different sounds. In addition to inventing this now obsolete script, Frere developed stereotyping methods he used to publish raised-print books. These methods, as well as Frere's experiments with the return line, were taken up by William Moon, whose career is explored in the Introduction. Mayhew misspells Frere's name as "Freer" in his interview with the blind reader.

5. For an important discussion of the pre-nineteenth-century history of the blind beggar trope, including its visual history, consult Barasch. Consult also chapter 2 of Klages's seminal study of blindness in nineteenth-century America, *Woeful Afflictions: Disability and Sentimentality in Victorian America*.

6. For a history of the Mendicity Society, consult Roberts and MacKay.

7. For a discussion of Edmund White and his sale of his poetry by subscription, consult my essay "Poet and Beggar: Edmund White's *Blindness*."

8. In 1840, *The Times* reprinted an article from the *Glasgow Courier* about the completion of the raised-print edition of the Bible. The *Glasgow Courier* had congratulated John Alston, the Bible's publisher, on having "for the first time in the history of literature, placed the complete Bible in the hands of the blind" ("Glasgow Asylum for the Blind").

9. To learn more about the nineteenth-century visual depiction of blind people, including blind people reading by touch, consult Tilley's "Portraying Blindness."

Chapter Two

1. For a discussion of the erotic dimensions of reading by touch in bed, and also of health concerns related to the transmission of contagious disease via the circulation of raised-print books, consult my essay "Between the Sheets: Contagion, Touch, and Text."

2. Eleanor Gertrude Brown's *Milton's Blindness*, published in 1934, is an early and influential study of Milton's blindness by a blind author. For examples of scholarship on the nineteenth-century literary legacy of Milton as a blind person, consult Maxwell and Nardo.

3. I am indebted to Mary Wilson Carpenter for this example, which she explores in a chapter dedicated to blindness in *Health, Medicine, and Society in Victorian England.*

4. Robert Meldrum, the author of *Light on Dark Paths* (1883), a guidebook for parents of blind students, featured an excerpt from the same prose passage on his book's title page, again misattributing it to Milton. It is possible that Levy was Meldrum's source.

5. The misattribution of this poem to Milton was the subject of an April 1856 letter to the Editor of the American monthly *The Guardian*. The magazine had published the poem in February 1856 under the title "Lines by Milton in his old age" without acknowledging that the author was not, in fact, Milton. The editor republished the poem, explaining "We were led wrong by others" and correcting the title to read "Lines On Milton in His Old Age." To read the poem and learn more about its attribution, consult *The Guardian*, April 1856, pp. 124–25.

6. As Thompson notes, her conception of "blindness gain" is inspired by H-Dirksen L. Bauman and Joseph J. Murray's notion of "deaf gain." To learn more, consult Bauman and Murray.

7. For a different reading of these passages by Johns, consult O'Farrell.

8. On the archetype of the blind seer and its role in the life and work of nineteenth-century American blind poet Frances Crosby, consult Cohen. Cohen's essay also engages the role Milton's poetry played in Crosby's career. For an historical overview and analysis of blind archetypes, including the blind beggar, consult Barasch.

9. For a comprehensive history of the education of blind students, consult Oliphant. For a nineteenth-century perspective, consult Armitage's *Education and Employment of the Blind* (1871). Consult also Tilley's essay "Portraying Blindness: Nineteenth-Century Images of Tactile Reading" in which she uses portraits of blind people reading to argue that "blind people actively used visual technologies to draw attention to their status as literate and educated, particularly through the practice of sharing their portraits with wider communities." She also explores, among other topics, differences in the visual depiction of male and female readers of raised-print books.

10. For a detailed discussion of Robinson's life and work, consult my essay "'Blindness clears the way': Edgar Robinson's *The True Sphere of the Blind* (1896)."

11. For a fascinating history of the Canadian Free Library for the Blind and the contributions made to it by Edgar Robinson and his wife, Marion Robinson, consult Friskney.

12. The violent deaths of three Victorian-era blind villains come immediately to mind. Those characters are: Dan Ogle from Arthur Morrison's *The Hole in the Wall* (1902), Stagg from Charles Dickens's *Barnaby Rudge* (1841), and Blind Pew from Robert Louis Stevenson's *Treasure Island* (1883).

13. A 1914 photograph of the American doctor and blind person J.W. Bolotin shows him seated at a desk reading from a braille book with his left hand at the same time that he uses his right hand to type. While the photograph, like

Hirst's account, documents interest in ambidextrousness in the context of blindness, the difference between Bolotin and Hirst's reader is that Bolotin, like other blind people, read at the same time that they either transcribed or took notes on a book, dedicating a hand to each task, this in contrast to Hirst's reader whose ability to read different material with each hand at the same time is exceptional.

14. Readers who wish to learn more about the concept of the supercrip can consult, in addition to Clare's *Exile and Pride: Disability, Queerness, and Liberation*, Kama and Scott.

Chapter Three

1. The raised-print sheet inserted at the start of this otherwise ink printed book features a passage from the Book of Isaiah. It reads: "And I will bring the Blind by a way that they knew not; I will lead them in paths that they have not known: I will make darkness light before them, and crooked things straight. These things will I do unto them, and not forsake them." Raised-print text at the bottom of the page identifies the printer of this sample sheet as N.B. Kneass, Jr. of Philadelphia. To learn more about Kneass and his career, consult my essay "Blindness and Design: Kneass' *Philadelphia Magazine for the Blind* (1899)."

2. In her introduction to the Penguin Classics edition of *The Moonstone*, Sandra Kemp observes that Collins's description of his reliance on an amanuensis are "exaggerated," explaining that "the manuscript is almost entirely in Collins's own hand" (x).

3. In "Henry James and Theodora Bosanquet: On the typewriter, *In the Cage*, at the Ouija board," Pamela Thurschwell shares a fascinating reading of James's collaboration with Bosanquet, his fiction, and communication technologies. Notably, nineteenth-century women authors seem to have made far less frequent use of secretaries than their male contemporaries.

4. For a discussion of Thackeray's habits when dictating fiction to his amanuensis George Hodder, consult Melville's *William Makepeace Thackeray: A Biography* (vol. 2, pp. 6–7). Consult also Hodder's autobiography. To learn more about Anne Thackeray Ritchie's life and career, consult Aplin.

5. For a discussion of Frances Browne and the bio-critical reading of her work as a blind poet and novelist, consult Tilley's "Frances Browne, the 'Blind Poetess': Toward a Poetics of Blind Writing."

6. The depiction of the body in *Poor Miss Finch* (which is featured in chapter 4) has been explored by a number of scholars. They include: Gregory Brophy on epilepsy, Jessica Durgan and Lillian Nayder on race, Tabitha Sparks on surgical cure, and Mary Ann O'Farrell and Martha Stoddard Holmes on blindness.

7. For an influential discussion of Bertha from *The Cricket on the Hearth*, consult Julia Miele Rodas's "Tiny Tim, Blind Bertha, and the Resistance of Miss Mowcher: Charles Dickens and the Uses of Disability." For a usefully focused exploration of the depiction of Bertha as a blind person, consult Elisabeth Gitter's "The Blind Daughter in Charles Dickens's *Cricket on the Hearth*."

8. While the text of the novel was complete at the time of his death, several illustrations were not. *Harper's* consequently opted to publish unfinished illustrations, found in du Maurier's sketchbooks, alerting readers they were works in progress.

9. To learn more about connections between blindness and the nineteenth-century development of writing machines, consult Kittler's chapter titled "Typewriter" in *Gramophone, Film, Typewriter* (1986), in which Kittler notes how the desire for writing tools for blind users energized and shaped the development of the typewriter. Kittler also offers a case study of Friedrich Nietzsche's partial blindness and typewriter use. Importantly, he observes regarding the design of early typewriters that "None of the models prior to Underwood's great innovation of 1897 allowed immediate visual control over the output. In order to read the typed text, one had to lift shutters on the Remington model, whereas with Malling-Hansen's—notwithstanding other claims—the semicircular arrangement of the keys itself prevented a view of the paper. But even Underwood's innovation did not change the fact that typewriting can and must remain a blind activity" (203).

Chapter Four

1. The slip of paper that Bridgman signs for Dickens, presumably as a souvenir, brings to mind the slips of paper handed out by the unnamed street reader whose interview with Henry Mayhew was featured in chapter 1. Desperate to support himself and his family, the street reader wrote Bible verses on slips of paper and handed them out to sighted passersby, circulating samples of his handwriting that were both collectible curiosities and proof of both his literacy and piety.

2. For a fascinating discussion of Laura Bridgman's literacy and Charles Dickens's response to it, consult Karen Bourrier's "Reading Laura Bridgman: Literacy and Disability in Dickens's *American Notes*." In it, Bourrier makes the important point that, for Bridgman, writing was a means for her "to communicate with her audiences without any mediation on the part of her teachers" (46).

3. Stamps were only one of a number of short-lived innovations that responded to the combination of, on the one hand, sighted educators' reluctance to embrace braille and, on the other hand, blind people's desire for a method to write tangible text. A comparable innovation was a string alphabet in which each letter of the alphabet was represented by a different kind of knot. This system was developed by two blind people in Glasgow, David McBeath and Robert Milne. A letter to, for example, a blind friend in another town would take the form of a series of knots along a length of rope. An inexpensive but time-consuming mode of communication, this method seems to have received more press coverage than real-world use.

4. For a detailed discussion of writing methods and tools, including stamps, consult chapter 3 of Heather Tilley's *Blindness and Writing: From Wordsworth to Gissing* (2018).

5. For an important discussion of both Gilbert's life and Martin's biography, consult Holmes's *Fictions of Affliction*. In it, Holmes explores, among other topics,

how Frances Martin's biography of Gilbert positions Martin as "both a sophisticated critic of emotional representations of blindness and an adherent to exactly this construction of her dear and recently deceased friend" (173).

6. Regarding the British debut of this machine, George Dodd recalled seeing "a blind man who, surrounded by sympathising visitors, printed his thoughts on slips of paper, which were distributed to those interested in them" ("Books for the Blind," p. 422).

7. Several years later, in 1859, when Gilbert wrote to the King of Hanover, who was a blind person, she opted first to dictate a draft of her letter and then to write a revised version in her own hand. Consult Martin, p. 176.

8. Notably, though Gilbert did not make use of braille in her own correspondence, she was an advocate for its wider adoption. She wrote, "I believe that the power of writing in some tangible form, with the greatest possible ease and rapidity, to be of the highest importance to the blind; and with this view I should like to see Braille's system in use in all our schools" (Martin 149).

9. David Bolt's influential work on literary representations of the suicide of blind people shares an extended analysis of sighted authors' investment in this troubling trope. Consult Bolt's "Caught in the Chasm: Literary Representation and Suicide Among People With Impaired Vision."

10. The depiction of blindness in *Poor Miss Finch* has been explored by, among others, Martha Stoddard Holmes, Heather Tilley, Tabitha Sparks, and Mary Ann O'Farrell.

11. Educated and socially privileged, influential representatives of the blind community, Gilbert and Fawcett were acquaintances; Fawcett served as a vice-patron for the Association for the General Welfare of the Blind. Though Fawcett was several decades younger than Gilbert, they died within months of one another. Though each of them managed extensive networks of correspondence, they had very different experiences of letter writing. Whereas Gilbert wrote hundreds of letters by hand, Fawcett chose to dictate his letters. Yet, like Martin's biography of Gilbert, Stephen's biography of Fawcett is prefaced by a frontispiece that pairs a portrait of Fawcett with a reproduction of his signature.

12. As is also the case with the life of Elizabeth Gilbert, Martha Stoddard Holmes shares an insightful discussion of Henry Fawcett's life in *Fictions of Affliction*. Holmes does not engage Ford Madox Brown's double portrait but her discussion of Henry and Millicent's marriage and specifically of Millicent's writing about her husband offer a valuable gloss to the painting.

For a different reading of this double portrait, consult Heather Tilley's "Portraying Blindness: Nineteenth-Century Images of Tactile Reading." Consult also chapter 1 of her book *Blindness and Writing: From Wordsworth to Gissing* for a reading of the painting focused on gender and on connections to Milton and his daughters.

13. The collection of the National Portrait Gallery includes a photograph of Henry Fawcett taken in a studio in Brighton in 1865. Notably, the NPG's collection also includes a chromolithograph of Fawcett, produced in the mid-1880s, that includes a reproduction of his signature written in pen.

Chapter Five

1. An earlier version of my work on this anonymous essay appeared in French in 2014; consult my essay "Comment un aveugle a vu l'Exposition international."

2. For information about the history of the object lesson, consult Sarah Anne Carter and Andrea Korda.

3. For an informative discussion of how deafness shaped Martineau's life and her published writings, consult D'Amore.

4. For a discussion of the history of the role played by models in blind people's education, consult Olsén. For a discussion of the role of touch in geographical studies, consult my essay "'Mountains might be marked by a drop of glue': Blindness, Touch & Tactile Maps."

5. To learn more about the history of touching in museum spaces, consult Candlin and Classen. For an important discussion of visual art, touch, and blindness, both historically and in contemporary art galleries, consult Kleege's *More than Meets the Eye*.

Works Cited

"About the blind." *Dundee Courier*, 7 May 1896, p. 4.

Allen, Edward E. "The Tangible Writing of the Blind." *New England Magazine*, vol. 3, no. 3, November 1890, pp. 320–29.

Allen, Grant. *Linnet: A Romance*. 1898. New York: New Amsterdam, 1900.

Alston, John. "On Printing for the Blind." *Proceedings of the Philosophical Society of Glasgow*, vol. 1, 1841–1844, pp. 239–42.

Alston, John. *Statements of the Education, Employments, and Internal Arrangements, Adopted at the Asylum for the Blind, Glasgow*. 1842. London: Sampson Low, Marston, 1894.

Altick, Richard. *The English Common Reader: A Social History of the Mass Reading Public, 1800–1900*. 1957. 2nd ed., Columbus: Ohio State University Press, 1998.

Anderson, Thomas. *Observations on the Employment, Education, and Habits of the Blind*. London: Simpkin, Marshall, 1837.

Aplin, John. *The Inheritance of Genius: A Thackeray Family Biography, 1798–1875*. Cambridge, UK: Lutterworth Press, 2010.

Aplin, John. *Memory and Legacy: A Thackeray Family Biography, 1876–1919*. Cambridge, UK: Lutterworth Press, 2011.

Armitage, T.R. *The Education and Employment of the Blind: What It Has Been, Is, and Ought to Be*. 1871. 2nd ed., London: Harrison & Sons, 1886.

Armitage, T.R. *On the Means Employed for Ameliorating the Condition of the Blind of Great Britain and Ireland*. London: Gilbert and Rivington, 1878.

Artman, William, and L.V. Hall. *Beauties and Achievements of the Blind*. 1854. Rochester, 1879.

Ashby-Sterry, J. "London Street Studies." *The English Illustrated Magazine*, September 1888, pp. 798–804.

Babb, Genie. "The Prosthetic Body." *Victorian Review*, vol. 35, no. 2, Fall 2009, pp. 9–13.

Babcock, Bertrand W., and Onoto Watanna [Winnifred Eaton]. "Eyes that Saw not." *Harper's Magazine*, no. 625, June 1902, pp. 30–38.

Baker, Charles. "Blind." *Chambers's Encyclopaedia*, vol. 2, London: William and Robert Chambers, pp. 224–30.

Baker, Charles. "Education of the Blind." *The English Cyclopaedia.* London: Sampson, 1859, pp. 200–217.

Barasch, Moshe. *Blindness: The History of a Mental Image in Western Thought.* Routledge, 2001.

Barnhill, Alexander. *A New Era in the Education of Blind Children.* Glasgow: Charles Glass, 1875.

Barrett Browning, Elizabeth. *Aurora Leigh.* 1861. Oxford University Press, 2008.

Bauman, H-Dirksen L., and Joseph J. Murray. "Deaf Gain: An Introduction." *Deaf Gain: Raising the Stakes for Human Diversity.* Minneapolis: University of Minnesota Press, 2014, pp. xv–xlii.

Bergen, Amanda. "The Public Examination of Deaf and Blind Children in Yorkshire, 1829–1890." *Northern History,* vol. 41, no. 1, March 2004, pp. 149–62.

"Blind Guy Fawkes." *All the Year Round,* 25 Nov. 1876, pp. 255–58.

"A Blind Man's Love." *Harper's New Monthly Magazine,* August 1857, pp. 336–44.

"The Blind." *The Times,* 20 May 1876, p. 7.

"The Blind." *The Youth's Magazine,* vol. 13, April 1850, pp. 157–65.

"Blindness and the Blind." *Southern Literary Messenger,* June 1842, pp. 415–19.

"A Blind Street-Merchant." *Chambers's Journal of Popular Literature, Science and Arts,* vol. 6, no. 269, 23 Feb. 1889, pp. 123–24.

Bolt, David. "The Blindman in the Classic: Feminisms, Ocularcentrism, and *Jane Eyre.*" *The Madwoman and the Blindman:* Jane Eyre, *Discourse, Disability,* David Bolt et al., editors. Columbus: The Ohio State University Press, 2012, pp. 32–50.

Bolt, David. "Caught in the Chasm: Literary Representation and Suicide Among People With Impaired Vision." *British Journal of Visual Impairment,* vol. 23, no. 3, 2005, pp. 117–21.

Bolt, David. *The Metanarrative of Blindness: A Re-reading of Twentieth-Century Anglophone Writing.* Ann Arbor: University of Michigan Press, 2014.

Bolt, David, et al., editors. *The Madwoman and the Blindman:* Jane Eyre, *Discourse, Disability.* Columbus: The Ohio State University Press, 2012.

Bourrier, Karen. *The Measure of Manliness: Disability and Masculinity in the Mid-Victorian Novel.* Ann Arbor: University of Michigan Press, 2015.

Bourrier, Karen. "Reading Laura Bridgman: Literacy and Disability in Dickens's *American Notes.*" *Dickens Studies Annual,* vol. 40, no. 1, 2009, pp. 37–60.

Bowen, B.B. *A Blind Man's Offering* 1847. New York, 1853.

Brantlinger, Patrick. *The Reading Lesson: The Threat of Mass Literacy in Nineteenth-Century British Fiction.* Bloomington: Indiana University Press, 1998.

Brontë, Charlotte. *Jane Eyre* (1848). Edited by Richard Dunn. New York: Norton, 1971.

Brown, Alexander [Shadow]. *Midnight Scenes and Social Photographs.* Glasgow: Thomas Murray and Son, 1858.

Brown, Eleanor Gertrude. *Milton's Blindness.* New York: Columbia University Press, 1934.

Bull, Thomas. *The Sense Denied and Lost.* Edited by B.G. Johns. London: Longman, Green, Longman, and Roberts, 1859.

Bulwer-Lytton, Edward. *The Last Days of Pompeii*. 1834. London: Dent, 1979.
Candlin, Fiona. "Rehabilitating unauthorised touch or why museum visitors touch the exhibits." *The Senses and Society*, vol. 12, no. 3, 2017, pp. 251–66.
Carpenter, Mary Wilson. "Blinding the Hero." *differences: A Journal of Feminist Cultural Studies*, vol. 17, no. 3, 2006, pp. 52–68.
Carpenter, Mary Wilson. "A Cultural History of Ophthalmology in Nineteenth-Century Britain." *BRANCH: Britain, Representation, and Nineteenth-Century History*, edited by Dino Franco Felluga, 2012. https://branchcollective.org/?ps_articles=mary-wilson-carpenter-a-cultural-history-of-ophthalmology-in-nineteenth-century-britain
Carpenter, Mary Wilson. *Health, Medicine, and Society in Victorian England*. London: Praeger, 2010.
Carter, Lorance. "Types for the Blind." *Macmillan's Magazine*, vol. 64, May 1891, pp. 51–55.
Carter, Sarah Anne. *Object Lessons: How Nineteenth-Century Americans Learned to Make Sense of the Material World*. Oxford University Press, 2018.
Carton, C. *The Establishments for the Blind in England: A Report to the Minister of the Interior and of Foreign Affairs*. 1838. London: Sampson, 1895.
"A Case for Commiseration." *The Standard*, 27 May 1874, p. 2.
Charlton Deas, J.A. "The Showing of Museums and Art Galleries to the Blind." *The Museums Journal*, vol. 13, no. 3, September 1913, pp. 85–109.
Chottin, Marion, and Hannah Thompson. "'Blindness Gain' as Worldmaking: Audio Description as a New 'partage du sensible.'" *L'Esprit Créateur*, vol. 61, no. 4, 2021, pp. 32–44.
"Circumstances of the Blind in Glasgow and Neighbourhood, On Roll of Glasgow Mission to the Blind." 1869. *History of the Society for the Blind in Glasgow and the West of Scotland, 1859–1989* by Helen Dunbar, Glasgow and West of Scotland Society for the Blind, 1989, p. 42.
Clare, Eli. *Exile and Pride: Disability, Queerness, and Liberation*. 1999. Durham: Duke University Press, 2015.
Clark. "Books for the Blind." *Wayside Gleanings for Leisure Moments*. Cambridge: Wilson, 1882, pp. 130–32.
Classen, Constance. *The Museum of the Senses: Experiencing Art and Collections*. London: Bloomsbury, 2017.
Cohen, J. Laurence, Jr. "Shining Inward: The Blind Seer, Fanny Crosby, and Education for the Blind in the Nineteenth Century." *Journal of Literary & Cultural Disability Studies*, vol. 11, no. 1, 2017, pp. 53–68.
Collins, Wilkie. *The Moonstone*. 1868. Edited by Sandra Kemp. Penguin, 1999.
Collins, Wilkie. *Poor Miss Finch*. 1872. Oxford World's Classics, 2000.
Common Touch: The Art of the Senses in the History of the Blind. Library Company of Philadelphia, 2016.
Craik, Dinah. "Blind!" *The Unkind Word and Other Stories*, vol. 2, London: Hurst and Blackett, 1870, pp. 1–12.
Craik, Dinah. *John Halifax, Gentleman*. 1856. New York and London: Harper & Brothers, 1903.

Crone, Rosalind. "Literacy." Victorian Literature, *Oxford Bibliographies*, August 2016, doi: 10.1093/obo/9780199799558–0140

Crosby, Frances Jane. "The Rise and Progress of the New York Institution for the Blind." *The Blind Girl and Other Poems*. New York: Wiley & Putnam, 1844, pp. 20–26.

D'Amore, Manuela. "Being 'excluded from the world of sound': Deafness, Invalidism and Resilience in Harriet Martineau's Writings (1834–1855)." *Cahiers victoriens et édouardiens*, no. 94, 2021, https://journals.openedition.org/cve/9580

Dark Days Brightened: A Selection of Poetry about and by the Blind. Edinburgh: Royal Asylum and School for the Blind, 1881.

Dickens, Charles. *American Notes*. 1842. Edited by Patricia Ingham. Penguin, 2004.

Dickens, Charles. *Barnaby Rudge: A Tale of the Riots of 'Eighty*. London: Chapman and Hall, 1913.

Dickens, Charles. *The Cricket on the Hearth and Other Christmas Stories*. Dover Thrift, 1994.

Dodd, George. "Books for the Blind." *Household Words: A Weekly Journal*, no. 171, 2 July 1853, pp. 421–25.

Du Maurier, George. *The Martian: A Novel*. London: Harper & Brothers, 1898.

"Editor's Preface." *The Star of Attéghéi; The Vision of Schwartz; and Other Poems*, by Frances Brown[e]. London: Edward Moxon, 1844, pp. vii–xxii.

"Education of the Blind." *The Times*, 24 June 1874, p. 12.

Eliot, George. *Romola*. 1863. Penguin Classics, 1996.

"English Magazines for January." *Daily Southern Cross*, 8 April 1863, p. 3.

Eriksson, Yvonne. *Tactile Pictures: Pictorial Representations for the Blind, 1784–1940*. Acta Universitatis Gothoburgensis, 1998.

Fawcett, Henry. Letter to Henry James Maine. 24 Mar. 1883, https://www.abebooks.com/paper-collectibles/Original-Handwritten-Letter-Signed-Economist-Henry/31374928583/bd. Accessed 9 Sept. 2023.

Fawcett, Millicent Garrett. Letter addressed "Dear Sir." 16 Oct. 1902, https://blackwells.co.uk/rarebooks/book.php?id=70773. Accessed 9 Sept. 2023.

Fenn, W.W. "Fingers versus Eyes." *Half-Hours of Blind Man's Holiday*, 2nd ed., vol. 2, London: Sampson Low, Marston, Searle, & Rivington, 1879, pp. 451–64.

Fenn, W.W. "My Own Story." *Half-Hours of Blind Man's Holiday*, vol. 1, London: Sampson Low, Marston, Searle, & Rivington, 1878, pp. 1–24.

Fenn, W.W. Preface. *Woven in Darkness: A Medley of Stories, Essays, and Dreamwork*, vol. 1. London: Kelly, 1885, pp. v–viii.

Fenn, W.W. "The Welfare of the Blind." *The Fortnightly Review*, April 1886, pp. 472–79.

Fenn, W.W. "What Touch Does for the Blind." *Woven in Darkness: A Medley of Stories, Essays, and Dreamwork*. London: Kelly, 1885, pp. 37–54.

Flint, Kate. *The Woman Reader: 1837–1914*. Oxford University Press, 1995.

"Foucault's Printing Key Frame, By Which the Blind May Write." *Leading American Inventors*, by George Iles. New York: Henry Holt, 1912, p. 327.

"Frances Browne." *Chambers's Journal*, vol. 15, no. 383, 4 May 1861, pp. 281–84.

Friskney, Janet B. "From Gleam of Light to Seedbed of a National Institute: The Canadian Free Library for the Blind, 1906–1918." *Papers of the Bibliographical Society of Canada*, vol. 50, no. 2, 2012, pp.187–237.

Fryer, Gavin. *Blindman's Mail: How the Blind have been Served by the Post*. 2010.

Gall, James. *An Account of the Recent Discoveries which have been made for facilitating the Education of the Blind*. 1837. London: Sampson Low and Marston, 1894.

Gall, James. *A Historical Sketch of the Origin and Progress of Literature for the Blind: And Practical Hints and Recommendations as to their Education*. Edinburgh: Hamilton, Adams, 1834.

Gitter, Elisabeth. "The Blind Daughter in Charles Dickens's *Cricket on the Hearth*." *Studies in English Literature, 1500–1900*, vol. 39, no. 4, 1999, pp. 675–89.

"Glasgow Asylum for the Blind." *The Times*, 28 Dec. 1840, p. 6.

Golden, Catherine. "Turning Life into Literature: The Romantic Fiction of George Du Maurier." *CEA Critic*, vol. 58, no. 1, Fall 1995, pp. 43–52.

Hammerton, J.A. "Wonders of the Blind and the Dumb." *The Temple Magazine*, vol. 5, Jan. 1901, pp. 339–44.

Haswell, D.O. *The Social Condition of the Blind*. 2nd ed., London, 1876.

Head, Francis Bond. *A Faggot of French Sticks; or, Paris in 1851*. New York: Putnam, 1852.

Hirst, Alfred. *My Dark World*. Reprinted from the *Sunday Magazine*, 19 April 1897. London: British and Foreign Blind Association.

Hirst, Alfred. "The Need of More and Cheaper Literature for the Blind in 'Braille' Type." *Report of the Conference on Matters Relating to the Blind*. London: Farmer & Sons, 1902, pp. 118–25.

Hirst, Alfred. *A Plea for the Study of Milton by the Blind*. Reprinted from *The Leeds Mercury*, 19 Dec. 1896. London: British and Foreign Blind Association.

Hodder, George. *Memories of My Time*. London: Tinsley, 1870.

Holmes, Martha Stoddard. "'Bolder with Her Lover in the Dark': Collins and Disabled Women's Sexuality." *Reality's Dark Light: The Sensational Wilkie Collins*, edited by Maria K. Bachman and Don Richard Cox. Knoxville: University of Tennessee Press, 2003, pp. 59–93.

Holmes, Martha Stoddard. *Fictions of Affliction: Physical Disability in Victorian Culture*. Ann Arbor: University of Michigan Press, 2004.

"How a Blind Man saw the International Exhibition." *Temple Bar*, January 1863, vol. 7, pp. 227–37.

Howe, S.G. "Education of the Blind," *North American Review*, July 1833, pp. 20–58.

Illingworth, W.H. *History of the Education of the Blind*. London: Sampson Low, Marston, 1910.

"Instruction of the Blind." *Penny Cyclopaedia*. London: Charles Knight, 1835, pp. 515–28.

James, Henry. "George Du Maurier." *Harper's New Monthly Magazine*, Sept. 1897, pp. 594–609.

John, Laurence. *A Blind Man's Love*. London: Henry Drake, 1895.

Johns, B.G. "Blind People." *The Quarterly Review*, vol. 11, no. 236, 1865, pp. 430–68.

Johns, B.G. *Blind People: Their Works and Ways*. London: John Murray, 1867.

Johns, B.G. "The Blind, their Works and Ways." *Edinburgh Review*, American Edition, vol. XCIX, January 1854, pp. 30–46.

Johns, B.G. *The Land of Silence and the Land of Darkness*. London: Longman, Brown, Green, Longmans, and Roberts, 1857.

Johns, B.G. "How the Blind Dream." *National Review*, vol. 5, no. 27, May 1885, pp. 309–19.

Johnson, Edmund C. *Tangible Typography: or, How the Blind Read*. London: J. Whitaker, 1853.

Johnston Ross, G.A. *The Story of a Working Man's Blindness*. Glasgow: John Calder, 1898.

Jones, Henry. "Behold! with wonder and amaze!" *Instructions for Teaching the Blind to Read* by T.M. Lucas, 2nd ed. London: Simpkin, 1837, pp. 48–49.

Jones, Mary Cadwalader. "The Education of the Blind." *Scribner's Magazine*, vol. 12, no. 42, Sept. 1892, pp. 373–87.

Kama, Amit. "Supercrips versus the Pitiful Handicapped: Reception of Disabling Images by Disabled Audience Members." *Communications*, vol. 29, no. 4, 2004, pp. 447–66.

King, Alice. "A Few Words about Blindness." *The Argosy*, vol. 38, September 1884, pp. 189–94.

King, Alice. "Our Blind Contributor—Alice King." *The Girl's Own Paper*, vol. 8, no. 389, 11 June 1887, pp. 577–79.

Kingsley, Charles. *Westward Ho!* 1855. London: Macmillan, 1911.

Kipling, Rudyard. "They." 1904. *Short Stories:1*. Penguin, 1971, pp. 93–116.

Kittler, Friedrich A. *Gramophone, Film, Typewriter*. Translated by Geoffrey Winthrop-Young and Michael Wutz. Stanford: Stanford University Press, 1999.

Klages, Mary. *Woeful Afflictions: Disability and Sentimentality in Victorian America*. Philadelphia: University of Pennsylvania Press, 1999.

Kleege, Georgina. *More than Meets the Eye: What Blindness Brings to Art*. Oxford University Press, 2018.

Kleege, Georgina, and Scott Wallin. "Audio Description as a Pedagogical Tool." *Disability Studies Quarterly*, vol. 35, no. 2, 2015, https://dsq-sds.org/index.php/dsq/article/view/4622/3945

Korda, Andrea. "Object Lessons in Victorian Education: Text, Object, Image." *Journal of Victorian Culture*, vol. 25, no. 2, 2020, pp. 200–222.

Langworthy, Jessica L. "Blindness in Fiction: A Study of the Attitude of Authors Towards their Blind Characters." *Journal of Applied Psychology*, vol. 14, no. 3, June 1930, pp. 269–86.

La Sizeranne, Maurice de. *The Blind As Seen Through Blind Eyes*. Translated by F. Park Lewis. New York: G. P. Putnam's Sons, 1893.

Lawrence, William. "Lectures on the Anatomy, Physiology, and Diseases of the Eye." *The Lancet*, 22 Oct. 1825, pp. 145–51.

Leach, Allan. "National Library for the Blind: Its past, present and prospects." *Health Libraries Review*, 1984, pp. 1–7.

Levy, W.H. *Blindness and the Blind: or, A Treatise on the Science of Typhlology*. London: Chapman and Hall, 1872.

"Literature for the Blind." *The Times*, 3 Jan. 1870, p. 5.

"Literature for the Blind." *The Times*, 27 Jan. 1870, p. 3.

Long, John Luther. "The Prince of Illusion." *The Century Magazine*, vol. 60, no. 5, September 1900, pp. 655–76.

"Lord Hatherley on Teaching for the Blind." *The Times*, 13 May 1873, p. 12.

M.M. "Teaching the Blind to Read." *Golden Hours*, no. 27, March 1866, p. 39.

Macculloch, Gilbert. *Story of a Blind Mute*. Edinburgh: James Gemmell, 1881.

MacKay, Lynn. "The Mendicity Society and Its Clients: A Cautionary Tale." *Left History*, vol. 5, no. 1, 1997, pp. 39–64.

Mannix, John Bernard. *Heroes of the Darkness*. London: S.W. Partridge, 1911.

Marston, Herbert J.R. "Education of the Blind." *The Times*, 15 June 1874, p. 13.

Martin, Frances. *Elizabeth Gilbert and Her Work for the Blind*. London: Macmillan, 1887.

Martineau, Harriet. "Blindness." *Household Words: A Weekly Journal*, no. 221, 17 June 1854, pp. 421–25.

Marx, Adolph Bernhard. *The Universal School of Music*. Louisville: American Printing House for the Blind, 1877.

Maxwell, Catherine. *The Female Sublime from Milton to Swinburne: Bearing Blindness*. Manchester and New York: Manchester University Press, 2009.

Mayer, David. *Playing Out the Empire*. Oxford: Clarendon Press, 1994.

Mayhew, Henry. *London Labour and the London Poor*, 4 vols. Dover, 1968.

McHenry, J. Howard. "Alphabets; or, Systems of Printing, Writing, and Notation of Music, Best Adapted to the Use of the Blind." Baltimore, 1870.

Meldrum, Robert. *Light on Dark Paths: A Handbook for the Parents of Blind Children*. Edinburgh: John Menzies, 1883.

Melville, Lewis. *William Makepeace Thackeray: A Biography*. London: John Lane, 1910, pp. 6–7.

Mills, P.V. "Thomas Lucas and his Embossed Stenographic Characters." *British Journal of Ophthalmology*, vol. 49, no. 9, 1965, pp. 485–89.

Mitch, David. *The Rise of Popular Literacy in Victorian England*. Philadelphia: University of Pennsylvania Press, 1992.

Moon, William. *Light for the Blind: A History of the Origin and Success of Moon's System of Reading for the Blind*. London, Longmans, 1873.

Morley, Henry. "At Work in the Dark." *Household Words*, 5 March 1859, pp. 321–24.

Morrison, Arthur. *The Hole in the Wall*. 1902. Okitoks Press, 2017.

"Museum for the Blind." *Daily News*, 3 Nov. 1886, p. 6.

Nardo, Anna K. "*Romola* and Milton: A Cultural History of Rewriting." *Nineteenth-Century Literature*, vol. 53, no. 3, 1998, pp. 328–63.

O'Farrell, Mary Ann. "Blindness Envy: Victorians in the Parlors of the Blind." *PMLA*, vol. 127, no. 3, 2012, pp. 512–25.

Oliphant, John. *The Early Education of the Blind in Britain c. 1790–1900: Institutional Experience in England and Scotland*. Lewiston, NY: Edwin Mellen, 2007.

Oliphant, John. "'Touching the light': the invention of literacy for the blind." *Paedagogica Historica*, vol. 44, no. 1–2, 2008, pp. 67–82.
Olsén, Jan Eric "Models for the Blind." *19: Interdisciplinary Studies in the Long Nineteenth Century*, vol. 19, 2014.
Pardon, George Frederick, editor. *Routledge's Guide to the International Exhibition of 1862*. London: Routledge, Warne and Routledge, 1862.
Plummer, John. *The Story of a Blind Inventor; being some account of the Life and Labours of Dr. James Gale, M.A., F.G.S., F.C.S.* London: William Tweedie, 1868.
"The Poor Blind Woman." *Day of Rest*, January 1881, pp. 51–58.
Pritchard, D.G. *Education and the Handicapped: 1760–1960*. Routledge, 1963.
Rainey, Frank. *Roman Letter*. Austin, Texas: Ben C. Jones, 1893.
Report of the Pennsylvania Home Teaching Society and Free Circulating Library for the Blind, 1904.
Ritchie, J.M. *Concerning the Blind*. Oliver and Boyd, 1930.
Roberts, M.J.D. "Reshaping the Gift Relationship: The London Mendicity Society and the Suppression of Begging in England 1818–1869." *International Review of Social History*, vol. 36, no. 2, 1991, pp. 201–31.
Robinson, E.B.F. *The True Sphere of the Blind*. Toronto: William Briggs, 1896.
Rodas, Julia Miele. "Mainstreaming Disability Studies?" *Victorian Literature and Culture*, vol. 34, no. 1, 2006, pp. 371–84.
Rodas, Julia Miele. "Tiny Tim, Blind Bertha, and the Resistance of Miss Mowcher: Charles Dickens and the Uses of Disability." *Dickens Studies Annual*, vol. 34, 2004, pp. 51–97.
Rose, Jonathan. "Education, Literacy, and the Victorian Reader." *A Companion to the Victorian Novel*, edited by Patrick Brantlinger and William B. Thesing. Blackwell, 2002, pp. 31–47.
Rose, Jonathan. *The Intellectual Life of the British Working Classes*. Yale University Press, 2001.
Rowe, Richard. "Pity the Poor Blind." *Life in the London Streets or Struggles for Daily Bread*. London: J.C. Nimmo and Bain, 1881, pp. 306–36.
Ruskin, John. "Letter XLIV: Notes and Correspondence." 6 June 1874. *Fors Clavigera. The Works of John Ruskin*, vol. IV. New York: John Wiley and Sons, 1886, pp. 118–19.
Rutherfurd, John. *William Moon, L.L.D, F.R.G.S., F.S.A. And His Work for the Blind*. London: Hodder and Stoughton, 1898.
Schaffer, Talia. *Communities of Care: The Social Ethics of Victorian Fiction*. Princeton: Princeton University Press, 2021.
Scott, Catherine. "Time Out of Joint: The Narcotic Effect of Prolepsis in Christopher Reeve's *Still Me*." *Biography: An Interdisciplinary Quarterly*, vol. 29, no. 2, 2006, pp. 307–28.
"Sir John Coleridge on Blind Institutions." *The Times*, 22 Oct. 1859, p. 7.
Sparks, Tabitha. "Surgical Injury and Narrative Cure in Wilkie Collins's *Poor Miss Finch* and *Heart and Science*." *Journal of Narrative Theory*, vol. 32, no. 1, 2002, pp. 1–31.
Stainsby, Henry. "Typewriting for The Blind." *The Blind*, no. 1, 20 Jan. 1898, pp. 18–22.

Stephen, Leslie. *The Life of Henry Fawcett*. London: Smith, Elder, 1885.
Stevenson, Robert Louis. *Treasure Island*. 1883. Penguin Classics, 2010.
Taylor, Charles Bell. "Notes on a case of apparently incurable blindness in which sight was restored." *The Lancet*, 11 Sept. 1897, p. 653–54.
Taylor, William. "Report on the various modes of Printing for the use of the Blind." *Report of the Seventh Meeting of the British Association for the Advancement of Science*, vol. VI. London: John Murray, 1838, pp. 87–102.
Thompson, Hannah. "Blindness Gain and the Art of Non-Visual Reading." *Blind Spot*, 5 Oct. 2018, https://hannah-thompson.blogspot.com/2018/10/blindness-gain-and-art-of-non-visual.html
Thurschwell, Pamela. "Henry James and Theodora Bosanquet: On the typewriter, *In the Cage*, at the Ouija board." *Textual Practice*, vol. 13, no. 1, 1999, pp. 5–23.
Tilley, Heather. *Blindness and Writing: From Wordsworth to Gissing*. Cambridge University Press, 2018.
Tilley, Heather. "Frances Browne, the 'Blind Poetess': Toward a Poetics of Blind Writing." *JLCDS*, vol. 3, no. 2, 2009, pp. 147–61.
Tilley, Heather. "Portraying Blindness: Nineteenth-Century Images of Tactile Reading." *Disability Studies Quarterly*, vol. 38, no. 3, 2018. https://dsq-sds.org/index.php/dsq/article/view/6475
Tilley, Heather. "The Sentimental Touch: Dickens's *Old Curiosity Shop* and the Feeling Reader." *Journal of Victorian Culture*, vol. 16, no. 2, 2011, pp. 226–41.
"'Tom Brown' For the Blind." *The Times*, 9 June 1879, p. 13.
"A Typewriting Office." *The Blind*, no. 1, 20 Jan. 1898, p. 14.
Vaughan, Agnes Laidlaw. "The Blind in the American Museum." *American Museum Journal*, vol. XIV, 1914, pp. 39–42.
Villey, Pierre. "Intellectual Work Among the Blind." *Annual Report of the Board of Regents of the Smithsonian Institution*, Government Printing Office, 1909, pp. 683–702.
Vincent, David. *Literacy and Popular Culture: England 1750–1914*. Cambridge University Press, 1989.
Vincent, David. *The Rise of Mass Literacy: Reading and Writing in Modern Europe*. Polity, 2000.
Warne, Vanessa. "Between the Sheets: Contagion, Touch, and Text." *19: Interdisciplinary Studies in the Long Nineteenth Century*, no. 19, 2014, pp. 1–9, https://doi.org/10.16995/ntn.715
Warne, Vanessa. "Blindness and Design: Kneass' *Philadelphia Magazine for the Blind* (1899)." *Cahiers victoriens et édouardiens*, no. 84, 2016, https://doi.org/10.4000/cve.2996
Warne, Vanessa. "'Blindness clears the way': E.B.F. Robinson's *The True Sphere of the Blind* (1896)." *Untold Stories: Disability History in Canada, edited by Nancy Hansen, Roy Hanes, and Diane Driedger*. Toronto: Canadian Scholars, 2018, pp. 53–65.
Warne, Vanessa. "Blindness: Creating and Consuming a Nonvisual Culture." *A Cultural History of Disability in the Long Nineteenth Century*, edited by Martha Stoddard Holmes and Joyce Huff. Bloomsbury, 2019, pp. 79–94.
Warne, Vanessa. "'Comment un aveugle a vu l'Exposition international': Specta-

teurs malvoyants dans la Grande-Bretagne victorienne." *Corpus: Revue de Philosophie*, no. 67, 2014, pp. 109–32.

Warne, Vanessa. "'Mountains might be marked by a drop of glue': Blindness, Touch & Tactile Maps." *Victorian Environments*, edited by Grace Moore and Michelle J. Smith. London: Palgrave Macmillan, 2018, pp. 97–114.

Warne, Vanessa. "Poet and Beggar: Edmund White's *Blindness*." *The Routledge Companion to Literature and Disability*, edited by Alice Hall. Routledge, 2020, pp. 181–92.

Warne, Vanessa. "'So that the sense of touch may supply the want of sight': Blind Reading and Nineteenth-Century British Print Culture." *Media, Technology, and Literature in the Nineteenth Century: Image, Sound, Touch*, edited by Colette Colligan and Margaret Linley. Ashgate, 2011, pp. 43–64.

"Waterloo Bridge." *Chambers's Journal*, no. 778, 23 Nov. 1878, pp. 750–52.

White, Edmund H. *Blindness; A Discursive Poem in Five Cantos*. London: James Martin, 1856.

Whiteley, Derek Pepys. *George du Maurier: His Life and Work*. Art and Technics, 1948.

Wilson, Henry J. "The Education and Employment of the Blind." *Journal of the Royal Society of Arts*, vol. 61, no. 3145, 28 Feb. 1913, pp. 406–19.

Woolmer, D.L. "The Chasing of the Shadows." *The Quiver: Annual Volume 1899*. Cassell, 1899, pp. 771–78.

Index